# OROMOCTO ADIEU

FOUR DECADES ON THE RIVER AND THE ORIGINS OF
NORTH LAKE PARISH

Rex Grady

Lilburne & Company, LLC

Lilburne & Company, LLC
51 E Street, Second Floor
Santa Rosa, California, 95404

Book Layout © 2016 BookDesignTemplates.com.

Cover Image: "Fredericton, N.B. from the Oromocto Road, 1837."
Hand-coloured lithograph on wove paper, by Robert Petley, British, 1812-1869, and originally appearing in Charles Joseph Hullmandel, Sketches in Nova Scotia and New Brunswick, J. Dickinson.

Image is currently part of the John Clarence Webster Canadiana Collection, New Brunswick Museum- Musée du Nouveau-Brunswick, Accession Number W3334.

Use of image is with the permission of the New Brunswick Museum- Musée du Nouveau-Brunswick

Oromocto Adieu: Four Decades on the River and the Origins of North Lake Parish/Rex Grady. -- 1st ed.
ISBN 978-0-578-52624-9

To My Mother

Jane Ellis Grady

# TABLE OF CONTENTS

Hugh and Almeda McMinn, c. 1870

## ACKNOWLEDGMENT

This book was undertaken many years ago in consequence of my search for tangible evidence of my family heritage. In the course of my search I have been fortunate to have received the help of many people. Greg Gossett, Gregg Hyde and their respective families, all of Ogden, Utah, extended hospitality for weeks on end while I laboured in the Family History Archives of the Church of Jesus Christ of Latter Day Saints in Salt Lake City. John Wood of Point Claire, Quebec and Beverly McMinn of Omaha, Nebraska provided the author with assistance in working out genealogical matters, as did Allen Boone, the incomparable antiquarian of Geary, New Brunswick, and the brothers Arlington and Basil Boone of Woodstock and Forest City, New Brunswick. The author's cousins Tom and Sam Collier, their wives Gladys and Delores, and Glady's sister Lois Gould, all of North Lake, New Brunswick, were especially generous, and they should know that the present volume could not have been written without their many acts of kindness. Tom and Sam were particularly helpful in providing information on the history of North Lake. They were not only able to introduce me to a plentitude of local lore, but also went far in revealing in their own words and manner the most authentic and admirable virtues of the native New Brunswicker. Other friends and relations who lent assistance were: Kathleen Holden of Laguna Nigel, California; my great aunts Nina (Kinney) Witham of Skowhegan, Maine and Lizzie (Kinney) Gould of Fosterville; Paul Farrell of Fosterville; Carl and Bertha Higgs of Forest City; Lawrence Farrell of Woodstock; and Glendon, Beth, Amanda and Erin Vye of New Maryland, N.B. The author's friend Jacques Vincent of Fredericton gave the author many moments of good cheer which will always be remembered with great fondness and delight. Denis Noel, also of Fredericton, has the special distinction of being not only a friend, but also an employee at the Provincial Archives of New Brunswick, and it was in the latter capacity that he was able to grant the author assistance in tracking down vital sources. The rest of the archival staff was equally helpful, and these individuals include Tom McCaffrey, Twylla Buttimer, Robbie Gilmour and Shioban Hanratty. The University of New Brunswick in Fredericton provided much assistance, which is gratefully recalled. Professor T.W. Acheson of the University of New Brunswick aided by reading early versions of the manuscript and suggesting needed changes. Finally, Michael Martino, of San Diego, California, extended useful editorial advice and encouragement.

In reflecting upon all of the assistance I received so many years ago, it dawns on me that some of those who aided me are no longer with us. They have joined the ranks of those of whom I've written, and they are, like them, a part of the history it is our duty, as those left behind, to recall and to record. Though I have shirked this duty for many years by neglecting the completion of this work, I believe that with its publication, my obligation, on this installment at least, is paid in full.

June 2019
Santa Rosa, California

# PREFACE

W.S. MacNutt once said that Canada's past has been one of parochialisms. Despite recent scholarly efforts to place provincial history into the broader context of national and continental affairs, MacNutt's characterization remains supremely true of New Brunswick. As late as 1864, when the Province was haphazardly moving toward acceptance of British North American Union, there were some, including the father of the aborted concept of Maritime Union, Lieutenant Governor Arthur Hamilton Gordon, who were struck by the Province's internal division upon sectional lines. Parochial New Brunswick was indeed a bundle of lesser parochialisms. Just how true this was, however, has never been adequately examined by historians, including MacNutt, who was rightfully more concerned with the discernment of those institutions and themes that contributed to the emergence of a coherent provincial establishment in the first eighty years of the Province's existence as a separate administrative entity. The conceit by MacNutt's successors, that New Brunswick was somehow attuned to and even leading national concerns, or at the very least represented a significant variant of national evolution, may well be warranted on one level, but it belies the essential genius of provincial existence — a genius which was denoted by unique and irascible localism. The historic inhabitants of New Brunswick, however much the modern academic protests that they conformed to a larger national pattern, were a distinct people, and though they shared some of the common attributes of the greater human family, their distinctiveness cannot be eschewed if a true rendering of their experience is ever to be forthcoming.

The present volume is an attempt at just such a rendering. It focuses upon the experience of a single community, examining its development following the initial stages of settlement up until the end of the colonial period. In the spirit of MacNutt, an effort has been made to discern the larger regional context, for it is believed that no true rendering of the sort which the author aspires to present can be achieved without demonstrating the link which the community in question had to the world of which it was so clearly an integral part. But the main focus is on the community itself, its peculiar historical foundations, its leaders and institutions, the deep and sometimes petty concerns of its people and the competition amongst them for control of land and timber. Such things are the stuff of any history, and they are to be found in surprising abundance in the surviving records of the day. Yet as important as these details are to the story at hand, they would be nothing without due consideration of the single greatest determinant of Nineteenth Century New Brunswick parochialism: geography. As Lieutenant Governor Gordon himself understood, provincial sectionalism was a function of provincial geography. This was true not only of the Province as a whole, divided as it was into St. John, St. Croix and Miramichi basins, but also of the several sections themselves. The community whose story is recounted in the following pages was undoubtedly part of a larger section, but its inhabitants' primary identification with each other and their own peculiar concerns, even to the detriment of greater administrative and social harmony, is as remarkable as it is unmistakable. Geography defined the community, placed strictures on its development and ultimately assisted in determining its fate. Thus, the story cannot be properly presented without the initial deference paid to the community's physical parameters.

And what of this community, the Oromocto? The author must admit that it was not for reason of its profound significance in the development of modern New Brunswick that he chose to make it the subject of his scholarly attention. Rather, it was an accident of heritage and a special compulsion the author felt regarding it that led him to focus his energies toward returning its experience to the full light of day. Some of his own forebears lived on the Oromocto, and it was in large part due to the permutations that occurred during the decades covered by the present volume that led them to depart for another locale. In attempting to understand their private migratory ordeal, the author was compelled to examine the community from which they sprang, in the course of which examination he discovered that they were part of a larger migration from the Oromocto which alighted, finally, upon the shores of East Grand Lake in the southern extreme of York County. How they came to make the decision to leave the

Oromocto became the author's special preoccupation, and in the course of pursuing an explanation it eventually became clear to him that the decision itself was intimately bound up in the greater history of the Oromocto community. Without understanding the development of the Oromocto, no understanding of the life and experience of the author's migrant ancestors could ever be had. The end result has been this book and the story told herein of the life of one of many peculiar settlements which dotted the countryside of Maritime Canada over a century and a half ago.

The present story is two-fold. On one level it is the history of the Oromocto community as a whole, its emergence from the wilderness, the origin of its institutions, the growth of local sectarianism, the rise of local political parties and the evolution of the local economy. On a second level, it is the story of a group of families, whose fortunes were linked unmistakably to the community to which they belonged. As time passed their own fate diverged from that of the community at large, in the main due to their inability to successfully adapt to changing circumstances. As they failed to fully conform to the changing context of the Oromocto, migration to the emerging parish of North Lake proved to be their best hope for maintaining themselves in some modestly comfortable fashion. In the end, the two stories compliment and reinforce one another, demonstrating each in their own way the vital truth that communal life is a paradox of fragility and strength.

Some readers may find this two-fold approach somewhat confusing, and might have preferred a more straightforward narrative, ungarnished by such complicated devises. To this the author can only say that while it may well be true that a more unburdened approach could have been employed, it would have been at the expense of historical veracity. Historians do a service to the reading public by breaking their subjects down into more digestible categories, but in so doing they as often as not distort the past beyond recognition. Life is neither neat nor always orderly, and certainly one never knows at any given moment what the next moment might bring. By imposing order upon events, the historian assumes a necessary outcome, one that may well have never been anticipated by the individuals who originally experienced it. There being a basic need, however, for some veneer of order, a compromise of sorts has been struck and the reader has been provided with overviews to four of the five subsequent chapters, each of which goes some way toward directing the two-fold accounts into a single narrative stream. No other aids will be forthcoming. No grand thesis will be presented. And no awe-inspiring conclusions will be drawn. Such things are left for the reader to discern; for the author, after toiling with his subject for years, has grown weary, and is presently in no condition to contemplate its long-familiar strains any longer.

# Chapter One

## THE RIVER OROMOCTO

In the heart of the St. John River basin, in the old county of Sunbury, lies a small tributary known as the Oromocto. Writing at the turn of the century, the basin's historian, William Obder Raymond, described the stream as beautiful and romantic.[1] So apparently obvious was the statement that Raymond did not deign it necessary to elaborate upon it in any greater detail. The Oromocto was beautiful, and, most likely, it was as picturesque in the 1830s as it was, decades later, when Raymond himself first visited it.

From the decks of passing river boats, as well as from the primitive steamers that were only then commencing to ply the waters between Fredericton and Saint John, the Oromocto's mouth became visible just as the shoals on the eastern side of the island that shares the stream's name begin to obstruct the course of navigation. Just to the west of the outlet and occupying a fertile slope first inhabited by the native peoples of the continent, was a small village, likewise called Oromocto. In the fourth decade of the Nineteenth Century, a second and third generation of Europeans tilled the soil here, and though they themselves knew little of their predecessors, they could hardly have been ignorant of their existence given the occasional unearthing by Oromocto farmers of shards of archaic clay pottery and partially mummified Indian remains.[2] By 1830 only a faint echo of that more ancient, aboriginal era remained — its meagre traces infrequently manifest in distant sounds emanating from the barrels of hunting rifles fired by transient native hunters. A lonely and mysterious breed, ghostly and

---

[1] W.O. Raymond, *The River Saint John: Its Physical Features, Legends and History from 1604 to 1784* (Reprint; Sackville: The Tribune Press, 1950), p. 17.

[2] Abraham Gesner, *Fourth Report on the Geological Survey of the Province of New Brunswick* (Saint John: Henry Chubb, 1842), p. 26.

elusive in their habits, these wandering neolithic souls only occasionally interacted with their European neighbours, and this usually only for the purpose of registering their kills and collecting their bear and wolf bounties at the county court house.[3]

The court house, known as the Burton Court House, loomed over the St. John River, about a mile downstream from the Oromocto's mouth, resting atop a knoll the ownership of which had been a source of some contention in the early days of the Loyalist settlement.[4] Of the many edifices fronting the river it alone stood desiccate in early spring, reclining placidly above the rush of waters caused by the melting ice, ever immune to the effects of the seasonal deluge as it carried away barns, houses, livestock and sometimes people toward its distant rendezvous with the Bay of Fundy. In the winter months, the Court House acted as the meeting place for the Court of General Sessions of Sunbury County, the members of which presided over cases brought before them by supplicants from all corners of the county. Throughout the rest of the year the building generally succumbed to the neglect of its tenants, who seemed to care less for maintaining basic repairs than for the operation of their licensed tavern in the Court House lobby.[5] Climate as well as negligence, however, must share responsibility for the premises' slow demise. Early in the 1830s, the locals would grow so disgusted with its sorry state that they demolished it and erected an entirely new, more suitable, structure.[6] The nearby gaol was equally derelict. So rundown did it eventually become that its rotting planks and rickety frame provided any number of escape routes for prisoners eager to elude the onus of

---

[3] General Sessions, Sunbury County Records, PANB, RS 157, A/2, 30 (1830), Bear Bounty Certificate of Peter Francis; RS 157, A/2, 32 (1832), Bear Bounty Certificate of John Say Bartus and Lolar Mark and Bear Bounty Certificate of Joseph Francis.

[4] William D. Moore, "Sunbury County: 1760-1830" (Unpublished M.A. Thesis, UNB, 1977), pp. 57-58.

[5] General Sessions, Sunbury County Records, PANB, RS 157, A/2. On April 4, 1831 John Scidmore Brown's yearly rent for occupation of the court house land and buildings was set at seventeen pounds, ten shillings.

[6] Ibid.

making good on delinquent debts.[7] In later years, when equity began to encroach upon the domain of law, an obstreperous din
would issue from the mouths of both rich and poor alike and take
the shape of demands for greater leniency in incarceration practices so as to allow poorer debtors to continue on with the work
that sustained the lives of their otherwise helpless dependents.[8]
In the 1830s such enlightened thinking seemed beyond the apprehension of local authorities. Thus, they remained in thrall to what
the rigid proclamations of the state defined as justice; compelled
not only to empower High Sheriff John Hazen to hunt down any
fugitives, but also, quite conceivably, to make advances of food
and clothing to families whose heads had been jailed after failing
to fulfil obligations to creditors.

It was fortunate for Hazen that his legal duties did not so frequently entail his pursuit of absconding debtors, for such
adventures would have been so labourious as to have prevented
his attendance to other responsibilities, not least of which involved the local Church of England establishment.[9] Like the Court
House, St. John's Church was slightly removed from the banks of
the Oromocto, its foundation having been laid on glebe land located at the right angle formed by the intersection of invisible
lines drawn from the St. John River and its lesser tributary. Built
in the 1790s through the labour and monetary subscriptions of the
then recent Loyalist settlers of Burton Parish,[10] the church long
languished as a minor outpost of the main county mission of the
Society for the Propagation of the Gospel at Maugerville, an

---

[7] William Scoullar vs. John Hazen (1832), Supreme Court Case Files,
1823-1835, Supreme Court Records, 1785-1835, PANB, RS 42. Other ex-
amples of prison escapes occur in General Sessions, Sunbury County
Records, PANB, RS 157, A/2.

[8] Petition of Charles Hazen et al., Records of the Legislative Assembly,
PANB, RS 24/1846/pc/file 14/no. 291.

[9] Vestry Minutes, Maugerville, 1784-1896, Archives of the Diocese of
Fredericton, PANB, MC 223, M3-1, and Financial Records of Burton
Church, 1820-1842, M3-3. Record books of St. John's Church indicate that
Hazen served as both a warden and vestryman.

[10] Ecclesiastical Return (1844), Archives of the Diocese of Fredericton,
PANB, MC 223, M3-3.

unending source of jealous pride for the people of that district who still smarted over the slight suffered upon them when the provincial government deprived them of the distinction of living in the county shiretown and sanctioned the erection of a new court house on the knoll so painfully visible from their forsaken northern shoreline. A scow had been procured to allow the Anglican missionary to commute from the parsonage in Maugerville to perform pastoral duties at St. John's,[11] but the frequent inclemency of the weather, as well as scandalous conflict with the faithful of his home parish, prevented greater assiduousness on his part.[12] Cursed with a Christian name that hardly inspired confidence or trust, this missionary, the Reverend Raper Milner, would stew in the religious caldron of Sunbury County for thirty years, sparking controversy in a district with a predilection for controversy, only to dissimulate his true feelings when confronted by his superiors with rumours that he wished nothing but the peace of reassignment to a less hectic post.[13]

Milner's occasional preoccupation with the complaints and criticisms of his parishioners naturally played into the hands of his rivals— notably the dissenting clergy and laymen who came to the river Oromocto at a very early date, preaching a Word of God free of the encumbrances of the hierarchy and elaborate ceremony so much more characteristic of the Anglican denomination. For the simple settlers of the wilderness, who were often so far removed from St. John's that weekly attendance was rendered impossible, the dissenters appeared as salvators of the lost city of Zion and its long-neglected and broken tabernacle. As St. John's Church decayed, as its glebe grew over with brambles and alder shoots and prospective tenants passed it by on their way

---

[11] Financial Records of Burton Church, 1820-1842, Archives of the Diocese of Fredericton, PANB, MC 223, M3-3.

[12] At least one of Milner's successors complained of such logistical difficulties in attending their scattered flock. See Society for the Propagation of the Gospel in Foreign Parts, PANB, MC 230, E, 1845.

[13] Id., Calendar of Correspondence, Volume 1, 1821-1848, p. 85 and Diary of Thomas O. Miles, PANB, MC 451, October 24, 1841 and August 14, 1842.

to settlement on cheap government lands,[14] the makeshift chapels of the dissenters rose in response to the call for bodily immersion in the living waters of the Lord. In an earlier era, New Light preaching had fulfilled the spiritual longings of the peoples of Maugerville and the surrounding countryside, only to recede like the tides of the Bay of Fundy, carrying all inspiration back to its source near the coils of Leviathan. Only one enclave remained, in Waterborough, Queen's County, where the Allineite pastor Elijah Estabrooks forged an eclectic congregation of settlers plucked from all along the middle reaches of the St. John River.[15]

To this congregation came several men whose families' influence upon the politics and economy of the Oromocto would be well established by the 1830s. The most significant of these was George Hayward, one of Sunbury's original settlers— a man whose desire for profit in the masting trade had brought him into alliance with Simonds, Hazen and White, and given rise to legal wrangles with their great competitor, William Davidson.[16] By the time of his death, he could claim to have at one time owned large sections of land on either side of the Oromocto River, from which places he had drawn labourers and neophytes into his twin allegiances to timber and dissent. Hayward's influence upon the Baptist community of the Oromocto was limited by his own apparent lack of initiative when it came to actually prosecuting the evangelical imperatives of the faith. Benjamin Glasier, his coreligionist at Waterborough, exercised greater responsibility in this regard. Taking into his own hands the crook of stewardship and bringing with him the New Light prejudices of the older Waterborough congregation, Glasier seems to have guided the nascent Oromocto flock following the departure of visiting missionary

---

[14] Ecclesiastical Return (1844), Archives of the Diocese of Fredericton, PANB, MC 223, M3-3.

[15] Ingraham E. Bill, *Fifty Years with the Baptists Ministers and Churches of the Maritime Provinces of Canada* (Saint John: imprint, 1880).

[16] William Davidson vs. James White (1786), Supreme Court Case Files, 1784-1822, Supreme Court Records, 1785-1835, PANB, RS 42 and the George Hayward Collection, PANB, MC 1396, Vol. 1.

John Landers.[17] Having accompanied the Reverend David Harris on a quest for souls along the stream in the last years of the previous decade,[18] Landers possessed a sterner view of the Baptist creed than many of his frontier charges, and when he abandoned the new congregation, he deprived them of the spiritual tutelage that might have forestalled their ultimate defection. In October of 1833 at a meeting place in Lincoln Parish on the west bank of the Oromocto, the small church nurtured by Harris and Landers, and now under the direction of Benjamin Glasier, formally reorganized according to the less rigid specifications of the Free Will successors of the Reverend Alline.[19]

Despite the diligence on the part of the dissenters, the appeal of their message was as yet unable to tempt the entrenched loyalty of many of the river's people to the tenets of Anglicanism. Great enthusiasm and kindness might greet the itinerant preachers of the Gospel, but nominal allegiance to the traditional faith remained substantially unshaken. Ravaged by an indifference originating in the salutary neglect of the official envoys of God and distracted by the insatiable demands of labour, the people of the Oromocto walked largely in the shadow of unredeemed mortality. This condition was bemoaned by Baptist missionary Edmund Manning, who, after his own inspection of the spiritual life of the river's inhabitants, could not refrain from berating the complacency of his colleagues in the more civilized townships of Nova Scotia.[20] But even Manning could not long stand to play the role of the solitary voice crying in the wilderness. He returned to his native land east of the Petitcodiac, leaving the damp bane of insobriety to overwhelm the people over whose sorrowful fate he had so profoundly fretted.

Near the mouth of the Oromocto four taverns catered to the

---

[17] New Brunswick Baptist Association, *Minutes of the Meeting of the New Brunswick Baptist Association* (Saint John: Henry Chubb, 1822).

[18] Bill, op. cit., pp. 577-8. Harris said of him: "God was with him and owned him as an instrument in the reformation."

[19] Records of the Lincoln Baptist Church, PANB, F7822. In the same year a second Free Will Baptist church was organized on the Rusagonis under the direction of the Reverend W. Pennington.

[20] Bill, op. cit., p. 137.

demands of the moderate tippler and guzzler alike,[21] giving the village the rudiments of a reputation for debauchery which the puritanical residents of the farming parishes of Maugerville and Sheffield could only look upon with a mixture of self-righteous disdain and reformist zeal. When even the youth of the region began to be drawn into "the vortex of dissipation," the newly formed Temperance Society of Sheffield agitated for a ban on the retailing of spirituous liquors, tenuously citing the feasibility of dry houses of entertainment and the great blessings that were sure to come to the wives and children of woodsmen once the canons of the teetotaller were enshrined in county regulations.[22] The quixotic ambition of the prohibitionists gained surprising support, but despite winning over several members of the Court of General Sessions, the movement to eliminate the habits of inebriation would not achieve victories of any significance until the latter half of the next decade, when the progress of Free Will Baptist evangelicalism would overcome the apathy and disregard of the greater part of the county's populace on either side of the St. John River.

However successful the prohibitionists became in the 1840s, their success proved nothing more than a transient epiphany. So pervasive would become the resulting illicit traffic in alcohol that the representatives of the Sheffield Total Abstinence Society could hardly disguise the evidence of their miscalculation merely by recourse to prosaic embroidery.[23] The Court's subsequent revocation of the short-lived temperance law was tempered by its munificent refusal to allow liquor sales on the north bank of the St. John River — an act of benevolence that soothed the pain arising from the fractured enthusiasm of that district's residents while simultaneously lifting the frail taint of illegality from the sottish inclinations of their southern neighbours. Again, the Oromocto's

---

[21] General Sessions and Minutes, Sunbury County Records, PANB, RS 157, A/1-2.

[22] Petition of the Members of Various Temperance Societies in the County of Sheffield, General Sessions, Sunbury County Records, PANB, RS 157, A/2/34 (1834).

[23] Petition of the Total Abstinence Society of Sheffield, PANB, RS 157, A/2, 47 a (1847).

taverns flourished as they had in years past and their proprietors, once again doing a lucrative business, virtually forgot the drought that had frustrated their finances and so mortally endangered their livelihood. In the 1830s, however, all this was still years away. The government still retained the good political sense to refrain from imposing upon the happiness of the people and thus, for the time being, prevented the birth of any substantive reasons why the men of the river should vent their frustrations against the status quo.

Equally placative to the potentially bitter feelings of the electorate was the final annulment of quit rents. A troubling and ancient feudal duty momentarily re-imposed in 1833 after a blundering misestimation of public passivity by Crown Land Commissioner Thomas Baillie, the quitrent was quickly and vehemently denounced by the people of the Oromocto. Intransigence characterized their refusal to offer up the required monies to the officers of the Crown,[24] in large part due to the people's inability to fathom that it ever could have been the intention of His Majesty to collect the foul tax "from those who fought the battles of their country, bled in defense of His cause and afterward suffered the severest privations in endeavouring to settle."[25] Recognizing the general contempt with which the obnoxious tax was held throughout the various settlements on the river and fully cognizant of the virtual lack of hard currency generally available to pay it, Assemblyman George Hayward, a grandson of the earlier mentioned bearer of that name, rose in defense of the protests of his constituency. Grateful for Hayward's intervention in upholding their rights in the matter of the oppressive tax, the people of the river proceeded to the polls in 1834 with none of the rancour normally preceding Sunbury County's traditionally scandalous legislative elections. George Hayward and his colleague, Thomas Obder Miles of Maugerville, went unchallenged. When no additional contestants appeared at the Burton Court House, High

---

[24] According to the quitrent receipts in the files of the General Sessions Records of Sunbury County (RS 157), only about forty inhabitants of the river paid their required assessments.

[25] Petition of Stephen Peabody et al., Records of the Legislative Assembly, PANB, RS 24, S43-P31.

Sheriff Hazen could do little else but cancel the impending contest and acclaim both Hayward and his fellow incumbent the county's duly chosen representatives in the provincial House of Assembly.[26]

Seven years earlier, the Lincoln Parish native had ridden into office atop a crest of popular support that was undoubtedly most pronounced along the Oromocto River.[27] A man of great integrity and patriarchal verve, Hayward had won the hearts of his constituents long before his venture into electoral politics through able conduct in several minor parish posts and a full and sincere display of those selfsame qualities of unpretentiousness in speech, methodical reasoning in thought, and grace, amity and humour when dealing with others that would later so impress a correspondent for *The Provincial Patriot*.[28] His colleague, Thomas O. Miles, exhibited similar refinement and could boast of an equally distinguished pedigree. Thoughtful as well as humane, confident in his abilities and possessed of a manner that evoked respectful deference from others, the Maugerville native divided his time between the north and south sides of the St. John River, upholding his responsibilities as county magistrate and pursuing the administration of his far-flung personal estate.[29] Both activities made him well known on the Oromocto, and his diligence in exercising his official capacity elevated him to a substantial level of popularity here that nullified the memory of his conservative father Elijah's bitter wrangles at the county polls with those notorious Oromocto favourites James Glenie and Samuel Denny Street.[30] He

---

[26] James C. Graves and Horace B. Graves, *New Brunswick Political Biography*, PANB, MC 1156, Volume 8, p. ii.

[27] Pollbooks, Sunbury County Records, PANB, RS 157, J/2/1 (1830).

[28] *The Provincial Patriot*, September 23, 1853.

[29] See Diary of Thomas O. Miles, PANB, MC 451.

[30] Moore, op., cit., pp. 133-134; Thomas B. Vincent, "Samuel Denny Street," *Dictionary of Canadian Biography* (Toronto: University of Toronto Press, 1987), Volume VI, p. 739-741; and D.M. Young, "Elijah Miles," *Dictionary of Canadian Biography* (Toronto: University of Toronto Press, 1987), Volume VI, pp. 504-505. Elijah Miles, as a candidate for the "Governor's Party" in 1816, defeated Street, thereby depriving the latter of his

was an energetic man who took on commitments in later years in the county agricultural and emigrant societies, and his spiritual outlook was unusually broad, allowing him to cross denominational lines and play active and constructive rolls in the Anglican, Baptist and even Catholic communities.[31] It was in part due to the influence of these two men— Hayward and Miles— as Justices of the Peace and as Assemblymen that the ancient combativeness of Sunbury's upper and lower sections was contained, and they, as much as or more than anyone else, can be credited with making the 1830s perhaps one of the more politically tranquil decades in the county's long and otherwise cantankerous history.

While the innate political skills of George Hayward and Thomas O. Miles may have contributed to the general accord that persisted in Sunbury County throughout most of the fourth decade of the Nineteenth Century, the placid state of affairs was perhaps more attributable to the impersonal forces of the market. The impassive axes of local lumbermen had already cut much of the best timber lying close to the banks of the county's great waterways, leaving, by the middle of the 1830s, a landscape of shrunken stands and every indication that the Oromocto's greatest era of exploitation had passed.[32] Never among the great timber producing regions of the Province, the Oromocto was now greatly depleted of its best timber, though increasing demand for sawed

---

seat. The upset led to a major controversy which culminated in a nasty brawl between the two contestants.

[31] Miles served as a vestryman in the Anglican Church and was a deacon (or elder) for the Baptists. In the 1850s, returned to the Assembly after a decade-long absence, he advocated on behalf of the Orange Lodge, urging his legislative colleagues to ignore the horror stories of Protestant extremism and to take into account the generally cordial relations that existed in the province between Orangemen and their Catholic neighbours. His lack of spiritual prejudice is reflected in his children as well. His son George became a Baptist pastor, while his son Obder was conspicuous in the assistance he lent the Catholic congregation of the Oromocto in moving their chapel from the North West Branch to the village in 1841.

[32] Graeme Wynn, *Timber Colony: A Historical Geography of Early Nineteenth Century New Brunswick* (Toronto: University of Toronto Press, 1981), p. 37.

logs and the rapid disappearance of the bias against sticks of either small or non-pine variety soon offset the forest's deepening penury. Activity in the woods thus continued only moderately abated, much to the pleasure and financial gain of local lumbermen, local merchandisers, and unseen capitalists in faraway Saint John. The extension of the viability of the Oromocto forest industry, however, did not completely prevent the occurrence of turmoil. As the serried flow of tens of thousands of harvested logs annually congested the river's various sluiceways and lesser tributaries, there arose confusion among proprietors and river hands over who owned which cache. By 1837 the situation on the water became so chaotic, and the various interested parties so frustrated, that the general clamour for a more orderly system of governing the business of the river could not be ignored by the provincial legislature.[33] In the winter of that same year, the Court of General Sessions of Sunbury County was granted discretionary power to devise and enforce rules pertaining to the local trafficking and navigation of timber.

Responding in similar fashion to the vigour of the economy, there arose a noticeable quickening of the sound of hammer falls emanating from several shipyards nestled in the safe, deep and sluggish waters just inside the mouth of the Oromocto. The workers here were a mixed bunch, some from Nova Scotia, others from Ireland. Many, however, hailed from the Oromocto — local men, both young and old, attracted by the wages that the newest yard owner, William Scoullar, paid his employees.[34] Scoullar's was not the only shipyard on the river, but it was certainly the most vital. In the 1830s, its progress far outpaced its oldest competitor, the ragged remnants of the firm of Simonds, Hazen and White, the only local active members of which had essentially ceased the bulk of their operations in the previous decade. Family patriarch John Hazen could only reminisce about the days when his clan had monopolized trade on the river and the nearby settlement of

---

[33] Petition of Thomas Mersereau et al., Records of the Legislative Assembly, PANB, RS 24, 1837/pe/file 7/no. 7.

[34] The make-up of the shipbuilders is an interpolation based on a reading of the data found in the 1851 Census of New Brunswick, Sunbury County.

Maugerville. In his family's place as chief supplier and employer of the scattered descendants of the Oromocto's first settlers stood Scoullar, who, with his brother-in-law, Henry Thomas Partelow, formed a partnership Hazen did not particularly admire.[35] His personal distaste for his family's successors in business was generally only moderately spiteful, and presumably he was able to ignore his discontent with the pair just as he ignored the hammering from the shipyard that no doubt could be heard from his place of abode.

Both Scoullar's shipyard and Hazen's home were numbered among several properties to be found on a fertile sheath of smooth, red, alluvial soil deposited over the centuries by the erosive and convective powers of the Oromocto. Not far from either parcel was a small ferry dock from which the Hazen family operated a small barge for the purpose of facilitating travel across the river.[36] In previous decades the interruption of overland traffic, compounded by the temperamental preferences and personal animosities of the ferryman, constituted only a local nuisance, suffered mainly by those few Oromocto farmers on the east bank of the river able to produce a surplus crop for sale at the more significant agricultural market in Fredericton.[37] The recent building of the Nerepis Road, however, magnified the annoyance into one of a more regional variety. Desires that a bridge be constructed to span the width of the river naturally arose, but while Sheriff Hazen graciously offered to relinquish a portion of his own land to allow for the building of the bridge's approaches, William Scoullar and lumberman George Morrow, less inspired by the spirit of good citizenship, made onerous demands upon the public purse, stubbornly refusing to allow the riverfront lands they owned to leave their possession without suitable compensation. In time, a reputed expert on the subject of bridges was contacted, and after consideration of various alternatives, a design characterized by sturdy piles and a forty-foot draw was finally agreed upon. Only the hopes of the penny pinchers met with

---

[35] See Chapter Two.

[36] Moore, op. cit., p. 134.

[37] Petition of Thomas L. Langen et al., Records of the Legislative Assembly, PANB, RS 24, S43-P37.

disappointment, as the initial claims that the bridge could be erected at little expense gave way to the actual expenditure of £1,800.[38]

The specific parcels on which the bridge's approaches were to be built represented but the smallest fragment of a larger geographic whole. Even the countryside immediately surrounding these lots and the homes and barns built throughout were but the terminus of a larger unified river system settled by successive waves of peoples beginning, in the days before history, with Micmac and Malecite and continuing on with Acadians, New England Planters, Loyalists and, finally, the Irish. The river's deep water and the red alluvial soil of its banks, as well as its obvious importance as an intersection of inland travel, first recommended it to the indigenous peoples, who established a small settlement at its mouth. Later, they were joined by Acadians, with whom they seem to have existed in relative amity. Following their common dislocation by the British, John Porteaus, a businessman of ever shifting interests, transformed himself from land speculator into an absentee landlord through diligent agitation of Parliament and Crown.[39] Construction of a blockhouse at the mouth of the river in what is now Burton Parish to accommodate troops entrusted with maintaining a suspicious surveillance of the disloyal populace of Maugerville seems to have improved his vacant property's worth. Settlers from the north side of the St. John soon signed leases to portions of his grant, hoping to find relief from the demographic pressures of the older communities of Sunbury County and secure escape from the freshets that had inundated them with annual regularity. Their tenure, however, was brief. Refugees from the American States began to arrive en masse in the early 1780s, prompting the government to escheat Porteaus' real estate, eject his tenants and re-assign the lots to families whose losses in the course of the late conflict represented a

---

[38] "Report of the Commissioners Appointed to Contract for the Erection of a Bridge over the Oromocto," Records of the Legislative Assembly, PANB, RS 24, 1840/zz/file 4.

[39] Moore, op. cit., p. 55.

tangible testament to their fidelity to King and country.[40] The fe-
cundity of the parcels at the mouth of the Oromocto required
stinginess when new property lines were drawn, and no grantee
(on the east bank at least) received much more than a hundred
acres.

Among those fortunate enough to gain title to land at the
river's mouth was the first of a number of men whose families
over the course of the decades preceding 1870 would experience
all the dishevelments of the locale and ultimately be compelled to
move on. The individual in question was William Carr, a man of
dubious military credentials, though clearly an escapee from the
revolution that had been so disruptive of life throughout the
American colonies.[41] His New England heritage[42] facilitated
friendship with the few older settlers who remained, particularly
with Benan Foster, who was a former rebel and possibly an early
leader of the Oromocto's Baptist community.[43] Contact with Foster brought him into communion with other old settlers, the most
notable of whom was Foster's father-in-law, Israel Kinney. Kinney was one of the blessed few of Porteaus' tenants allowed to
retain at least a portion of their land;[44] quite a surprising fact considering his prominence in Maugerville's rebellious uprising in

---

[40] Moore relates that Porteaus' tenants were not necessarily ejected following escheat. They were extended a period of grace during which re-
application for their lots could occur, otherwise the land would be
granted away to other applicants. See Moore, op. cit., p. 55.

[41] Petition of William Carr (1785) and Petition of Benan Foster et al.
(1788), Land Petitions, PANB, RS 108.

[42] Eugene Campbell, whose facts have been known to be incorrect, has
stated that Carr was from Massachusetts. See his book, *French Lake* (Oromocto: imprint by author, 1981).

[43] New Brunswick Baptist Association, *Minutes of the Meeting of the New
Brunswick Baptist Association* (Saint John: Henry Chubb, 1822). A Benjamin Foster acted as a member of the Association Missionary Committee,
the purpose of which was to deliver "the glorious Gospel of the Blessed
God to many of the destitute settlements throughout the province."
Whether this man was the same as Benan Foster, who eventually settled
in Carlton County, is not immediately clear.

[44] Moore, op. cit., p. 58.

1775.[45] Not long after his arrival, Carr married Kinney's niece, a woman who proved nearly as fertile as the Oromocto's red soil, producing children as regularly as the earth produced its copious reward.

Carr's wife's prolific womb eventually became less a temporary haven for the nascent fruits of pleasure than a source for increasing worry. An extensive account with Hazen and White guarded Carr and his family from the more common plight of the majority of settlers less fortunate to have salvaged something of their former means before coming to live in the residue of British North America.[46] Limitations on the size of his land, however, boded ill, both for his growing family's immediate sustenance, and the legacy they would inherit following Carr's death. He might have moved further upstream to French Lake, thereby following the example of his Foster and Kinney kinsmen, but access to still ungranted parcels in this vicinity had become barred by a desperate band of nameless squatters.[47] With his freedom of movement on the river obstructed, Carr faced a dilemma common among the families of the area, and when discussion of the problem became more general he found himself in sympathetic company. After flames destroyed his home and quite possibly demoted him to the status of a bankrupt, he sold off his valuable yet constrained river-front parcel and, in the company of a group of men in similar straights, removed into the poorly charted wilderness in the rear of the first tract of settled lots. Here they established a new settlement wherein three hundred acre parcels were easily justified on account of the reputed bareness of a country once visited by fire.[48] Carr was the first of the company to proceed into the back-country, where, according to one of his sons, he became the original pioneer of the settlement that, for a

[45] Raymond, op. cit., p. 215.

[46] Hazen and White and Company Records, York/Sunbury Historical Society Collection, PANB, MC 300, M38, files 1-4.

[47] Petition of Benan Foster and William Carr (1788), Land Petitions, PANB, RS 108.

[48] Petition of Benjamin Rockwell et al. (1802), Land Petitions, PANB, RS 108. Reports of the Deputy Surveyors in the 1840s and 1850s confirm the occurrence of fires in this area, as do those of Abraham Gesner.

reason still not entirely clear, came to be known as Geary.[49] Other settlers soon followed, cashing in on a bounty of remaining timber that rapidly grew in value as the years passed and foreign enemies made British commerce with northern Europe a dangerous and expensive exercise. Taking up lots first in Geary and later in an adjacent settlement slightly to the north known as Farnham, William's sons eagerly joined in the scramble for profits in the new industry. When timber berths became subject to competitive bidding, they hastily made their way to Fredericton, where they gained rights to cut pine on a stream called Brizely Brook that originates posterior to Geary in the rolling and then largely unexplored hills of the Oromocto watershed's ultimate frontier.[50]

Among Carr's many grandchildren was Frederick A. Carr, a young man who seems to have tired of the crowded life on the family farm and returned to the mouth of the Oromocto, where he found work in Scoullar's shipyard.[51] Among his co-workers here was James Scovill Frost, whose presence on the river is surprising if only for the reason of his distinguished heritage. He had been born in Kingston, King's County, the son of that noteworthy scourge of the rebels, William Frost.[52] Following his capture by and subsequent escape from the clutches of the rebels, the elder Frost had become a notorious figure of legend and dread, who led raiding parties into the countryside outside the confines of British-held New York and terrorized his former Stamford neighbours to such a degree that his name became anathema in those parts and he himself was forbidden, on pain of death, from ever returning.[53] With his wife, Abigail Scoffield, the keeper of a

---

[49] Petition of William Boone et al. (1810), Land Petitions, PANB, RS 108. The name Geary was a corruption of New Niagara, the origin of which is unclear.

[50] Petition of Edward Carr, SU 1818; Petition of Edward Carr, SU 1819; Petition of Alexander Carr, SU 1819, Timber and Saw Mills, 1817-1865, Timber and Saw Mill Records, RS 663a.

[51] 1851 Census of New Brunswick, Sunbury County.

[52] Will of William Frost (1827), King's County Probate Court Records, PANB, RS 66; King's County Registry Office Records, X1/109, PANB, RS 89; and the Frost Papers, PANB, MC 382, file 2.

[53] Raymond, op. cit., p. 256.

now famous diary, he sired seven children, the fourth of whom was James — named in honour of the Anglican pastor who guided the little Connecticut refugee colony on the Kingston Peninsula in its early years of struggle in the wilderness. While one of his brothers went on to Saint John to make his fortune as a merchant,[54] James stayed with his father, clearing virgin lands and giving every indication that he intended to permanently remain in that vicinity.[55] His father's death in 1827 seemingly released him from any loyalty he had to the parish of his birth and allowed him to journey alone upriver until he came to the Oromocto. What specifically drew Frost here is presently unknown: certainly ship building, with its good pay and relatively distinguished character, were considerations, but so too, it seems, was the presence of a Kingston woman with whom he had spent his childhood. Her heritage obscure, her immediate antecedents uncertain, Abigail Jones is said to have fled her home and family following the onset of a pregnancy conceived out of wedlock. In her wanderings she found herself on the Oromocto's red soil, where she received sympathy and hospitality from Mr. and Mrs. William Carr. A combination of innate good-heartedness and Christian conscience most likely mandated they overlook the inconveniences stemming from their own already unwieldy brood to administer pre-natal and post-partum care to the unfortunate woman and her infant daughter.[56] By the time James S. Frost appeared on the river, Abigail's daughter and the Carr's son, William Jr., lived together as man and wife, while Abigail herself, following at least one additional and equally fruitful liaison, had come to be known by the people of the river as the "Old Tramp Lady." Whatever the attraction may have been that drew him toward her, Frost married

---

[54] Frost Papers, PANB, MC 382, file 2.

[55] Petition of William Secord et al. (1810), Land Petitions, PANB, RS 108.

[56] Frost's wife's story survives to this day in the memories of the people of the Oromocto. The details were related to the author by Geary folklorist and genealogist Allen Boone. Her Kingston origins are attested to by her child's surname, Whelply — a family that closely associated with the Frosts following their settlement in Kingston Parish.

her,[57] and then took up for a time on property Abigail's Carr benefactors had conveyed to her in the trollopy days of her
spinsterhood. Tending a handful of grazing animals[58] and earning
a living in Scoullar's employ, Frost soon confirmed that his wife's
age had depleted neither the fertility of her soil nor the generosity
of her love.

It was on the ruddy earth of the village of Oromocto that the
Frosts' daughter Margaret grew up. Here she attended school and
had as playmates the children of another tenant of the river by the
name of Thomas McMinn.[59] Like Frost, McMinn was not a native
of the Oromocto, but had presumably been drawn there by a
growing shipbuilding industry. His native land was Georgia,
where his father had settled, possibly from Pennsylvania, only to
be driven out in the early stages of the bloody civil war waged in
the back-country of the southern colonies during the first years of
the American Revolution.[60] Seeking vengeance upon his enemies
for their rather rude interruption of his private affairs, the senior
McMinn joined a loyal militia and fought for most of the war, only
to experience the anguish of a surrender made all the more painful by the death of his wife. Left alone to raise his children,
McMinn followed the stream of refugees escaping to British-held
East Florida, where he intended to put together the fragments of
his broken life. When Florida was ceded to Spain, McMinn again
was forced to move, this time forsaking the warm climes of the
south for the colder latitudes of Nova Scotia, where rocky, inhospitable soil, impersonal and unfeeling magistrates and miserly

---

[57] Elizabeth Sewell, *Sunbury County, New Brunswick, Marriages (1766-
1888), Volume One* (imprint by author, 1987), # C461. Stephen Peabody,
the justice of the peace who performed the marriage, however, had the
bothersome habit of reporting the marriages he sealed without mention
of the female spouse's maiden name.

[58] He leased his animals to a Mr. Lawson in 1839. See Sunbury County
Registry, PANB, RS 95, 16/214.

[59] School Returns, General Sessions, Sunbury County Records, PANB,
RS 157, A/2, various years.

[60] Petition of Thomas McMinn (1786), reproduced in Peter Wilson
Coldham's *American Loyalist Claims*, Volume I (Washington: National
Genealogical Society, 1980), pp. 274-276.

task masters made life virtually impossible for him to bear.[61] Even compensation, after several years of desperate petitioning and impatient waiting, did little to relieve him of heavy heart, as he was forced to endure what then might have been considered to be the indignity of accepting land in a tract reserved for Negro settlement.[62] Prosperity was not, however, beyond his grasp; for upon the flinty soil of New Scotland he eventually was able to scratch a living and provide for the future of his children. His son Andrew became a stone mason,[63] while his more bellicose son Hugh made his way as a seafarer and merchant, the proprietor of his own vessel and a licensed privateer in arms against the unprotected foreign mercantile fleets doing business with Napoleanic France.[64] When McMinn died around 1801, his eldest son Andrew inherited most of his remaining legacy, leaving nothing of the fruits of a lifetime of hardship and toil for the enjoyment of his youngest son and namesake.[65] His heritage denied him, the younger Thomas departed for Saint John, where he briefly entertained thoughts of permanent settlement.[66] Failing here to gain title to Crown land, Thomas continued on until he came to the Oromocto.

With neither acquaintances nor family in the area and bereft of financial assets, Thomas McMinn was compelled to earn his bread and board by the sweat of his brow: manning road crews[67] and selling the grass he hayed from his rented lot near the mouth of

---

[61] Petition of Thomas McMinn (1787), Public Archives of Nova Scotia (PANS), RG 5, Series A, Volume 2, no. 90.

[62] Grant to Thomas Young et al. (1787), PANS, RG 1, Volume 373, no. 13 (cross referenced as Book 19, Page 14).

[63] 1827 Census of Nova Scotia, Halifax County, PANS.

[64] Letter of Mark dated September 8, 1800, to the schooner *Sir William Parker*, master Hugh McMinn, in Volume 13 of the *Nova Scotia Historical Society Collections*. Thomas McMinn Sr.'s son, John, also pursued a maritime career.

[65] Thomas McMinn Sr. died intestate. To settle matters, his property was auctioned in 1801.

[66] Petition of Thomas McMinn, Land Petitions, PANB, RS 108.

[67] General Sessions, Sunbury County Records, PANB, RS 157, A/2.

the river.[68] His family's maritime background and his own present proximity to the Oromocto's shipyards hint at his probable employment there in some capacity. When he married, he chose to remain within the bounds of his own Anglican faith through an alliance with Elizabeth Grass. She was the daughter of German expatriate Jacob Grass, who had survived both the bitterness of the Southern Campaign as a member of the New Jersey Volunteers and a failed bid to settle the upper reaches of the Oromocto. Retreating to the river's mouth, Grass had found not only a more pleasing situation on a tract of interval land, but also heartening proofs of his enduring potency through marriage to the pubescent daughter of a fellow Loyalist gentleman by the name of John Mills.

The addition of the venerable New England Mills stock to that of McMinn's via the providential union of Thomas and his Grass bride provided the transplanted Nova Scotian a degree of familial lustre otherwise elusive in those first uncertain days in the watershed. Yet the scars of the late American tumult were hardly absent from the Mills heritage, as pater Mills himself had managed, despite his distinguished roots, to suffer his share of the general privation resulting from revolution and war. When the rebellion flared up in his native Stamford, Connecticut, and suspected Tories were being mercilessly persecuted, Mills had found it expedient to declare his solidarity with the rebels.[69] Governor Tyron's march through the country, however, presented him with the opportunity to flee a conflict that was becoming increasingly disturbing in its overtones and unthinkable in its implications. By 1776 he was safely within the confines of British-held New York and restored to the pastoral care of Stamford's former Anglican minister, the Reverend John Sayre. Here, Mills joined the New Jersey Volunteers, fought throughout the Middle Colonies and took part in the Southern Campaign, during which he suffered imprisonment and the subsequent presumption by his comrades of

---

[68] Hazen and White and Company Records, York/Sunbury Historical Society Collection, PANB, MC 300, MS 38, files 1-4.

[69] E.M. Wicks and V.H. Olson, *Stamford's Soldiers: Genealogical Biographies of Revolutionary War Patriots From Stamford Connecticut Area* (Stamford: Stamford Genealogical Society, 1976).

death in battle.[70] Mustered out of service in New York, he joined Sayre's Stamford emigrant company, afterward settling in Kingston, New Brunswick, upon a sterile lot which he abandoned as soon as Sayre removed to the Oromocto.[71] Following in his spiritual mentor's wake, Mills settled on land below French Lake, where he reasserted his former status as a gentleman, only to run afoul of the irascible James Glenie.[72] He died in the 1830s at an extremely great age, outliving his son-in-law Jacob Grass by several years, undoubtedly convinced of the future viability of his prodigious spawn and able to take some comfort in his progeny's continuing attachment to the river he had come to call home after so many troubling convulsions.

McMinn's marriage was a fruitful one, not only in the sense that it tied him to a vast and well-established network of kinship and extended him a sense of belonging, but also in that his children were many. By the end of the 1830s three of them were parish ratepayers,[73] of whom the youngest, Hugh, was soon to disappear for an immediate destination that perhaps will always remain a mystery. The eldest of McMinn's children was George, a skilled carpenter who probably passed for a time as a shipyard worker. If so, he would have laboured along-side of James Frost, whose daughter he would marry in 1853. His brother Henry and sister Mary Jane exercised greater haste than he in regard to matrimony, as both became espoused by the end of the 1830s. Mary Jane's

---

[70] British Military and Naval Records, Index, Harriet Irving Library (HIL), RG 8, I, Series C; and Murtie June Clark, *Loyalists of the Southern Campaign of the Revolutionary War* (Baltimore: Genealogical Publishing Company, 1981), Volumes 1-3.

[71] Petition of John Mills (1785), Land Petitions, PANB, RS 108.

[72] James Glenie vs. John Mills, 1792/1798 and John Mills vs. Gabriel DeVeber, Supreme Court Case Files, 1784-1822, Supreme Court Records, 1785-1835, PANB, RS 42. Their legal battle dragged on for years, Mills audaciously counter suing Glenie's ally Sheriff Gabriel DeVeber when the later seized his goods by order of the court. His gentlemanly status is attested to in the records of his land sales, wherein he was careful to distinguish himself from the common farmer and yeoman.

[73] General Sessions, Sunbury County Records, PANB, RS 157, A/2/40a (1840).

marriage took place a year later than her brother's, far from the Oromocto in the parish of Brighton, Carleton County.[74] Her betrothed was a restless and voluntary exile by the name of Daniel James Wood. Drawn from his home in Waterborough, Queen's County, Wood exhibited all the traits of flotsam and jetsam in his movements along the St. John River, never knowing real and enduring stability until his final relocation near the American border many years later. His father Moses had been a cooper of the Washedemoack, whose humble status masked an uproarious history as a refugee raider, who rejected the rebellious path of his father and brothers in Westchester County, New York, and remained loyal to the Crown. His father paid a financial penalty for the son's choice, and the son, with his loyal sister Elizabeth and her Loyalist husband Daniel Hoyt, paid the price of exile.[75] They took out leases to adjacent parcels on the same day near Gagetown in 1787, but both eventually moved on: his sister and her family to York County, and Moses himself, after an autumnal marriage to Elizabeth Perry, into the Queen's County hinterland.[76]

Further upstream, some ways from those reaches of the Oromocto more familiar to William Carr, James Frost and Thomas McMinn, is the area known as French Lake. Referred to for convenience sake as a lake, it is in fact merely the deeper portion of a vast swamp fed by a series of smaller tributaries and vernal upwellings. To the east lies the Geary and Rockwell streams, the latter named for one of William Carr's fellow pioneers of Geary Settlement. To the west lies the Rusagonis, a large network of canals, the two main branches of which diverge near the centre of the old Hazen and White ground and disappear into the interior. An intractable wilderness in the 1780s, Hazen and White had

---

[74]George Hayward, *Carleton County, New Brunswick, Marriage Register (1832-1887)*, Volume I (Fredericton: published by author), housed in PANB, MC 80/871.

[75] *Public Papers of George Clinton, First Governor of the State of New York, 1777-1795, 1801-1804*, Volume VI (Albany: J. B. Lyon Company, 1902), at pp. 495-496.

[76] See Queens County Registry Office Records, PANB, RS 92, B-251 and D-445 and Gagetown Parish, Anglican Church Records, sites.rootsweb.com/-nbqueens/gagear.

erected a sawmill here, not far from the Rusagonis' juncture with the Oromocto. The partners employed the mill in the cutting of shingles and ship's timber until selling it, along with half of their enormous land grant, to their kinsman, Stephen Peabody. Not long afterward, in 1807, the Loyalist Thomas Smith erected a second mill on the stream's South West Branch, thus beginning a short and eventful period of more intensive exploitation that resulted, with the aid of the great fires of 1825, not only in the eventual enervation of the mill and the flight of a significant portion of the Smith clan across the Oromocto to Geary, but also the near complete exhaustion of the once rich stands of Rusagonis timber. The sounds of splitting wood during this brief yet lively era became a clarion call to a vast army of lumberjacks from throughout the Oromocto watershed. What remained after the recession of their advance was a swampy interval subject to the steady redemptive deposits by nature of fine arable soil,[77] a process of reclamation that soon encouraged the arrival of settlers long deterred by Hazen and White's monopoly on its now decimated forests. By the 1830s the Rusagonis had become a showplace of well-manicured farms laid out atop and between low rolling hills of long and lazy amplitude.[78]

While Hazen and White had controlled much of the western portion of the central Oromocto's vast wetland, their one-time associate, the elder George Hayward, managed to snatch up a large part of its eastern portion.[79] One of the men Hayward employed in the exploitation of this territory was undoubtedly the young refugee William Boone, son of a Rhode Island Loyalist whose nativity in a township named Kingston seemingly conditioned him to association with the major company of Stamford Loyalists that alit in New Brunswick shortly before the British abandonment of New York City. Not content to remain with his Connecticut friends and comrades at their chosen home on the Kingston Peninsula, the elder Boone moved northward, up the St. John, landing

---

[77] Abraham Gesner, *Fourth Report on the Geological Survey of the Province of New Brunswick*, p. 25.

[78] Ibid.

[79] The George Hayward Collection, PANB, MC 1396, Volume One.

along the shores of Grand Lake,[80] and then attempting to settle the savage country watered by the upper Oromocto. Deterred in this endeavor by the challenges posed by the environment, Boone took the bulk of his family to the Keswick. Remaining behind on the Oromocto were his sons William and Samuel, who apparently summoned the courage and strength to subdue a wilderness that had bested their somewhat more impatient father. Within several years William had so ingratiated himself with old Hayward that he received from him the hand of his daughter and title to several hundred acres of land on the lower side of French Lake.[81] Under Hayward's influence, the Boones gravitated toward the Baptist faith— a process epitomized by the ordination of William's brother James as a minister of the Gospel. In these early years, the bonds between William Boone and others of probable Baptist pretension likewise strengthened, particularly those between himself and William Carr. Thoughtfully observing Carr's successful subjugation of Geary, Boone joined two of Carr's sons (men who would soon become his sons-in-law) in an effort to settle waste lots just east of French Lake.[82] The initial result was not entirely promising, though Boone did succeed in carving out a modest niche of back-country wholly suited to the nourishment of his hopes for a protracted occupation.

Like Carr, William Boone had a large entourage of sons, the oldest of whom were coming into their majority in the first several decades of the nineteenth century. George, the eldest, moved with his father into Geary. While the elder Boone managed to purchase land from earlier settlers, youth and nonexistent savings prevented the younger man from making a similar acquisition.[83]

---

[80] Petition of Simon Loose et al. (1785), Land Petitions, PANB, RS 108.

[81] The George Hayward Collection, PANB, MC 1396, Volume One. Samuel Boone, on the other hand, choose to remain on the North West Branch of the Oromocto, where he became the founder of a rather large branch of the family.

[82] Petition of William Boone et al. (1810), Land Petitions, PANB, RS 108.

[83] Petition of George Boone (1819), Land Petitions, PANB, RS 108. Boone's request for a lot on the northern bound of Geary Settlement was rejected.

Illegal occupation and tenancy were his alternative fates, but as work in the surrounding woods was increasingly plentiful, the limited potential for lawful independence as a yeoman farmer was hardly too upsetting. In the 1830s he lived on a lot in Geary's upper reaches owned, it seems, by one of William Carr's numerous progeny.[84] One of his closest neighbours here was James Till, a Saint John native whose father had experienced both the initial exultant pride and the final despair of Burgoyne's Hudson River Valley campaign.[85] While Till's brother William inherited the estimable portion of their father's legacy — becoming a Baptist pastor in Saint John and the progenitor of a dynasty of printers — James inherited the remnants of their father's degradation.[86] Unable to measure up to the example of his closest kin, James Till departed his place of birth and exiled himself to the Oromocto, where he was not content, it seems, until he had removed as far into the New Brunswick wilderness as possible. His initial effort to settle the Oromocto's North West Branch was aborted,[87] and by some strange coincidence he found himself in Geary, retracing the route taken by William Boone, whose daughter he soon found himself bound to in matrimony.

Directly northwest of the land settled upon by George Boone and James Till is a ridge that juts out just above the upper portion of French Lake Settlement, bounded on the north by the southern perimeter of the lake after which it takes its name. This southern shore is a wide interval, exhibiting soil reminiscent of the ground at the Oromocto's junction with the St. John. In the 1830s it was so highly esteemed as grazing land that people from all over the surrounding countryside brought their cattle and livestock to it

---

[84] Sunbury County Registry Office Records, 12/234, PANB, RS 95.

[85] David Russell Jack, "Biographical Data Relating to New Brunswick Families Especially of Loyalist Descent" (Collation; Saint John: Saint John Free Public Library, 1980).

[86] His son, William Till Jr., oversaw the publication of *The New Brunswicker* during the 1850s and 1860s, and became the author of a prize essay on immigration policy.

[87] Petition of James Till (1810), Land Petitions, PANB, RS 108.

following the annual retreat of the frost.[88] Unmindful of property lines and incapable of common respect, the unthinking beasts abandoned the roads leading to the pastures and invaded the farms and private meadows of the local populace, forcing the latter to erect a gateway to regulate the entry of grazing animals to the lush meadows beyond. The Acadians had been the first to come to the area and build homes, the sunken basements of which have since become the petty finds of amateur archaeologists.[89] These original French inhabitants had abruptly departed and their buildings were presumably torched by a patrol under Colonel Arbuthnot's unsteady command as a prelude to the English settlement of Maugerville and the rest of the St. John River Valley in the years preceding the American Revolution.[90] By the time the Loyalists arrived the evidence of the Acadian presence had nearly disappeared under several layers of sediment deposited by the spring freshets, giving the first prospective Loyalist settlers of the area the impression that it was an overgrown wilderness little changed since time immemorial.

The first English settlers here were in fact less English in origin than German. Martin Oltz and Elias Faus could each recall homes in Germany: the former most likely in Hesse, the latter in Waldeck.[91] Rented out by their respective masters to the King of England in that monarch's improbable quest to subdue his rebellious American colonies, both Oltz and Faus came to North America as mercenaries charged with the waging of a war the details and genesis of which, from their perspective, were completely irrelevant. Oltz had suffered grave injury as a result of the conflict, forcing him to rely on the patronage and protection of New Jersey-born aristocrat Lawrence Van Buskirk.[92] When Van Buskirk quit the Province, Oltz sedulously aspired to end his own wanderings and took up with Faus and a disbanded member of

---

[88] Petition of John Foss et al., General Sessions, Sunbury County Records, PANB, RS 157, A/2/32 (1832).

[89] E. Campbell, op. cit., p. 27.

[90] See Raymond, op. cit., p. 125-6.

[91] Petition of Elias Faus et al. (1787), Land Petitions, PANB, RS 108.

[92] Petition of Martin Oltz (1785), Land Petitions, PANB, RS 108.

the King's American Regiment by the name of Nathaniel Howe for the purpose of advancing their common desire for land. The alliance was a natural one, not only because of the ethnic affinity of Oltz and Faus, but also because of the sympathy the three men had for each other's misfortune.[93] Together, they explored the Oromocto, in the course of which they discovered, on the southeast side of French Lake the vague remains of the old Acadian clearing. More inclined to place security above independence and haste before clearly demarcated property lines, the three men erected their cabins in suffocating proximity to one another.[94] Lacking influence, either in the newly organized county government or the amorphous bureaus of the equally nascent provincial administration, basic relief in the form of planks, shingles and items of clothing to ease their initial privation was not forthcoming.[95] Oltz soon abandoned his lot, leaving his son to sell to Faus his share of a six hundred acre grant to which he and his two comrades had received collective title.[96] The irritation Howe felt over the selectivity of Oltz's conveyance, which may well have been based solely on ethnic loyalties, was natural, if not justified, and further compounded his probable sense of aggravation stemming from his recognition of the ill-advisedness of his location-- a recognition renewed each time he surveyed it and saw nothing but a vast wetland.

Howe's initially poor judgement rapidly gave way to technical ingenuity and agricultural savvy. Aided by what remained of the prior efforts of unknown French-speaking benefactors, Howe cleared some twenty-five acres, purchased cows, sheep and pigs in the space of five short years and then managed to convince the government of his just claim to an adjacent lot containing

---

[93] Oltz himself had been denied land on grounds of the prior claims of others, while Faus and Howe had had the bad luck to take an interest in land that had already attracted the speculative fancy of George Hayward.

[94] A surveyor's plan accompanying the Petition of Elias Faus et al. (1787) indicates the close proximity of the cabins the men constructed.

[95] Petition of Elias Faus (1785), Land Petitions, PANB, RS 108.

[96] Sunbury County Registry Office Records, 12/51, PANB, RS 95.

hundreds of additional acres.[97] His desire to possess the vacant land was as much the result of spite as it was of pure ambition. Yet while his ambition brought him success, it also inspired the revulsion of his neighbours, one of whom found it all too easy to accuse him of malicious conspiracy in the suspicious deaths of several prize animals.[98]

Like others along the river, Howe was eventually lured into pursuit of the wavering riches to be found in the timber trade. And as others overextended themselves in this venture and entered the ken of financial turmoil, so too it seems did Howe. By 1823 mounting debts had compelled him to sell virtually all of his extensive land holdings. So desperate did he become in his old age that he was forced to bait his son-in-law, James Mills, with the entirety of his remaining estate as a means of assuring proper accommodation for himself and his equally aged wife.[99] The fact that the terms of the agreement rather unfairly impelled Mrs. Howe to labour for her keep led her to depart with her husband's war pension following Nathaniel's death to more hospitable quarters occupied by her son John in Maugerville.[100] Her eldest son, Nathaniel Jr., had already passed away, having first been driven to a desperate search for vacant land on the upper Oromocto following his father's bankruptcy. Another son, George, still lived, but his station as a menial labourer employed by the local magnates at the river's mouth hardly bespoke well of his fortunes. Of all the Howe sons, only William remained in French Lake, dissembling his disappointment over a nonexistent inheritance and living on the bounty and land of others until, in the following decade, he would finally brave the wilderness and begin life as a proprietor with his wife, children and the gratifying if delusory

---

[97] Petition of Nathaniel Howe (1790), Land Petitions, PANB, RS 108.

[98] William Crandlemire vs. Nathaniel Howe, 1823, Supreme Court Case Files, 1823-1835, Supreme Court Records, 1785-1835, PANB, RS 42.

[99] Sunbury County Registry Office Records, 12/69-71, PANB, RS 95.

[100] Petition of John Howe, Records of the Legislative Assembly, PANB, RS 24, 1847/pe/file 2/no. 54. John, by the way, had for some time been employed as a trusted hand by Assemblyman Thomas O. Miles. In his diary, Miles had occasion to mention Howe's activities, most of which related to the upkeep of the Miles properties.

title of "colonel," the exact origin of which remains, to this day, unknown. Following him in this direction would be John Howe, an American national who seems to have been drawn to the Oromocto by the one-time prosperity of his expatriate Howe relations.[101] Dubbed "Yankee John" by his neighbours to distinguish him from several others bearing his name, John Howe made his home in Geary, where he warmed up to and probably rented a house from members of the expansive Boone clan.[102] Proximity with the Boones gave him access to a bevy of nubile young Boone women, one of whom he not surprisingly married before making his way into the lonely uplands watered by a small tributary of Brizley Brook, named to commemorate his short-lived and ill-fated occupation of that country.

The Howes' sad fall from grace and the privileges that come from a wealth in excess of subsistence contrasted sharply with the enduring bounty of the meadow lands further upstream. Originally granted to a group of disinterested Shelburne speculators, the land had long lain fallow, soggy and unkempt, subject to seasonal invasion by a wide array of wildfowl and finally, it seems, to escheat. Its commercial potential had once been recognized by none other than James Glenie, and it was only the temperamental Assemblyman's truculent relations with the Lieutenant Governor at the time that barred the establishment here of a large and potentially lucrative cattle ranch.[103] In the more tranquil and settled days of the 1830s, inhabitants from either extremity of the river brought their herds to its rich ground, some even going so far as to travel to Fredericton in order to negotiate leases on meadow lands for more or less exclusive use.

Wild grass grew lush here even in the most dry of seasons,

---

[101] No outright proof of Yankee John Howe's kinship with the French Lake Howe's has yet surfaced, but the likelihood that there was a connection is great given the coincidence of his settlement along the Oromocto.

[102] His residence in Geary at this time and afterward is attested to in the statute labour returns in the General Sessions, Sunbury County Records, PANB, RS 157, A/2.

[103] See W.G. Godfrey, "James Glenie," *Dictionary of Canadian Biography* (Toronto: University of Toronto Press, 1983), Volume V, pp. 348-9.

attracting in these times grazing animals from an even wider radius of country. Twenty miles upstream these extensive meadows begin to narrow and are bisected by an invisible line drawn by the surveyors of the Crown Land Office in 1834 to mark the boundary between the older Parish of Burton and the newly partitioned one named Blissville.[104] Beyond the demarcation line, the narrowing of the meadow lands intensifies, particularly as the forks marking the juncture of the North West and South Branches of the Oromocto are approached. To the east lay the outlet of Brizley Brook, down which the Carr brothers had driven logs in the early years of the timber craze, and down which others presently continued that precipitous ordeal. To the west lay a maze of eddies and channels-- the outlines and guardians of a series of grassy islands, at the base of which was the shore known as Pride's Landing. Named for a humble bookkeeper who had migrated to the area from Gagetown after the coming of the Loyalists, the Landing was once the location of a small shipyard, where local woodsmen and carpenters constructed timber rafts, canoes and even small schooners.[105]

As indicated by its name, the North West Branch of the Oromocto flows toward the forks along a northwest course. Punctuated by rapids which increase in frequency as the river nears its source, it had been the scene of a series of ancient fires that left the low interval on its southern bank largely defoliated and charred. The first Loyalist settlers of the river found the scorched countryside a depressing sight, while its anthracitic-looking soil, free of the insulating cover of the forest's luxuriant growth, proved hospitable only to the frosts that visited the region each year with frightening prematurity.[106] A second fire had ravaged the north bank of the river in 1825, destroying numerous homes and livestock and exposing something of the slate and carboniferous limestone so long hidden beneath shrub, tree and a

---

[104] "Bill to Divide the Parishes of Lincoln and Burton," Records of the Legislative Assembly, PANB, RS 24, 1834/bi/file 3/no. 15.

[105] Katherine DeWitt and Norma Alexander, *Days of Old: A History of Fredericton Junction* (Fredericton: Sunbury West Historical Society, 1987), p. 16.

[106] Petition of Solomon Tracy (1811), Land Petitions, PANB, RS 108.

decaying membrane of branches and leaves. A sallow ridge followed the course of the river on this northern bank, drooping into the interior with a precarious crown formed by the blackened remains of several species of conifers. A melancholy and ghostly reminder of the beauty that in earlier days had been a source of enchantment for traveler and inhabitant alike,[107] the fire-scarred country haunted two reconstructed settlements that had shared its incendiary fate.

Hartt's Mills was the first of these settlements. Its founder, Thomas Hartt, bore the woeful burden of a rumour that it had been men in his employ who had inadvertently sparked the flames that had brought so much ruination to the land and its inhabitants.[108] Many years before, Hartt had left his birth-place in Maugerville with the intention of constructing a mill that nurtured the distant promise of allowing him to wrest economic dominance from the magnates stationed closer to the river's mouth. Preeminence along the Oromocto was not to be, but as the Rusagonis relinquished its riches, Hartt managed to become a regular supplier of timber and lumber for use at the Hazens' shipyard.[109] Satisfying the demands of shipbuilders also had the effect of ingratiating him with the poor, who flocked to the banks all along the river's length to salvage the slabs his sawyers carelessly flung aside.[110] His generosity was wholly unintended, and certainly it did little to benefit the quality of life of the alewives

---

[107] Abraham Gesner, *Fourth Report on the Geological Survey of the Province of New Brunswick*, p. 71.

[108] Miriam L. Phillips, *Tracy and the Little Lake Area: Facts and Folklore* (Imprint by author, 1985), p.1.

[109] Hazen and White and Company Records, York/Sunbury Historical Society Collection, PANB, MC 300, MS 38, files 1-4.

[110] Hartt complained to the Assembly that refuse from Tracy's Mills was filling up his millpond, but the fact that a number of people upstream from him simultaneously requested the Assembly not to pass a law preventing such dumping indicates that Hartt, whose mill was further downstream, was also making a practice of it. See Petition of the Inhabitants of Sunbury and Petition of the Mill Owners of Blissville, Records of the Legislative Assembly, PANB, RS 24/1840/pe/file 6/nos. 209-210.

and gaspereau that had traditionally sustained the existence of their species in waters now choked with sawdust and barricaded by a nearly impermeable mill dam. Concern for the environment and the continued feasibility of supplementing spare rural liveli-hoods through fishing sparked debate throughout the watershed. Old men, recalling the days before the arrival of Hartt, told tales of the convergence of as many as eighty fishing boats, each trav-ersing the waters with net and rod and returning fully loaded to moorings at places as far away as Fredericton. Prompted by the soulful reminiscing of the aged, protests against the carelessness of Hartt's operation and demands that a sluiceway be constructed to allow fish to pass to their spawning ground in distant Great Oromocto Lake were lodged with the Court of General Ses-sions.[111] Aggravated by popular pressure and subjected to an inquisition at the Burton Court House, Hartt responded favoura-bly,[112] and thereby gained the admiration of Dr. Abraham Gesner, who passed through the country during the latter part of the dec-ade while conducting his famous geological survey. Ignorant of Hartt's earlier recalcitrance, Gesner could only judge the man by the fruits of his recent corrective labours, inviting him afterward to peer into his microscope to view the ancient remains of long-extinct flora he had found in the barrow Hartt's men had erected in the process of their excavation.[113]

Hartt's great rival on the river was Jeremiah Tracy, after whom the second casualty of the 1825 fire, Tracy Settlement, took its name. Tracy and his brothers Jonathan, Israel and Solomon had come to the North West Branch in 1802, apparently at the behest of their father. A strong-willed, domineering man, the elder Tracy

---

[111] Petition of the Inhabitants of the North and South Branches of the Oromocto, Sunbury County Council General Sessions, PANB, RS 157, A/2/33a (January, 1833).

[112] The King vs. Thomas Hartt, Sunbury County Council General Ses-sions, PANB, RS 157, A/2/35 (January 1835) and Sunbury County Council Minutes, RS 157, A/1/3 (1830-37). Jeremiah Tracy was likewise charged and convicted, the people of the river coming out in droves to testify against them.

[113] Abraham Gesner, *First Report on the Geological Survey of the Province of New Brunswick* (Saint John: Henry Chubb, 1839), pp. 70-71.

had shirked his kinfolk's conformity with the cause of rebellion in an act of defiance that cost him his home in Goldsboro, Maine. But while he forsook the privilege of remaining in his native country, Tracy earned the gratitude of his King, who, through his minions, granted him land near the Oromocto. Legend ascribes to him a sawmill here,[114] and the legend find some confirmation in the accounts of Hazen, White and Company.[115] Prosperity in business in time proved no match for the bounty stemming from his loins, hence his probable encouragement of his maturing sons to depart from the river's mouth. Hazen and White's stranglehold on the Rusagonis prevented immediate settlement in that direction, thus the Tracy brothers made their way to the North West Branch, mindful that the land there, though partially burnt, could be justifiably petitioned for in large quantities. The brothers were correct in their assumption, as they quickly gained title between them to over one thousand acres. Later purchases expanded the amount of land in the family's possession; and when the great boom in timber occurred and the success Hartt was having in culling the unscorched forest along nearby tributaries was too obvious to ignore, young Jeremiah Tracy began, with the help of outside investment,[116] to construct a mill of his own.[117] No sooner was the mill completed than the fire of 1825 destroyed it, forcing him to cultivate a habit of borrowing for the purpose of rebuilding his demolished enterprise that would grow to such obscene proportions that he became the subject of countless lawsuits aimed at retrieving delinquent loans.[118]

---

[114] C. Tracy McFarland, "Genealogy of the Tracy Family" (typescript by author, 1966).

[115] Hazen and White and Company Records, York-Sunbury Historical Society Collection, MC 300, MS 38, files 1-4.

[116] Sunbury Country Registry Office Records, PANB, RS 95, 11/433. The investment came from George P. Nevers, a son of Assemblyman Samuel Nevers and a distant relation of Assemblyman George Hayward.

[117] Id., 11/431. Dated July 30, 1821, the deed records that Jeremiah had already erected the frame to his saw mill on his brother Jonathan's land.

[118] See Supreme Court Case Files, 1785-1835, Supreme Court Records, 1785-1835, PANB, RS 42.

Despite his tumultuous beginnings, Tracy prospered. His prosperity came as a result of the expanding traffic in deals-- an occurrence that commenced just as he began his operations and continued through the decade of the 1830s. As Hartt had gone beyond the main course of the North West Branch, so too did Tracy, who competed with his rival for reserves on such streams as the Yoho and Lyon. When travelling through the district, Gesner found every rivulet flowing into the upper North West Branch a testament to the efforts of the two men and others like them. Each minor stream and creek was interrupted by sluices and dams, reposing like apparitions in a landscape devoid of human inhabitants. The absence of a sustained human presence here was a sad sight, redeemed, in Gesner's mind, only by the hope that one day, when the lumbermen had cleared the country of all its arboreal cover, true civilization might come to the valley, populating it with a race of hardy mechanics and miners employed in the operation of textile mills and entrusted with the task of unearthing the vast mineral wealth thought to be buried beneath successive layers of sawdust and ash.[119] Small outcropping of coal and ornamental porphyry formed the basis of this never to be realized vision, a vision the people of the region entertained no doubt with a mixture of wonderment and scoff. Everyone knew that timber was the only treasure of this forsaken country, and as each year passed lumber crews moved further into the interior until, finally, they tumbled into the basin of Great Oromocto Lake. Flanked on the south by a ridge of hills that formed the Magagaudavic divide, the lake possessed such unrivalled stands that even crews in the employ of lumbermen from over a narrow portage road leading to distant St. Andrew's and the Bay of Fundy began, in the 1830s, to be attracted by its prospects for profit.

East of the southern bend of the Oromocto's North West Branch lay a vast uninhabited district, much of the lumber on which was beyond easy conveyance by water or beast of burden. For many miles this wilderness extends, rocky and mountainous, until it terminates abruptly on the narrow interval of the west bank of the South Branch Stream. Here, stretching from the point

---

[119] Abraham Gesner, *First Report on the Geological Survey of the Province of New Brunswick*, p. 71.

at which the stream joins the main course of the Oromocto to a place many miles southward, lay South Branch Settlement, a collection of some 160 farms. Flanked on either side by steep ridges, the settlement had been nurtured by the valley's rich soil, the discovery of shells in which were thought to be proof of the existence of an ancient inland sea that had once covered the entire South Branch lowlands. The settlement was a prosperous one, and though its people fervently clung to a belief in the magical properties of the divining rod and frequently sped into the surrounding forest in search for hidden caches of treasures rumoured to have been deposited there by their ancestors, it preserved a reputation for the otherwise solid virtues of peace and good government.[120] Anglicanism was virtually unheard of here, as the missionaries of the established church felt disinclined to leave the relative certainty of life in the fractious spiritual community of Maugerville. In the resultant spiritual vacuum, the Baptists had made great inroads, winning souls with steady and inspired preaching, but visiting all too infrequently to satisfy the cravings of the local spirit. While some of the people of the North West Branch marked their allegiance to a newly adopted Calvinist creed in the formation of a congregation not far from Hartt's mill, the people of the South Branch wandered blindly in the wilderness before finally embracing the liberating message of the Free Willers, whose evangelical tours in the area are attested to only by the warnings of more mainstream dissenters.[121] With no regular conference to either gauge their beliefs or appeal to for regular and irregular preachers of the Gospel, the spirit of the Lord moved over the face of the waters of the river, inspiring men of more indigenous origins to take up the mantle of the Levites and lead the people in the rebuilding of the fallen temple. Imagining perhaps that his name was a secret indication that he was the chosen one to minister to the wayward flock, the Irish-born Loyalist Levi Parsons accepted the onus of a spiritual calling and became the first known permanent Free Will Baptist pastor of the South

---

[120] Abraham Gesner, *Fourth Report on the Geological Survey of the Province of New Brunswick*, p. 25.

[121] Bill, op. cit., p. 137.

Branch.[122] In the fashion of the Levite-sprung prophet Moses, Parsons expired before his people could fully enter into the promised land of faith, but no sooner had his bones been put to rest in 1838 than did a formal meeting house rise under the direction of the itinerant Reverend Boone.[123]

The origin of the South Branch's peaceful and attractive settlement lay, rather ironically, in the disorderly arrival of the Loyalists. Finding the lower sections of the Oromocto under occupation, aspiring settlers, most of whom had failed in their efforts to gain title to land elsewhere in the province, began to accept the imperative of a more thorough exploration of the river. The first to brave a reconnaissance of the upper Oromocto was John Mersereau, a Staten Island Loyalist who had led a refugee company to the city of St. John and was himself soon to become a Justice of the Peace of Sunbury County.[124] Accompanied by Dr. Joseph Clark, Mersereau journeyed upstream via canoe, passing the forks and entering the South Branch. Perhaps taking a tip from Israel Perley, who had traveled through the area two decades earlier on his way to survey the future site of Maugerville, the two men focused their attention on a thin band of interval on the stream's west bank. Upon their return to the mouth of the river, word of the arableness of the South Branch spread infectiously to several of Clark's fellow Connecticut refugees. Led by James Scoffield, they made an inspection tour of their own — a tour that resulted in their laying claim to a tract adjacent to the one explored by Mersereau.[125] Threatened by a desperate bid from a small band of provincials commanded by Sergeant Hezekiah Wyatt, Scoffield's party succeeded in convincing sympathetic magistrates of the justness of their cause, thus winning recognition of their prior occupation, as well as the now germinating seeds the interlopers had sown in their haste to perpetrate their

---

[122] Sharon Knorr, "Hoyt Pioneer Cemetery," PANB, MC 80/642. Upon Parsons' death in 1838, Clapman Smith Jr. took over duties as pastor.

[123] Records of the Patterson Baptist Church, PANB, F8114.

[124] John Wood, "John Mersereau, Loyalist," *Generations*, no. 32 (June, 1987), pp. 28-34.

[125] Petition of James Scoffield et al. (1785), Land Petitions, PANB, RS 108.

fraud.

Among the members of the Scoffield party was Solomon Tucker, a Stamford native who, like other Stamford settlers of the Oromocto, had bypassed Kingston, where the majority of their former neighbours had settled.[126] Tucker had served in the King's American Regiment under the immediate command of Sergeant Wyatt, an experience that certainly must have weighed heavily upon him as he, Scoffield and the others fought to secure the sergeant's ejection from their chosen tract. With Wyatt's expulsion, Tucker seems to have developed an ambivalence that slowly resolved into a sense of alienation, engendering perhaps the thought that the prize had less value when possessed than when merely desired. Quitting his land, Tucker repentantly joined his former sergeant and several other one-time members of the King's American in an exploratory survey of prospective farmland. Wyatt's party retreated further upstream, pressing on until they came to a suitable location some thirty miles from the main river's juncture with the St. John. As it was spring, the men eagerly set to work clearing their land of obstacles to more uniform cultivation, planted seed, and won the recommendation of their former commander, Colonel Abraham DePeyster.[127] Taking advantage of the initial vulnerability of the party's claim was a man named William Smith, who accused them of stealing his improvements, forced a court of inquiry and then arranged matters so as to conveniently exclude his antagonists from attendance. Wyatt's fierce rejoinder following the meeting caught the attention of Surveyor General George Sproul, who, upon a review of the facts, could not help but rule in Wyatt's favour. For this Wyatt, Tucker and the others expressed thanks, but Tucker himself would not long enjoy the fruits of the Surveyor General's benevolence. Already a mature man at the time of his arrival in the province, he died in the first decade of the nineteenth century.

After his demise, Solomon Tucker's sons sold their father's land and ran off in search of more definite prospects elsewhere on

---

[126] Lorenzo Sabine, *Biographical Sketches of Loyalists of the American Revolution* (Reprint; Port Washington, New York: Kemikat Press, 1966).

[127] Petition of Hezekiah Wyatt et al. (1785), Land Petitions, PANB, RS 108.

the river. By the late 1830s Solomon Jr. was apparently dead, having spent his days pawning apples to John Hazen,[128] sleeping in the Burton gaol[129] and living off the charity of friends.[130] After a brief attempt to gain title to Crown land,[131] Solomon Jr.'s brother Robert may have settled on the demesne of his father-in-law Stephen Buckingham. In the 1830s, however, Robert too apparently died, leaving in the wake of his departure several children, including a son William, who seems to have divided his time between French Lake and South Branch, working, no doubt, as a hired hand for one or more of the river's major lumbermen.[132] While in French Lake, William married Lydia Mills, granddaughter of John Mills and widow of Nathaniel Howe Jr.[133] It was not the most advantageous of alliances, as it forced him to take in a collection of fatherless children whose surname he did not deign to change, but for whose upkeep he was indefinitely responsible. Nor did he deign to alter the state of the wilderness, as he forsook the improvements his new wife's late husband had been in the process of making at the time of his death, thus leaving behind their overgrown and rotting remnants as a doleful reward for desperate Irish emigrants.[134]

---

[128] Hazen and White and Company Records, York/Sunbury Historical Society Collection, PANB, MC 300, MS 38, files 1-4.

[129] Draft Minutes, 1830-1837, Sunbury County Records, PANB, RS 157, A/1/1.

[130] Ralph Jarvis vs. Solomon Tucker, 1833, Supreme Court Case Files, 1823-1835, Supreme Court Records, PANB, RS 42. Given tenancy on a lot his "beloved friend" Richard Fenn had purchased from Jarvis, Tucker benefited from the misfortune of Jarvis' former tenant John Dew, whom Fenn had illegally evicted.

[131] Petition of Robert Tucker (1812) and Petition of William Smith et al. (1815), Land Petitions, PANB, RS 108.

[132] General Sessions, Sunbury County Records, PANB, RS 157, A/2. Tucker's name appears on a number of French Lake statute labour lists during the early 1830's.

[133]George H. Hayward, *York County, New Brunswick, Marriage Register, Volume One: 1812-1837-- A transcription of the original* (Fredericton: published by author, 1986).

[134] Petition of Arthur Connally (1839), Land Petitions, PANB, RS 108.

Just below the grant to Wyatt and his associates was a tract of land that once had been the possession of the Honourable Philip Livingston, at least until its proprietor decided to shed himself of the burden of obedience to the Crown, on which occasion the land was escheated. As if responding innately to the removal of its rebellious former owner, a strange menagerie of Loyalist refugees resolved to settle it. Chief among them was Everet DeWitt, a scion of a distinguished Dutch family of New York that counted Old World military heroes and New World explorers among its ranks. Several of his sons fought in the war — one as a member of the King's American, another with the New Jersey Volunteers. Everet himself hadn't enlisted in a formal regiment, being perhaps too old, but when the city of New York became subject to piratical attacks he joined a longboat company and cruised the waters around Staten Island with ever watchful vigilance.[135] His first attempt to settle in New Brunswick ended disappointedly, yet when his comrades in failure, the Boones, made their way to the Oromocto, he obligingly followed suit.[136] A complex tangle of attachments, acquaintances and friendships led him and his sons into contact with the Stamford Seelys and Southern Campaign veteran Jacob Grass.[137] Together they ventured to the South Branch, where the claims of several members of their company were disqualified by an unusually methodical agent of the Crown.

Everet DeWitt was among those fortunate enough to gain title to South Branch land, but the struggle to acquire it was hardly any more taxing than the struggle to improve it. His industry, however, allowed him the luxury of an account with Hazen and White, compelling frequent travels downstream to purchase supplies.[138] During one such journey Everet, along with his son John, met an untimely end as the boat they were travelling in

---

[135] DeWitt and Alexander, op. cit., p. 49.

[136] Petition of Simon Losee et al. (1785), Land Petitions, PANB, RS 108.

[137] Petition of Everet DeWitt et al. (1785), Petition of Everet DeWitt et al (1786), Land Petitions, PANB, RS 108.

[138] Hazen and White Papers, Collections of the York/Sunbury Historical Society, MC 300.

capsized.[139] John DeWitt left a widow and seven children, all of whom were charitably taken in by his father-in-law, former King's American corporal Charles Durose.[140] One of the seven eventually went to French Lake, where the upkeep of a hotel became his custom in life.[141] Son Charles, on the other hand, remained with his mother and eventually inherited a portion of her estate. Included in his inheritance was his father's former property and a parcel of land once owned by his maternal grandfather encompassing the upper portion of Back Creek. Young Charles DeWitt's virtues were many, and these undoubtedly allowed him to win the confidence of his peers, as well as repeated election to a variety of parish posts.[142] The great prize of Justice of the Peace eluded him, but success in the timber business did not. Borrowing money from William Scoullar, DeWitt extended his operations onto a berth purchased from the government, hired men to work it and reaped moderate profits as a result.[143]

As Charles DeWitt expanded his activities he began to accumulate additional holdings. One such holding formerly belonged to Abigail Anderson, the sister of his late mother.[144] Prior to her inheritance of a portion of her father's estate, Abigail had married a mysterious man by the name of John Anderson, who may have been a member of the King's American Regiment, but whose date of arrival on the Oromocto is unknown. Anderson settled on a lot opposite DeWitt, and having cleared it, passed it on to his like-named son following his own premature death. When Robert Tucker attempted to usurp title to the land, John Anderson Jr. had

---

[139] DeWitt and Alexander, op. cit., p. 49.

[140] Ibid.

[141] Moore, op. cit., p. 150.

[142] General Sessions, Sunbury County Records, PANB, RS 157, A/2.

[143] His dependence on Scoullar for capital to fund his activities is indicated several places, notably in a judgement against him for 410 pounds in 1840. See Sunbury County Registry, 16/365, PANB, RS 95. In 1835 he purchased a license to cut a specific number of tons per annum. See *Journals of the Legislative Assembly (1838), Appendix 3.*

[144] Abigail's paternity is implied in her joint sale with Phebe Durose to Phebe's son Luke of one of Charles Durose's original grants. See Sunbury County Registry, 11/459, PANB, RS 95.

little choice but to appeal to the magistrates at the Court of General Sessions to vouch for his family's just right to retain it.[145] Finding protection for his claim in the comforting embrace of patronage, Anderson possessed little additional means of sheltering himself and his kin from the chilling effects of poverty. However, when the merchants and lumberman of the Oromocto began in the 1830s to contemplate the untapped commercial possibilities of the upper watershed, reason for entertaining a more optimistic outlook suddenly presented itself. Recognizing the advantages of a mill to process timber severed from the vast and unexploited hinterland of the South Branch, William Scoullar moved to make arrangements to construct the much-needed edifice just beyond the furthermost point of settlement. As Scoullar moved, so too did Anderson, who sold his improved land to his kinsman, Charles DeWitt, and took up on a small parcel hemmed in between a bend in the river and a large lumber tract originally owned by DeWitt's brother John.[146]

Anderson's move onto the South Branch frontier did not occur in the absence of company. Moving with him, with a slightly higher degree of initiative, was another old family of the river, the Buckinghams. Like Solomon Tucker and Charles Durose, Stephen Buckingham had served under Hezekiah Wyatt in the King's American Regiment. Not long afterward, he married Wyatt's daughter; and when Wyatt died in the early 1800s, it was Buckingham who was entrusted with administering the deceased's estate on behalf of Buckingham's son William, whom Wyatt had designated its soul beneficiary. While conducting the duties incumbent upon a Surveyor of Highways in a district seemingly avulsed from the main currents of civilization by the engulfing tide of the forest,[147] Buckingham supplemented his income with periodic forays onto his son's inevitable inheritance for the purpose of harvesting timber.[148] Sanctioned by the provisions of his

---

[145] Petition of John Anderson (1812), Land Petitions, PANB, RS 108.

[146] Sunbury County Registry Office Records, 16/157, PANB, RS 95.

[147] General Sessions, Sunbury County Records, PANB, RS 157, A/2.

[148] Will of Hezekiah Wyatt (1807), Sunbury County Probate Court Records, PANB, RS 72.

father-in-law's will, his depredations did little to lift him and his family out of the ranks of the rural poor, though some consolation must have come from the unoppressiveness of his civil obligations in the form of a minimal rate of tax.[149] When finally coming of age, William Buckingham fared better than did his father, as he inherited the Wyatt farm and built up an economic base that eventually qualified him for the franchise. Dissatisfied with their own inheritance following Stephen's death, William's siblings began to give signals that a move upstream, beyond the mill-site contemplated by William Scoullar, was an increasingly attractive option. As early as 1832, Stephen's son Solomon purchased a portion of John DeWitt Jr.'s old lumber lot[150] and embarked upon an attempt to convince the rest of his clan of the rewards to be gained by the total divestment of old Stephen's legacy. In this Solomon was successful. In 1838, the land was sold and the clan, accompanied no doubt by the surviving Tuckers, completed its relocation to the upper limits of settlement beyond Scoullar's now operative mill.[151] Of the children of Stephen Buckingham still living on the river, only daughter Deborah declined to move. She remained, for the time being, with her husband William Howe at French Lake.

In the rear of the small settlement now begun by the heirs of Charles Durose, John Anderson, Hezekiah Wyatt and Stephen Buckingham, lay what must have appeared to them the veritable end of the earth. Impassable, intractable and virtually unexplored, the forest that lay beyond their emerging homesteads still awaited the day when the adventurous spirit of risk would steal the heart of some as yet unsuspecting entrepreneur. Continuing prosperity in the 1830s, enduring demand for wood products and the erection of a mill at the very doorstep of the great forest empire of the upper portion of the river basin were all encouraging signs that the imposing wall barring entry would finally be breached and the rich palaces within ransacked of their treasure. But even to think of doing so now imposed heavily upon the mind and strained the imaginations of the most enthusiastic of men. Wild, obstructed channels, unnavigable even by canoe, prohibited easy

---

[149] General Sessions, Sunbury County Records, RS 157, A/2.

[150] Sunbury County Registry Office Records, 14/479, PANB, RS 95.

[151] Id., 16/21.

movement, while roads through the district were nonexistent. Those who had caught even the vaguest glimpse of the lake at the furthest end of the watershed across the county line in Charlotte were no doubt few, and surely none had yet dared cut wood upon its pristine shores. The day was fast approaching, though, when the feat would be accomplished, and when it was it would strain the entire community of the river from the South Branch all the way to the village of Oromocto, causing strife and disjuncture on many fronts and pitting settlement against settlement. More important than any conflict that would arise would be the long-term implications the opening of the South Branch would have on the fortunes of the people who lived along the greater river's course. South Branch Lake represented the last great lumbering frontier of the Oromocto, and once it was gone the bonds of attachment holding settlers firmly to the river would loosen, a process that could be slowed but not prevented by the movement of timber activity into the hinterland away from the river's main waters. In the decade of the 1840s, this would begin to occur, and life on the river, particularly for the families of Anderson, Boone, Buckingham, Carr, DeWitt, Frost, Howe, McMinn, Till, Tucker, and Wood, all of whom had in one way or another become largely dependent on the prosperity of the timber industry, would never again be the same.

# Chapter Two

## ENTREPRENEURIALISM & EXPLOITATION

While the 1830s were a period of relative stability and peace, conflict characterized the Oromocto community during the 1840s. Following the removal of most of the watershed's best timber, competition erupted not only between individual settlers, but between the river's major entrepreneurs as well. Institutions such as the Anglican Mission, the Free Will Baptist Church and the Court of General Sessions, a unifying geography and common participation by the River's inhabitants in a timber-oriented economy continued to act as cement to the larger river community, but cracks in the solidarity among both its members and leaders in this tumultuous era quickly developed, spawning bitter controversies over shrinking resources that would rage throughout most of the decade. Strife flared up throughout the entire watershed, but nowhere did the major contenders exhibit more enmity than on the South Branch, where the River's last great repository of timber lay yet unharvested. It was over the question of who would control the flow of timber on this stream that the great defining battle of the decade would be fought, giving added impetus to the formation of factions and providing a group of reputed reformers led Thomas O. Miles and George Hayward with the quintessence of corruption in the person of William Scoullar.

The tribulations arising from competition over diminishing resources and political leadership were severely compounded by a series of debilitating depressions and crop failures that had the effect of limiting capital, lowering employment levels, devaluing wages and making life on the River increasingly difficult, if not less viable. Though much of the best timber had been extracted from the South Branch, and though the more benevolent and beneficial aspects of free enterprise seemed stunted as a result of the emergence of George Morrow as the River's dominant patron, a degree of stability, if not prosperity, returned by the end of the decade. Despite this stabilization, a large segment of the River's people, convinced of the obvious uncertainties of life, would begin to search for new alternatives to safeguard themselves from any recurrence of bad times. And while timber's prominence as a staple would remain and the traditional economy based upon it would subsequently flourish, the stage, at decade's end, would be set for a great period of land settlement embarked upon by many of the less fortunate members of families whose perseverance on the River after so troubling an era was testimony to their commitment and identification with a larger river community.

≈≈≈

William Scoullar was a man of impressive deportment. Standing above the average height, with balding temples and a handsome countenance, Scoullar must have captured the immediate attention of his peers.[1] Laughter came easily to him, and his humour, more pithy than profoundly riotous, had a subtleness that enamoured those around him, lulling them into a state wherein they found it all too easy to accept the shallowness of his expressed thought for more than mere sophistry. His slight Scottish burr, diluted by years of residence in the colonies, only added to his charm, giving him a natural advantage over others less blessed by fate and the ambiguous grace of heredity.

Though William Scoullar's father was apparently a man of some means in his native Lanark,[2] he found it more expedient to send his son to Saint John, New Brunswick, where the boy's uncle, James Scoullar, had begun to make his fortune as a merchant-tailor. A man of genuine religious convictions and a kindliness that stemmed in part from an innately humane disposition,[3] James Scoullar seems to have taken his young nephew into his home, where he initiated him into the mysteries of his business and introduced him into a circle of acquaintances and friends whose influence proved significant in kindling William's aspirations.

---

[1] *The Provincial Patriot*, September 23, 1852.

[2] J.C. & H.C. Graves, Volume 7, p. 44; and *The New Brunswick Courier*, October 9, 1830.

[3] William Scoullar, New Brunswick Museum Branch Records, Vertical Files, PANB, RS 184.

They were a close-knit group, sharing a Scottish emigrant past and an interest in commerce so stereotypical of their race. Conscious of their peculiarity and their growing strength in the nascent economic life of the city, they formed the St. Andrew's Society in 1798.[4] Ostensibly an organization aimed at preserving the cultural interests and identity of the Scottish emigre community, the St. Andrew's Society, with a membership role that included the names of Hugh Johnston, Robert Crookshank, Andrew Kinnear and William Pagan, became one of the most important social clubs in the province. Dazzled by his countrymen's wealth and prestige and encouraged by his uncle, young William eventually set himself up as a petty merchant. In this capacity he slavishly mimicked his elder kinsman: buying and selling goods and property, financing mortgages, making loans, even going so far as attempting to develop a country estate along the narrowing upper reaches of the Kennebecasis River.[5]

William Scoullar's middling success and his comfortable mode of life changed in 1825. In the midst of the construction of a new building from which he planned to conduct his expanding business, James Scoullar took ill. To alleviate his ailing condition, James journeyed to New York for a recuperative holiday, only to be jostled and fatigued by the discomfort of an ocean voyage and measurably weakened in his bodily strength.[6] In July of 1825 he died, leaving a wife, seven children, a large stock of unsold merchandise and creditors who grew in number and boldness as word of his demise spread throughout the province. James Scoullar's death left his nephew in the awkward position of simultaneously mourning his uncle's passing and foreseeing the day when the wings of opportunity might be his own to don. Dreams of claiming his uncle's place in the economic life of the

---

[4] See I. Allen Jack, *History of the Saint Andrew's Society of St. John, New Brunswick, Canada, 1798-1903* (St. John: J & A. McMillan, 1903).

[5] Petition of William Scoullar (1818), Land Petitions, PANB, RS 108, and various records of transactions found in the Saint John Registry Office Records, PANB, RS 94 involving Scoullar and assorted parties, including individuals who mortgaged properties to him.

[6] William Scoullar, New Brunswick Museum Branch Records, Vertical Files, PANB, RS 184.

city became more vivid as he commenced administration of the deceased man's estate.[7] The responsibilities of executorship, however, eventually proved less a blessing than a burden, as William not only faced the task of running his uncle's affairs, but also of fending off a horde of claimants to the estate's assets.[8] As his legal troubles grew, William's mind likely drifted toward thoughts of a career free of the turmoil in which he now found himself drowning and guaranteed of the kind of success he had come to envision for himself. Ironically, it was his uncle's increasingly onerous business that provided the avenue of his escape. Caught in the cultural and financial orbit of Hugh Johnston, James Scoullar had followed a similar path of investment. Like Johnston, Scoullar's clients included the petty merchants and retailers of the Oromocto, the foremost of whom was John Dow. Ship builder, lumberman and shopkeeper, Dow had long contracted with Saint John interests to build vessels intended to advance the Caribbean trade.[9] Among the merchants Dow had occasion to deal with in this regard was none other than James Scoullar.[10] Dow's retirement toward the end of the decade left a vacuum of enterprise opportune for one, such as the younger Scoullar, to forge an identity of his own, well removed from the big pond and voracious big fish of the regional entrepot.

In 1829 Scoullar moved to the Oromocto, buying a house-lot near the River's mouth[11] and beginning his entrepreneurial activities by opening a small retail establishment, where he sold fish, pork, molasses and liquor to quench the hunger and thirst of the

---

[7] Estate Papers of James Scoullar, St. John County Probate Court Records, PANB, RS 71 and the Day Book of William Scoullar, York/Sunbury Historical Society Collections, PANB, MC 300, Ms. 41/20.

[8] The large number of files involving Scoullar to be found in the records of the Supreme Court of the province is evidence enough of this.

[9] Moore, op. cit., p. 88.

[10] Day Book of William Scoullar, York/Sunbury Historical Society Collections, PANB, MC 300, Ms. 41/20.

[11] Sunbury County Registry Office Records, PANB, RS 95, 12/629.

local lumbermen.[12] Oozing smoothery and a gregariousness that bordered on the disingenuous, Scoullar both charmed and irritated a populace whose Loyalist pretensions and nativist sentiments contrasted with his own emigrant enthusiasm. Scoullar's natural personableness and his seemingly desperate effort to assimilate into the older community partly ameliorated the innate resentment of his hosts, allowing him a rather orderly entry into the vestry of St. John's Church,[13] into business along the River, and into the heart of a woman born on the Oromocto's banks. The woman was Mary Kinney, a daughter of a minor lumberman, bear hunter and a notoriously corrupt Burton Parish constable.[14] Scoullar's marriage to her in 1831 proved beneficial for his young, motherless son, as well as politically expedient for himself, as it placed him at the centre of a vast web of relations stretching the entire length of River, thus creating a natural constituency no mere emigre, however wealthy, could otherwise have hoped to accrue.[15] New kinsmen bearing the names of Kinney, Grass, Mills, McMinn and Carr now bustled around him, noisily looking for patronage and employment, quickly accepting him as one of their own and forgetting the fact that he shared neither their experience nor the experience of their fathers and grandfathers in those lean

---

[12] "Account of the Parish of Burton with William Scoullar for Sundries furnished Paupers by Order of Mr. Dow, Overseer of the Poor, 1829," General Sessions, Sunbury County Records, PANB, RS 157, A/2/34 (1834). The General Sessions papers and the Draft Minutes also records Scoullar's applications for license to retail liquor at his store.

[13] Vestry Minutes of Maugerville and the Financial Records of Burton Church, Archives of the Diocese of Fredericton, PANB, MC 223, M3-1 and M3-3.

[14] Petition of Nathaniel Kinney, SU-1823, Timber and Saw Mills, 1817-1865, PANB, RS 663a; Bear Bounty Certificates of Nathaniel Kinney, General Sessions, Sunbury County Records, PANB, RS 157, A/2/30 (1830); Bear Bounty Certificates of Nathaniel Kinney, General Sessions, Sunbury County Records, PANB, RS 157, A/2/32 (1832); and Moore, pp. 134-35.

[15] *New Brunswick Courier*, May 21, 1842. The date of the marriage is problematic since no record of Scoullar's previous wife has been found, and the dates of the births of his children indicate little space to admit the death of one wife and his marriage to another.

days subsequent to war and painful exile.

For all of Scoullar's efforts to ease his way into the society of the River, traces of resentment still lingered among the older residents, particularly among the older elites. Staid in their thinking and intent on guarding their various rankings in Sunbury County's petty hierarchy, the elites initially tolerated the presence of the newcomer. But this general state of tolerance could only be preserved with the greatest exertion of civility, and thus would, at the slightest prodding, succumb to the meaner instincts of men who perceived a dire threat to their often trivial distinctions within the community. When Scoullar appeared in court as a witness on behalf of another foreign-born merchant then residing at Oromocto, his testimony so irritated the exalted plaintiff, High Sheriff John Hazen, that the latter's charge of misconduct soon echoed in the halls of justice in both Fredericton and Burton Parish. Not content merely to expound upon the newcomer's verbal distortions in a strictly official forum, Hazen took it upon himself to educate the populace regarding the conniving and exploitative ways of the unscrupulous, smooth-talking Scotsman. Denouncing Scoullar as "a damned perjured villain," Hazen used the universal deference his office commanded to assist him in his conduct of a private war of aspersion, pleading his concerns so formidably as to convince the locals that the only proper course of action to rectify the wrong done him was to strike at Scoullar's very livelihood through the imposition of a boycott. Charges of slander and a request for damages in the amount of a thousand pounds formed the brunt of Scoullar's own efforts to redeem his faltering business and restore his tarnished reputation. Hazen's befuddlement upon Scoullar's victory in court was rivaled and surpassed only by the Sheriff's growing enmity, a feeling that so prejudiced him against his antagonist that the subsequent accusation made by Scoullar that Hazen had allowed a man from whom Scoullar hoped to recover unpaid debts to escape custody seemed inordinately plausible. Fortunately for Hazen, disorganization on the part of Scoullar and the faint-heartedness of the latter's assembled witnesses prevented the charge from ever getting a proper hearing before the Supreme Court. Over the protests of legal counsel, Scoullar's suit was discarded. Grudgingly burying their dislike for one another, the two men returned to the Oromocto, each to resume conduct of his own peculiar affairs while attempting to carry out, for the sake of internal peace and communal amity, that often inconceivable Christian responsibility to love one's neighbour.[16] That the two men were in fact immediate neighbours could not have made the dictates of their common faith any less difficult to uphold.

Throughout his legal ordeal with Sheriff Hazen, Scoullar's chief ally was his business partner, Henry Thomas Partelow. Born in Saint John in 1804, the son of a shoemaker and grandson of Loyalists, Partelow spent the majority of his life in the shadow of his more famous elder brother, John.[17] Bereft of his brother's superior accounting skills, Henry nevertheless possessed a suitable intellect, as well as a decent mind for business. When his old acquaintance Scoullar committed himself to building a new life on the Oromocto, Partelow opted to join him in the endeavour.[18] Taciturn, less flamboyant in his speech and actions, with a gelid sense of public-spiritedness and a mild interest in history and antiquities,[19] Partelow's temperament admirably complimented his partner's and facilitated a business alliance that was cemented with his marriage to Scoullar's recently immigrated sister.[20] While marriage ended prematurely with the death of Partelow's young wife after the birth of their second child, the alliance and affection that had grown between the two men abided.

Upon his arrival at the River's mouth, Partelow quickly began

---

[16] William Scoullar vs. John Hazen (1832), Supreme Court Case Files, 1822-1835, Supreme Court Records, 1785-1835, PANB, RS 42.

[17] J.C. & H.C. Graves, Volume 8, p. 36 and S.W. MacNutt, "John R. Partelow," *Dictionary of Canadian Biography* (Toronto: University of Toronto Press, 1976), Volume IX, p. 622.

[18] The Scoullars and Partelows had indeed been long acquainted. When James Scoullar died it was John R., then a clerk in the employ of Hugh Johnston, who was directed by the Probate Court to make an inventory of the deceased man's estate.

[19] It was Partelow who revealed to Dr. Gesner the traces of aboriginal habitation near the mouth of the Oromocto, and it was he who relinquished to Gesner a number of artifacts local farmers had lately uncovered in the course of their plowing.

[20] *New Brunswick Courier*, October 9, 1830.

collaborating with his new partner. After Scoullar purchased the old Dow shipyard on the east bank of the river,[21] not far from Oromocto Village in 1834, Partelow acted as co-contractor for the building of ships for a number of Saint John merchants. In the early days of their operation, the two men procured the timber for ship construction from the River's various lumbermen, but it was not long before inflated prices forced upon them the realization that it would be more economical if they eliminated all dealings with middlemen and became their own supplier. As the North Branch was already crowded with competitors, they selected a site on the South Branch on which to build a double sawmill. Once the site was procured, the first of two mills was erected.[22] Anticipating a steady harvest of timber to readily flow from nearby land leased directly from the government, the partners soon discovered that the main stream and its more significant tributaries had already been heavily subjected to the restless axes of local woodsmen. To remedy the imminent threat of scarcity, Scoullar sent parties to explore the upper reaches of the South Branch, instructing them to proceed through the tangle of uncharted forest until reaching the stream's headwaters.[23] When they returned with reports of pine and spruce scattered amidst large stands of hardwood, Scoullar was greatly pleased, though the removal of a great number of impediments from the River, the erection of dams and the construction of roads and camps would, by his own calculation, likely run as high as 500 pounds.[24] For the sake of ensuring himself of a reliable source of timber exempt from the profiteering of independent suppliers, he was more than willing to undergo initial financial hardship, though he would

---

[21] Sunbury Counry Registry Office Records, PANB, RS 95, 14/535.

[22] Petition of William Scoullar and Henry Partelow, SU/1835, Timber and Saw Mills, 1817-1865, Timber and Saw Mill Records, PANB, RS 663a; Petition of William E. Perley, SU/1841, Timber and Saw Mills, 1817-1865, Timber and Saw Mill Records, PANB, RS 663a.

[23] Petition of William Scoullar, SU/1843, Timber and Saw Mills, 1817-1865, Timber and Saw Mill Records, PANB, RS 663a.

[24] Petition of William Scoullar and Henry Partelow, SU/1835, Timber and Saw Mills, 1817-1865, Timber and Saw Mill Records, PANB, RS 663a.

first require guarantees from the government that the countryside his investment would make accessible to provincial enterprise would be his alone to exploit.

To his great disappointment, Scoullar soon learned that two St. Andrew's speculators, Samuel Abbot and John Wilson, had already explored the region and, having found it to their liking, filed a claim for the choicest section at the Crown Land Office.[25] To compensate for the frustration of his efforts to gain control of the softwood around South Branch Lake, Scoullar picked up title to a reserve on Shin Creek not far from his mill; but, as the land had already been exposed to the industry of local lumbermen, the supply obtainable from it was hardly adequate to satisfy the demands of the saw blades of his mill and the special needs of his shipbuilding concern.[26] The purchase of logs from neighbouring woodsmen made up the subsequent resource deficit, driving costs upward and no doubt aggravating Scoullar to no end whenever he examined his accounts. Yet while inflation proved to be a source of some anxiety, the premiums paid to his humble suppliers in return for modest caches of timber seem to have had its own special reward. Indeed, so grateful were the people of the River for a patron to whom to regularly sell their wood that they were more than pleased to cast their vote for Scoullar's partner when he ran for a seat in the Legislative Assembly late in the summer of 1837.[27] The significance of Partelow's election could not have been lost upon Scoullar, and he no doubt expressed great confidence that, with Partelow in Fredericton to lobby from within the government on behalf of their shared business interests, possession of a suitable source of timber in the watershed would soon be assured.

That Partelow's victory in the election of 1837 was disruptive to the political stability of Sunbury County there could be no doubt. For more than a decade Assemblyman George Hayward of Lincoln, representing the County's southern section, and Assemblyman Thomas O. Miles, representing the north, had

---

[25] Petition of William Scoullar, SU/1843, Timber and Saw Mills, 1817-1865, Timber and Saw Mill Records, PANB, RS 663a.

[26] Ibid.

[27] Pollbooks, Sunbury County Records, PANB, RS 157, J/2/2 (1837).

fashioned an accord between Sunbury's warring communities. With Miles' defeat and replacement by a man from the Oromocto who possessed neither appreciation for the delicacies of internal relations, nor any sympathy for the constituencies opposite the Oromocto in Maugerville and Sheffield, the peace quickly disintegrated. Miles himself, convinced that Partelow (and, Scoullar) had perpetrated fraud by encouraging unenfranchised individuals to cast ballots, introduced a formal complaint in the House of Assembly. Partisanship orchestrated by Partelow's distinguished brother, however, yielded a ruling in Partelow's favour.[28] Miles returned to his Maugerville home to brood over his ill-treatment at the hands of his former colleagues, while Partelow retained his newly won seat, glorying, at least temporarily, in the acclaim of a body of grassroots support distinctive in the main in its uniquely sectional quality. He had won high office, and he and his partner had secured the influence in government their interests demanded, but only at the price of future controversy.

While Scoullar and Partelow appeared indifferent to the alienation Partelow's victory had produced throughout the northern portion of Sunbury County, they seemed equally ignorant of the fact that not everyone inhabiting the Oromocto watershed was pleased by the electoral outcome. Of those most disturbed by it was the French Lake lumberman, George Morrow. Though sharing with the two ship builders a similar migrant background, George Morrow was a man cast from a markedly different mould. Born in Ireland in 1801, he came to New Brunswick at the age of eighteen.[29] Rugged, rough, perhaps a little stern, he steadfastly adhered to the Methodist creed, channeling the energy normally reserved for the prosecution of the Wesleyan evangelical imperative into a zealous quest for salvageable timber along the various branches of the Oromocto. His outward crudeness encased a native intelligence of surprising depth, compensating for a marked lack of refinement that was perfectly suitable for life in the wilderness. He married as well as could be expected of an unconnected young man in a country not his own, taking as his wife the

---

[28] "Reduced List of Votes for Miles and Partelow," Records of the Legislative Assembly, PANB, RS 24, 1838/zz/file 1.

[29] The 1851 Census of New Brunswick, Sunbury County.

daughter of a moderately successful lumberman residing on the southern side of French Lake.[30] Upon a piece of property adjacent to the Oromocto's eastern bank which he had purchased from his father-in-law, Morrow built himself a house and a store. Very soon, Morrow began to make trips to Saint John for the purpose of replenishing his stock. It was on one of these trips that he first met William Scoullar. Morrow kept an account with Scoullar's uncle, and when the uncle died, Scoullar himself continued on in his uncles' place, supplying wholesale goods to the dour Irishman.[31]

So long as Morrow obtained what he desired, relations between the two men remained cordial. But when Scoullar moved to the Oromocto with the intention of transforming himself into a local magnate, cordiality abruptly ended. Scoullar's ambitions were simply incompatible with Morrow's; for while Morrow had few, if any, of the cultural pretensions of the class to which Scoullar belonged, he, like Scoullar, entertained hopes for great personal accomplishment on the river. His fledgling store provided many of the river's people with useful and necessary food and sundry items, as well as the liquor so indecorously craved by the lumbering segment of the population. His own activity as an employer of timber crews was only just beginning when Scoullar arrived on the scene, but by 1832 Morrow had been able to entice North West Branch miller Jeremiah Tracy into an alliance in which Morrow quickly became the dominant partner.[32] Morrow's diversification safeguarded him from the vagaries of the boom and bust nature of the timber economy, as did his catering to the predominantly inelastic demands of the eating and drinking public. Unlike Tracy, his business kept him relatively debt free, allowing him to gain access to timber berths on the North West Branch for which even his mill-owning competitors lacked the capital to purchase. Thomas Hartt was particularly offended by Morrow's intrusion into the affairs of a portion of the river on which the

---

[30] John Wood, "Daniel Wood of French Lake, Chronology Notes, Typescript, 1990, PANB, MC 80/1513.

[31] Day Book of William Scoullar, York/Sunbury Historical Society Collections, PANB, MC 300, Ms. 41/20.

[32] George Morrow vs. Jeremiah Tracy (1832), Supreme Court Case Files, 1822-1835, Supreme Court Records, 1785-1835, PANB, RS 42.

Irishman had no visible or tangible interest. While he himself managed to preserve a large share of the business of the stream, his son, Thomas Hartt, Jr., and son-in-law, David L. Kelley, faced imposing difficulties resulting from Morrow's presence there. When Thomas Sr. deeded them rights to a small mill that the previous spring's freshet had left inoperable, the two men rebuilt it, only to find, when operations recommenced, that Morrow, in cahoots with Tracy, had already gained possession of the best remaining chances. Attempts to dislodge Morrow failed, as Tracy obediently circulated a petition to the settlers of the river and disingenuously uttered fearful predictions of the imminent arrival of the antichrist of monopoly if Hartt and Tracy succeeded in their designs.[33]

Morrow's snopesian penchant for prevailing against his competitors, of using subterfuge, subtle threat and even manipulation to this end, revealed a determination of particularly uncompromising character that is nowhere better illustrated than in his debasement of George Phineas Nevers. The son and grandson of former assemblymen and a kinsman of George Hayward,[34] Nevers owned sawmills on the Rusagonis River and Rockwell Stream and, since 1821, possessed a substantial interest in a portion of Tracy's North West Branch milling establishment.[35] Since the early days of timbering, Nevers' eminence in the commerce of Burton Parish had given him a leverage over the settlers of the region not unnoticed by the predacious Morrow. Recognizing the benefits to arise from interest accrued and the possibility that a

---

[33] Petitions of David Kelley and Thomas Hart Jr. (1842), Land Petitions, PANB, RS 108.

[34] George H. Hayward, *The Nevers Family of Sunbury County* (Fredericton: published by author, 1991), PANB, MC 80/984, and J.C. & H.C. Graves, Volume 8, p. 35. The Graves' information on George P. Nevers' father is incorrect. They confused the Honourable Samuel Nevers with his cousin Samuel Nevers Jr., who had left the county for Wakefield as early as 1794. George H. Hayward does not consciously correct the error, but his extensive research provides the evidence to thoroughly discredit the Graves' account.

[35] Sunbury County Registry Office Records, PANB, RS 95, 11/433. Fire destroyed the mill in 1825, but Nevers apparently continued to hold a share in it following its reconstruction.

peculiar habit of financing operations through borrowed money might well lead to his rival's ruin, Morrow craftily took it upon himself to provide Nevers with the sums he required. His strategy was unwittingly abetted by his own brother-in-law, John Wood, who seems to have found work for himself as a jobber conducting the bulk of Nevers' affairs while Nevers himself reclined in semi-retirement at his home on the banks of the lower Oromocto. Nevers' propensity for indebtedness in time became so great that even the gentle winds of prosperity that blew through the pine and spruce stands of the province during the early and middle years of the 1830s could not lift him above that ultimately ignominious fate of all those unable to fulfil their financial obligations. When the inevitable collapse occurred, Morrow swooped down upon the fresh carrion, joining with his father-in-law and the great Saint John merchants Robert Rankin and Ralph Jarvis in the dismemberment of the choicest portions of the body of Nevers' modest empire.[36] Unable to remunerate his creditors for debts still outstanding, Nevers looked on helplessly as Sheriff Hazen seized his most lucrative assets and sold them at public auction. Jeremiah Tracy, whose joint occupation with Nevers of their North West Branch mill-site enmired him in the general predicament, managed to escape (no doubt through Morrow's connivance) the more devastating effects of Morrow's legal thrust, and was thus able to re-purchase Nevers' portion of the establishment.[37] George Hayward bought the Geary mill, saving his kinsman from the despair of watching it pass into less friendly hands, at least until 1836,[38] when George Morrow would finally acquire it from Hayward and thereby assure himself of total control of the trade in deals within the minor watershed formed by Rockwell Stream.[39]

Given Morrow's hawkish protection of his financial interests and the merciless and methodical way in which he slowly

---

[36] George Morrow vs. George P. Nevers & John Wood (1834); and Robert Rankin et al. vs. George P. Nevers & John Wood (1833), Supreme Court Case Files, 1822-1835, Supreme Court Records, 1785-1835, PANB, RS 42.

[37] Sunbury County Registry Office Records, PANB, RS 95, 14/547.

[38] Id., 15/169.

[39] Id., 15/173.

expanded his dominion, William Scoullar's arrival on the Oromocto must have instilled within Morrow's heart an almost
primal fear that, as with animals in the wild when faced with a
mortal threat, became channeled into an instinct for self-preserva-
tion. As Morrow was aggressive by nature, his basic manner of
defense naturally was aggression. But Morrow himself would not
be drawn so easily into a fight, at least not one in which he himself
could be justifiably identified as the instigator. In such times, prudence ameliorated his aggressive tendencies, auspiciously
derailing what might otherwise have been an ill-considered and
ill-omened pursuit of profits and victory. Putting haste aside and
assiduously anchoring his resentment within the confines of his
own stalled intentions, Morrow awaited the opportunity to waylay his rival in the full, redeeming light of the law. His patience
received its due reward in the summer of 1834 when men in Scoullar's employ on the North West Branch inanely snatched eighty
sticks of white pine timber conspicuously inscribed with Morrow's mark from a pond not far from Hartt's Mills.[40] Morrow's
reaction was swift. Claiming damages amounting to less than 200
pounds, Morrow clearly intended merely to warn the trespasser
that he could not lumber along the North West Branch unless he
wished to further test Morrow's resolve. Not being a belligerent
man, and mindful of other, less contested, opportunities for profit,
Scoullar heeded the warning. He moved his main operations over
to the South Branch, where construction of his mill was nearly
complete and pristine stands beckoned with a voice largely devoid of the harsh and competitive tones to be found elsewhere
along the river.

Scoullar's relegation to the South Branch Stream came at a time
when it appeared that the country immediately surrounding it
was relatively free of significant competition. As attested to by the
interest of Abbot and Wilson, there existed, however, a popular
acknowledgement of the potential profits to be made from exploitation of the woods around South Branch Lake. When the two
Charlotte County gentlemen encountered difficulties in meeting
the schedule of payments established by the Crown Land Office

---

[40] George Morrow vs. William Scoullar (1834), Supreme Court Case
Files, 1822-1835, Supreme Court Records, 1785-1835, PANB, RS 42.

and then demonstrated an inability to mount even a single expedition to harvest South Branch timber, there emerged a general understanding that the Lake's shores would soon revert to Crown control and thus be available for competitive bidding by the public at large.[41] Scoullar, in particular, was quite anxious to make advantageous use of the occasion, though he was by no means unique in this regard.

Indeed, a young farmer, then in his early twenties, named William Edward Perley viewed recent developments on the South Branch with more than modest ardour. His interest in the South Branch and in the river's primary industry was hardly surprising given the fact that he had grown up in the region. His grandfather was the notable Israel Perley, who had traveled up the Oromocto in 1761 and 1762 on his way to survey the best site for a prospective settlement that would eventually take the name Maugerville.[42] The elder Perley's service to that community landed him a seat in the Nova Scotia Assembly, but distance and rumours of war prevented him from availing himself of the opportunity to represent his respectful peers. Given his New England heritage and his close familial relations with General Israel Putnam (after whom he was named), it is not surprising that Israel Perley took an active role in organizing for rebellion, in which activity he proved so stalwart that he was later tried for treason by vengeful agents of the Crown.[43] Once the case against him was dismissed for lack of sufficient evidence, Perley quickly resumed his standing in the community, becoming both a county magistrate and a Deputy Surveyor in the employ of the provincial government. Among his many children was son William, the father of William Edward. By virtue of his birth into one of the County's first families, William embarked upon a course that may well have led him to high office if not for the mortifying effects of an illness contracted while still in the prime of life.[44] Fortune took

---

[41] Petition of William Scoullar, SU/1843, Timber and Saw Mills, 1817-1865, Timber and Saw Mill Records, PANB, RS 663a.

[42] Raymond, op. cit., p. 141.

[43] Moore, op. cit., p. 28.

[44] William Perley, like many young men of his social standing, held a number of minor parish posts. He owned a number of valuable

a kindly interest in the well-being of his heirs, providing a fine husband for his widow in the person of an upstanding South Branch Baptist gentleman by the name of James Bailey. Already saddled with a numerous brood from an earlier marriage to a sister of Charles DeWitt, Bailey showed no reluctance in seeing to the upbringing of his new wife's three children, whom he afforded every luxury and every opportunity youngsters growing up in the placid South Branch community in the first decades of the Nineteenth Century could have been expected either to want or require.

By the time young William Edward Perley entered into his majority, the tranquility of the South Branch succumbed to a blithesome prosperity. Scoullar's mill and high prices abroad for colonial timber quickened lumbering activity all along the river's navigable length. Caught up in the excitement generated by the economy, Perley's ambitions as a lumberman fully matured, prompting him, following his marriage to a daughter of North West Branch miller Thomas Hartt Sr., to bid on several small timber berths: one on the Waasis Stream in Lincoln Parish, the other on the Lyon.[45] So committed was he to the success of his nascent enterprise that he disdained even ties of blood and joined George Morrow's league of complainants against the reputed conspiracy of his own brothers-in-law, Thomas Hartt, Jr. and Edward L. Kelley, to consolidate a number of scattered timber berths into a

---

properties, including lots on Oromocto Island, which put him into partnership with some of the most prominent men in the County, including Elijah Miles, George Hayward, Francis Peabody, William Wilmot, Samuel Nevers and his own brother Solomon and cousin Amos Perley — an impressive list of names considering the fact that five of them were at one time or another Assemblymen. Perley was always at the centre of local power. The Court of the General Sessions frequently had recourse to his inn and tavern for the purpose of holding its periodic meetings. What he may have become had he lived is, of course, impossible to say. Certainly, it is conceivable he could have followed in the footsteps of his cousin Amos Perley, who served with Elijah Miles as Member of the Assembly from Sunbury County from 1820 to 1822.

[45] Petition of William Perley, YO/1840; Petition of William Perley, SU/1841, Timber and Saw Mills, 1817-1865, Timber and Saw Mill Records, PANB, RS 663a.

single mill reserve to be held by themselves alone. Though
Perley's opposition to his kinsmen's efforts helped him to maintain his hold on his small Lyon Stream berth, it most assuredly
guaranteed him rough treatment when he failed to honour a debt
owed to his father-in-law, the elder Thomas Hartt. Hartt's extrac-
tion from Perley of £320 via a civil suit did much to hinder Perley's
immediate objective,[46] which was to build a sizeable store of investment capital, and certainly damaged his capacity to follow
through on his discrete intention to employ his accumulated savings toward the preemption of the river's more established
lumbermen by laying hold of the timber around South Branch
Lake.

Alone, with his savings depleted, he could not act; thus he approached his uncle, Assemblyman George Hayward,[47] with an
offer of partnership that he undoubtedly argued would be of
enormous benefit to them both. Others had dismissed his plans to
improve the navigation of South Branch Lake as pure madness,
citing the ruggedness of the terrain and impenetrable density of
the forest as perpetual impediments to the introduction of man's
industry.[48] Yet, while others scoffed, George Hayward listened.
Mulling over the claims of his determined nephew, weighing
them against the doubts harboured by his neighbours, carefully
considering the expense of the operation and the sources of capital
available to him as a member of the Board of Directors of the Central Bank of New Brunswick,[49] and contemplating, finally, the
profit that would likely accrue to himself and the community at
large should the enterprise succeed, Hayward assented to his
nephew's pleas, but only on condition that he be granted some
form of security should the venture fail. After mortgaging his
farm to his uncle for several hundred pounds[50] and enlisting the

---

[46] Sunbury County Registry Office Records, PANB, RS 95, 17/192.

[47] Hayward was married to old Israel Perley's daughter Charlotte.

[48] Petition of George Hayward, William E. Perley & Duncan W. Perley,
SU/1845, Timber and Saw Mills, 1817-1865, Timber and Saw Mill Records, PANB, RS 663a.

[49] J.C. & H.C. Graves, Volume 8, p. 17/b.

[50] Sunbury County Registry Office Records, PANB, RS 95, 17/194 &
18/65.

assistance of his equally ambitious though more volatile younger brother Duncan, William E. Perley commenced his career as one of the major capitalists of the Oromocto.

For all of his youthful enthusiasm and ebullient powers of persuasion, William Perley was helpless against the unremitting vehemence of the great economic disruption of the province that occurred even as he began planning for the excavation of the upper reaches of South Branch Stream. Rocked by a series of devastating fires and fearful of the effects of a threatened and imminent reduction of the timber preference that for so long had extended the Province a modicum of prosperity, the people of the bustling entrepot of Saint John were overcome by a wave of panic.[51] Hardly confining itself to the city, the panic spread outward, traveling up the St. John River, crossing the portages and inundating the basins of the Miramichi and St. Croix with devastating results. Even before the full effects of the ailing economy were manifest, Lieutenant Governor Sir William Colebrooke devised a policy of "Association Settlement" to woo the errant economy away from its subservience to the uncertain whims of timber and reorient it according to the steady pace of the plough.[52] The Oromocto became a target for Colebrooke's experimentation following the encouraging reports of Emigrant Agent Alexander Wedderburn[53] and, more particularly, of Provincial Geologist Abraham Gesner, whose exploration of the region in the previous decade had convinced him of the land's promise as a safe haven for the sedentary vocation of farming.[54] Proceeding on Colebrooke's orders, Deputy Surveyor Amasa Flaglor made his way to a tract of forested earth in the rear of Geary. Ringed by marshy ground, an apparently limitless forest to the south and east and the lingering scars caused by an ancient fire, the tract Flaglor rather clumsily surveyed was dubbed Victoria Settlement in honour

---

[51] W.S. MacNutt, *New Brunswick, A History: 1784-1867*, p. 283.

[52] Id., p. 284, and Acheson, *Saint John: The Making of a Colonial Urban Community*, p. 86.

[53] Alexander Wedderburn to Sir Howard Douglas, August 19, 1840, Executive Council Records, PANB, RS 7, pp. 2551-4.

[54] Abraham Gesner, *New Brunswick: With Notes for Emigrants*, p. 158.

of the young ruler of the British Empire.[55] Unconvinced of Victoria's fertility and skeptical of its accessibility to major markets, Colebrooke's candidates for resettlement shunned it, and thereby presented the unadored settlement's agent, Abraham Gesner, with a rather glum prospect of ever populating it. By the end of the winter in the early part of 1842, Gesner did manage to convince ten desperate and unemployed mechanics to relocate there, but after taking a first-hand look at the lonely country that was to be their new home, not one of them remained to so much as bid at auction on the land.[56]

The Oromocto's permanent residents suffered to a degree comparable to that of the ephemeral settlers of Victoria. Cursed by a late freshet in the spring of 1841, the people of the river pushed the normal agricultural calendar forward a month. A premature harvest had little ill-effect on wheat grown in upland places like Geary, but a persisting dampness of the lower interval soils nurtured a rust that infected the potato crop and diminished the returns for lumberman-farmers who supplemented their subsistence diets with a high quantity of starch.[57] The consequent scarcity became all the more intense as the gloomy course of the downturn in business continued unchecked. While no one starved, certain amenities of life were sacrificed, including the ongoing construction of the much-debated drawbridge at the mouth of the river. Intended to span the Oromocto's width and fuse two portions of

---

[55] Survey of Victoria Settlement, Sunbury and Queen's County Flat Book (65), no. 6, 6/14, Crown Lands Branch Maps and Plans, PANB, RS 656, 17r/203.6.

[56] Abraham Gesner to Sir William Colebrooke, February 16, 1842, *Journals of the House of Assembly* (1842), p. 114. Gesner never commented upon his failure to locate settlers in Victoria, but his failure is all too evident from the records of settlement found in land petitions and surveys of the period. Gesner, it should be noted, also took an interest in another prospective settlement at a place called Enniskillan, on the banks of Back Creek. Led by William Miller, the settlers were all Saint John mechanics. Like so many others in the Association Settlement program, they encountered tremendous bureaucratic difficulties, Gesner's intercession on their behalf notwithstanding.

[57] Rev. Raper Milner to John M. Wilmot, January 1, 1842, *Journals of the Legislative Assembly* (1842), Appendix clxxxv-vi.

the great road connecting Fredericton with Saint John, the unfin- ished bridge silently awaited the arrival of Keswick timber required for its completion.[58] The delay was perplexing to no one more than Sheriff Hazen, on whose land the bridge's approaches lay half completed, and on which the bridge's foreman lan- guished morosely, occupying his long, idle days with the superfluous rearrangement of his building materials as if they were deckchairs on the proverbial sinking ship.

A poor harvest and the delays in completion of the bridge were, of course, of profound interest to the community as a whole, but equal (if not greater) attention was undoubtedly paid to the exigencies of William Scoullar. Having operated much of his busi- ness on advances from his Saint John clients, Scoullar, in the midst of this economic depression, found himself unable either to sell his timber or complete construction of a ship at his ship yard whereby he might have generated a return satisfactory to both himself and his creditors. Unable to pay his debts unless he sold his product, unable to sell his product without additional invest- ment, Scoullar solicited his brother George for a loan of £750 and invited him to join himself and Henry Partelow as a more or less equal partner.[59] Though younger than William, George Scoullar possessed a certain level-headedness that eluded his elder brother, and while he had never mixed in the same elevated cir- cles William had, he certainly exhibited a greater sense of political sagacity in choosing a mate from the ranks of the distinguished Sayre clan of Westmoreland County.[60] The marriage seems to have helped him gain a foothold in the timber trade of the Petitcodiac River,[61] but when his brother's plea came to his atten- tion, George deferred the prospects opened in that locality and journeyed with his wife and children to a new home on the Oro- mocto.

---

[58] Petition of David Brown, Records of the Legislative Assembly, PANB, RS 24, 1845/pe/file 4/no. 128.

[59] Sunbury County Registry Office Records, PANB, RS 95, 17/42.

[60] Theodore M. Banta, *The Lineage of Thomas Sayre, A Founder of South- ampton* (New York: The De Vinne Press, 1901), p. 347.

[61] Petition of George Scoullar, SU/1839, Timber and Saw Mills, 1817- 1865, Timber and Saw Mill Records, PANB, RS 663a.

Despite William Scoullar's hopes to the contrary, his brother's presence on the river did nothing to halt his own financial descent.  As the crisis bottomed out, the sums of money borrowed from his brother were quickly expended; thus he mortgaged hundreds of acres of valuable Rusagonis farm properties to cover additional operational costs.[62] With much of his landed wealth given up to indenture and facing the real possibility that the inevitable recovery would not remunerate sufficiently to allow him to liberate his assets, Scoullar experienced additional anxiety as his partner Henry Partelow's popular esteem sharply declined. Indeed, with the ruin of the Province's finances, a profound dissatisfaction with the entire House of Assembly had taken root, animating the people with a new appreciation for the legislature's irresponsible method of allocating government revenues, and instilling a consciousness of the real possibility that this irresponsibility, however immediately beneficial to the people at large, had been a fearsome provocateur of the present state of economic distress. As early as the summer of 1841, at the semi-annual meeting of the County Inferior Court of Common Pleas, amidst the swearing of oaths and the venting of petty lawsuits, Sheriff Hazen had shed any pretension of non-partisan demure and rose to fulminate against the excesses of the House of Assembly. That the partner of his old enemy was a main target of his attack could not have been doubted by his deferential audience.[63] Attentive to the Sheriff's diatribe against the treacherous actions of the legislature and, by implication, of Partelow, the people approved of his call for a comprehensive discussion of the matter in a more formal and appropriate setting.

By the middle of July a meeting was convened at the Burton Court House. In attendance were the elites of both sides of the St. John, each of whom carried with him his own private objective and simultaneously contributing to a delay that lasted three hours as they scurried about the building's interior, probing their fellows' humours and likely amenability, searching in this way for

---

[62] Sunbury County Registry Office Records, PANB, RS 95, 17/179 & 17/181.

[63] *New Brunswick Courier*, July 31, 1841.

leverage in the advancement of their individual ambitions.[64] As one commentator said, it proved a "mean, miserable, paltry, one sided affair," dominated by the tasteless conceit of a group of self-styled reformers led by the normally reasonable Thomas Obder Miles. Still very much disgruntled with Partelow for the latter's role in his ouster from the Assembly four years earlier, Miles allowed himself to become unfettered of his good sense by declaring his intention to stand for election in opposition to the corruption and incompetence of the present members — a declaration all the more ill-advised considering the presence at the meeting of his good friend, incumbent Assemblyman George Hayward.[65]

Though Miles was the dominant figure among the so-called reformers, the primary speaker for their cause was Maugerville's Calvin Luther Hatheway, a son of a distinguished Loyalist settler of Burton Parish. Early in life Hatheway had won appointment as a Deputy Surveyor, in addition to high rank in the provincial militia.[66] Unfortunately, these distinctions adversely affected his emotional and intellectual balance, contributing not only to the inflation of his self-esteem beyond all reasonable levels, but also to a growing obsession with land settlement as a cure-all for the ills of the province. In the mid-1830s, he had stumbled upon some useful information favouring British claims in the disputed territory to the west, yet the sincere thanks of successive Colonial Secretaries to whom he communicated his astounding findings disappointed his obvious craving for more tangible honours, titles and imperial privilege.[67] Failure as a sawmill proprietor on the Musquash prompted his return to Sunbury County,[68] where he

---

[64] Ibid.

[65] Ibid.

[66] J.M. Whalen, "Calvin Luther Hatheway," *Dictionary of Canadian Biography* (Toronto: University of Toronto, 1990), Vol. XII, pp. 374.

[67] Petition of Calvin L. Hatheway, Records of the Surveyor General, PANB, RS 637, 7/j/2/a.

[68] Petition of Calvin Hatheway (1835) and Petition of Calvin Hatheway (1836), Land Petitions, PANB, RS 108. The files include extensive correspondence regarding Hatheway's efforts to gain control of Crown land to facilitate his milling operations.

began to cull his wide experience in preparation for a treatise reviewing the history of New Brunswick and the Province's prospects for further advancement.[69] As a public man he had great aspirations, though he was forever banished from solidarity with the common folk upon whom public men are so dependent by a high flown yet ultimately vacuous volubility that made him hopelessly incapable of restraining himself from pronouncing even upon subjects of which he knew naught.[70]

Hatheway's condemnation of Partelow from the court house podium met with little objection, save from Partelow himself, who apologized for nothing, minimized the size of the crises at hand and held out the promise of a great windfall soon to alight upon the heavily encumbered Province through the agency of the New Brunswick and Nova Scotia Land Company.[71] Hayward, on the other hand, maintained his diffidence, as well as his dignity, throughout the course of the gathering, allowing his nephews to come forward in his defense. The mercurial Duncan Perley, however, hardly helped his uncle's cause. His unambiguous verbal assault on the Sheriff inspired so sharp a rebuke from his target[72] that Perley was compelled to brutally waylay him later that day at a local pub.[73] More mindful of the penalties that await the intemperate enemies of lash-bearing magistrates possessing the discretionary powers of official punishment, William E. Perley used greater moderation in echoing his brother's sentiments, criticizing the legitimacy of the meeting and asserting the possibility

---

[69] See Calvin Luther Hatheway, *The History of New Brunswick from its First Settlement* (Fredericton, James A. Phillips, 1846).

[70] Even Hatheway's good friend and long-time neighbour, Thomas O. Miles, felt this way about him. Miles said of him following a speech Hatheway delivered to a meeting of the County Agricultural Society: it was "not the trouble of going five rods, no information whatever imparted." Another, less sympathetic, critic referred to him and ilk as "political quacks."

[71] *New Brunswick Courier*, August 14, 1841.

[72] Id., July 31 and August 14, 1841.

[73] Diary of Thomas O. Miles, PANB, MC 451, July 13, 1841. It may well have been for this impertinence, on June 22, 1842, that Duncan Perley was publicly flogged.

that the thirty or forty assembled men could hardly speak defini-
tively for the County as a whole.[74] His expression of confidence in
his uncle, though, was undermined by the testimony of Hayward
himself, who, having realized the damage done his reputation
and having already privately acknowledged his own culpability
in the problems now facing the Province, delivered an address to
the assembled crowd that was punctuated by an admission of personal fallibility and blame.[75]

His admission proved damning not only to his own immediate
political future, but also to that of Partelow. As the health of William Scoullar's financial interests depended in large part on his
partner's access to power, Partelow's likely consignment to the
tartarean depths of political exile would be a fate which Scoullar
himself would be forced to endure as well. Some relief came when
Lieutenant Governor Colebrooke, after receiving from Thomas O.
Miles a petition of the freeholders of Sunbury County requesting
the disbanding of the present legislature and the holding of a new
election,[76] decided that so drastic an action as a means of achieving greater Responsibility in the House of Assembly would be
premature. Less than a year later, however, dissolution came, and
the same agitators for reform who had gathered so earnestly at
the Burton Court House in 1841 now clumsily coalesced into a faction united more by their animosity toward Partelow and the
interests he represented than by any higher principles of constitutional government. Conscious of his having been irredeemably
discredited, Partelow deemed it best to withdraw in his partner's
favour.  Being personally exempt from charges of corruption and
political incompetence, candidate Scoullar could reasonably an-
ticipate the support of the very same constituencies on the
Oromocto that had been instrumental in electing Partelow five
years before.

Unable now to vindicate himself personally against his old foe,
Miles transferred his animosity to Scoullar and tried, using all
those powers of conciliation that had helped him previously to

---

[74] *New Brunswick Courier*, July 31 & August 14, 1841.

[75] Id., August 14, 1841.

[76] Diary of Thomas O. Miles, PANB, MC 451, September 27, 1841 &
April 11, 1842.

build an ecumenical bridge between dissent, conformity and popery, to cement an accord among the many divergent elements in the nascent reform faction. As a means of fostering a general spirit of altruism and thus setting for his peers a suitable example to follow, Miles withdrew his previous declaration of candidacy. His subsequent backing of the respectable but largely unknown Sheffield farmer Whitehead Stickney Barker, however, upset the ambitions of Calvin Hatheway, who, to remedy this affront, held a caucus at his home for the purpose of engineering, through the orchestrated exclamations of several well-placed followers, his own nomination to a place on the reform ticket.[77] Realizing that the presence in the race of two men from the north side of the St. John River would risk conceding potential reform votes on the Oromocto to Scoullar, Miles leapt opportunely just as George Horatio Nelson Harding was preparing to present Hatheway's name for nomination and advanced, instead, that of Barker, who was subsequently acclaimed by an overwhelming majority of those present. His glorious thunder stolen, Hatheway suffered Harding's rather lukewarm introduction, which was hailed by a single puny voice whose withered resonance was immediately smothered in the embrace of the profoundest silence. As a more suitable candidate to stand with Barker, Miles preferred George Morrow, whom he probably viewed as the only man on the Oromocto who could challenge Scoullar for the political loyalty of the watershed's inhabitants. For a man such as Morrow, obsessed with the crack of breaking timber and convinced that the road to wealth lay not through the jungle of influence and patronage at the highest levels of government and finance, but through hard and persistent labour, it was difficult to grasp the allure of office. Dazzled briefly by the vision of himself adorned in the robes and wigs reserved for the great men of the land, and perhaps encouraged by his own personal animosity toward Scoullar, Morrow allowed himself to accept Miles' entreaty to enter the race.[78] Morrow's mental preoccupation with the affairs of business, however, soon reasserted itself, leaving Miles and the reformers no other choice but to accept Calvin Hatheway as the only viable reform

---

[77] Id., September 23, 1842.

[78] Id., September 21, 1842.

alternative on the Oromocto to the candidacy of William Scoullar.

As the reformers struggled with materials still too insufficient to allow for the construction of a platform sound enough to bear their combined weight, Scoullar embarked upon a whirlwind tour of the river, throughout which he undoubtedly diminished the importance of the greater problems of the economy and the question of responsible government and offered, instead, tangible proof, in the form of a very liberal dissemination of personal largesse, of his own suitability as an agent of prosperity. So powerful was Scoullar's influence upon the Oromocto that Miles could not delude himself into discounting the reality of Scoullar's seeming invulnerability. That Barker could garnish support there was unlikely, as he possessed no connection with the people and was almost wholly unknown to them. When Miles took the opportunity to introduce Barker to an assembly of the local militia at the annual training frolic on the North West Branch, Barker was greeted with polite inquiry but little in the way of rousing and positive acclaim.[79] The nature of Hatheway's reception there is not known, but it was more than likely attended by steady and derisive laughter.

With the reform campaign on the Oromocto stalled, Lieutenant Governor Colebrooke made an appearance in support of a cause which promised to be amenable to his own efforts to enact provincial Responsibility. Taking a detour while en route to the Province's north shore,[80] Colebrooke stopped in with his wife and daughter at the Burton Court House, where Sheriff Hazen, Justice Miles and the assembled dignitaries of Sunbury County read addresses and sang praises, but ultimately failed to advance the interests of reform.[81] By December, Scoullar's victory seemed foreordained, inspiring the most desperate of his opponents to hold out against all odds for the requisition of George Hayward.[82] Hayward, though, could not be dislodged from his commitment to return to private life. Not surprisingly, then, when the balloting

---

[79] Id., September 20, 1842.

[80] *New Brunswick Courier*, October 15, 1842.

[81] Diary of Thomas O. Miles, November 8, 1842.

[82] Id., December 19, 1842.

commenced, Scoullar swept the Oromocto and rode into office on the votes of the likes of Thomas McMinn, James Till, the Carr clan and many more. So resoundingly did he trounce his opponents that the nearly universal abstention of the folk of the upper Oromocto (for reasons probably related to the commencement of the lumbering season) did not effect the final tallies. In the end, his column recorded 156 votes, compared to the 134 garnered by his closest competitor.[83]

When Scoullar and his newly elected colleague, Whitehead S. Barker, took their seats in the Assembly in January of 1843, the economic situation of the Oromocto remained unchanged. Scoullar's own personal exigencies remained unaltered as well, and were hardly modified for the better by the presence on the Executive Council of his greatest creditor, John R. Partelow. In the midst of an impossible attempt to solve the deficits of both the Province and the city of Saint John, Partelow could spare little tolerance and absolutely no sympathy for Scoullar's personal plight, despite any familial ties that might have bound them together. The very presence of Scoullar in the Assembly seemed to hasten the expiration of Partelow's restraint in the matter of Scoullar's broken promises and prompted Partelow's recourse to the courts.[84] After suffering the obloquy of a short residence in the county jail, Scoullar emerged only to face a barrage of additional suits filed by his shipyard foreman and a group of Saint John merchants too impatient to await any longer the upturn in business that would surely have been Scoullar's salvation.[85] The upturn came, but all too late for Scoullar's good, as the plaintiffs arrayed against him won a total of over £2,000. Unfriendly litigation only compounded a general problem that had already obliged him to ignore both the limitations of his finances and the stipulations of the law by sending his men onto crown land near Shin Creek without proper sanction. Scoullar's indiscretion did not escape detection, and the subsequent investigation determined the precise extent of the illegal harvest and the precise amount of the

---

[83] Pollbooks, Sunbury County Records, PANB, RS 157, J/2/3 (1842).

[84] Sunbury County Registry Office Records, PANB, RS 95, 17/238.

[85] Id., 17/240 & 17/293.

penalty to be exacted.[86] A pittance compared to the sum already wrung from him by order of the Court, the penalty imposed upon him reaffirmed his growing impotence along the Oromocto and the rising perception that the river's destiny was increasingly less susceptible to the crafting power of his formerly grasping hands.

A new reality of economic power on the river became evident by the summer of 1843. With the occurrence of a boom in timber prices following the announcement by the British Government that it would not abolish the preference outright, but, instead, reduce it gradually over the course of the next several years, the collective despair accumulated over the past year and a half was swept away. The great bridge, so long frozen in a state of metaphorical encumbrance to match its literal encirclement by winter ice, now emerged complete, just in time for English traveler James Silk Buckingham to see it from a passing riverboat on his way to Fredericton, and to comment upon its attractive lines rising above shipyards then in the throws of renewed activity.[87] Rediscovering the value of the crown lands, young men below the age required for legal application disguised their immature years before magistrates at the Burton Court House and purchased settlement lots, befuddling Deputy Surveyor Andrew Blair and outraging recently reinstated Surveyor General Thomas Baillie, who, with inflated statistics to match his inflated passion, declared an ineffectual war on squatters throughout Sunbury County.[88] The problem of squatting equally perturbed the wardens of St. John's Church, who could point to only a single tenant on its otherwise forsaken estate and the continued circumvention of the church glebe by new settlers for unclaimed portions of the royal

---

[86] "Statement of Lumber cut and hauled by persons in the employ of William Scoullar," Timber and Saw Mill Records, PANB, RS 663a/e/1/d.

[87] James Silk Buckingham, Canada, Nova Scotia, New Brunswick and Other British Provinces in North America, With a Plan of National Colonization (London: Fisher, Son & Company, 1843), p. 415.

[88] Andrew Blair to Thomas Baillie, September 6, 1843, Records of the Surveyor General, PANB, RS 637, 2/d/30 and Journals of the Legislative Assembly (1843), pp. 44-46.

preserve.[89]

Despite the enduring hibernation of the landed wealth of the Church, a great revival in belief swept the Oromocto in concert with the recovery of the economy. Overcoming the objections of certain members of the missionary hierarchy, the English-born Reverend J.M. Sterling succeeded the late Reverend Milner in the spring of 1843.[90] Pleasantly lacking Milner's combativeness and exhibiting a greater attentiveness to the spiritual needs of the people of the southern side of the St. John River, Sterling still could not overcome the obstacles imposed upon him by nature and an inadequate government. Poor roads, inclement weather and the frequently turbulent and dangerous state of the St. John impeded the fulfillment of his missionary mandate. Still, regardless of these impositions, his efforts overcame the lethargy and animosity of a great segment of the population of the lower Oromocto toward the saving rituals of the Church and the graceful instruction of its preachers.[91] Sterling's preoccupation with the restoration of a mission ravaged by years of neglect sadly did not extend so far as to allow him to administer attention to the back settlements, where dissenters continued to thrive in relative isolation.[92] On the Rusagonis, the heirs of Deacon Glasier led the dissenting population to contemplate the construction of a new meeting house, "open to all denominational preachers of good character and standing" and, presumably, to all sectarians;[93] even the likes of the Deacon's son, lumberman Stephen Glasier, who, according to Thomas O. Miles, possessed "strange ideas respecting many passages of scripture."[94] On the North West and South Branch streams Baptist sentiments continued to predominate, but they lay sunken in a puddle of uncertainty that only deepened with the

---

[89] Ecclesiastical Return (1844), Archives of the Diocese of Fredericton, PANB, MC 223, M3-3.

[90] Society for the Propagation of the Gospel in Foreign Parts, Calendar of Correspondence, Volume 1, 1821-1848, p. 85, PANB, MC 230.

[91] Ecclesiastical Return (1844), Archives of the Diocese of Fredericton, PANB, MC 223, M3-3.

[92] Ibid.

[93] Diary of Thomas O. Miles, PANB, MC 451, December 5, 1843.

[94] Id., February 16, 1846.

defection of the North West Branch's deacon to the banner of the Free Willers.[95] County Cork native Thomas Magee broke the negligent silence in the fall, impressing the people of the river with his pure spirit and upright conduct and winning a number of converts at the church near Hartt's Mills.[96] His visitation, however, had little impact on the people of the South Branch, who generally attended Free Will meetings supervised by the successor of the late Levi Parsons— the middle-aged farmer Clapman Smith, Jr.[97] A son of a former Justice of the Peace and husband of a sister of Charles DeWitt, Smith soon withdrew in favour of a more permanent preacher of the Word in the person of Abner Mersereau.

As great as was the relief experienced by the general population of the Oromocto, nothing could match that felt by William Edward Perley as the dark days of depression succumbed to the light of recovery. Taking enormous pleasure in Scoullar's troubles, and convinced that Scoullar, in his present predicament, would be unable to offer resistance, Perley, his uncle George Hayward and his brother Duncan hired a crew of men to begin the long-awaited process of opening the last great lumbering region of the Oromocto River. Labouring under the special incentive to begin harvesting as soon as possible so as to maximize profits before the final elimination of the Preference took effect, Perley's men toiled throughout the summer and early fall, clearing the main stream of obstructions, blasting over a hundred rocks and boulders, building dams and camps and driving a road twelve miles deep into the uninhabited forest.[98] Given the magnitude of the operation, it is hardly surprising that Perley's activity did not go unnoticed by Scoullar. Convinced that his own recovery was entirely dependent on gaining a stable source of timber for his mill, Scoullar, with his partners' assistance, resolved to

---

[95] Fragment of an Account of the Baptist Church of the North West Branch, John Nason Collection, PANB, MC 431, File 4.

[96] Ibid., and I.E. Bill, op. cit., p. 386.

[97] Sharon Knorr, "Hoyt Pioneer Cemetery," (typescript by author, 1986).

[98] Petition of George Hayward, William E. Perley & Duncan Perley, SU\1845; Petition of William E. Perley, SU/1846, Timber and Saw Mills, 1817-1865, Timber and Saw Mill Records, PANB, RS 663a.

undermine Perley's efforts. For the time being nothing could be done toward achieving this end, as the Abbot Grant had not yet been annulled. Thus, until annulment occurred, Scoullar could only wait, but his anxiety grew so great in consequence of the delay that he began dedicating his spare time to harassing and obstructing his competitors in every conceivable way. A lawsuit aimed at recovering a minor sum ignited Perley's displeasure,[99] but did not sufficiently weaken the man's resources so as to prevent him, through the agency of his uncle, from acquiring a small berth on the shores of South Branch Lake when the same was put up for sale at auction.[100] When George Morrow, who had taken no active role in Perley's enterprise, followed suit,[101] it was Partelow's turn to take aim. Partelow's release of a flurry of legal grievances against both Perley and his brother, however, amounted to nothing more than a general nuisance.[102]

The discomfort Perley and his partners felt on the occasion of Partelow's obvious persecution only magnified in intensity as the Perleys' petition for a second berth on South Branch Lake, encompassing an even larger section of the Abbot tract, was tabled on account of complications involving the final vestiges of Abbot's claim.[103] It was clear to all concerned that the delay presented Scoullar with the opportunity to locate the sums he would need to make good on any application for a mill reserve, as well as provide him with additional chances to further unnerve his rivals. So infuriating did the wait become that Duncan Perley rushed off with vengeance in his eyes to confront Partelow's innocent

---

[99] Sunbury County Registry Office Records, PANB, RS 157, 17/267.

[100] Petition of George Hayward, William E. Perley & Duncan W. Perley, SU\1845, Timber and Saw  Mills, 1817-1865, Timber and Saw Mills, PANB, RS 663a; Petition of George Hayward, SU/1845, Timber and Saw Mills, 1817-1865, Timber and Saw Mill Records, PANB, RS 663a.

[101] Petition of George Morrow, SU/1843, Timber and Saw Mills, 1817-1865, Timber and Saw Mill Records, PANB, RS 663a.

[102] Petition of Duncan W. Perley, (1843), Records of Lt. Governor Sir William McBean George Colebrooke, PANB, RS 345, B/4.

[103] Petition of William E. Perley, Records of the Legislative Assembly, PANB, RS 24, 1847/pe/file 11/no. 386.

brother-in-law, Edward Allison Clowes, after being apprised of the man's presence at the Blissville home of Justice of the Peace William Hoyt.[104] Striking him in the face in plain sight of the esteemed magistrate, Perley quickly retreated, but only for the purpose of summoning his brother so that they might together plot further acts of violence. After observing the Perleys and one of their henchmen loudly planning their malicious scheme in the middle of the road immediately outside the Hoyt home, Clowes pleaded with the Justice for protective escort to the river's mouth, but Hoyt, displaying clear sympathy for his Blissville neighbours' ignoble cause, refused to comply. When Clowes' companion George F. Wilmot (an employee of William Scoullar) attempted to ward the tormentors off, William Perley, overcome by a desperate thirst for blood made all the more uncontrollable by his brother's barbaric example, lunged at him, knocked him to the ground, leapt atop him and delivered a furious barrage of well-placed blows that only ended when his fury abated and his downed opponent was incapable of further response.

Realizing the utter savagery of his action, William Perley went into hiding, though his brother shamelessly paraded himself around the watershed, only to be apprehended by the local constabulary. Confined to the Burton gaol, he was no doubt surprised to find among his fellow inmates no less a personage than Henry Partelow, who had just been consigned there on account of a suit filed by one of his and Scoullar's innumerable creditors.[105] Seemingly ignorant of the ignominy of his own incarceration, Partelow did not shrink from exercising even from the dampness and indignity of his prison cell his prerogatives as a county magistrate by calling a hearing into the complaints he, as a private citizen, had already filed against the person of his incredulous jailmate. Upon his release Duncan Perley hurried to Fredericton, where his and his brother's berth was scheduled to be sold. To his great chagrin, Perley discovered the depth of Scoullar's resourcefulness. Desperate to halt his rivals' progress, Scoullar had apparently

---

[104] Petition of Edward A. Clowes, (1843), Records of Lt. Governor Sir William McBean George Colebrooke, PANB, RS 345, B/3.

[105] Petition of Duncan W. Perley (1843), Records of Let. Governor Sir William McBean George Colebrooke, PANB, RS 345, B/4.

instructed his brother George to acquire the berth at all costs. In compliance, George Scoullar sent his agent, one Charles McCormick, to place a competing bid too exorbitant for the Perleys to match. And though he himself did not, in fact, possess the sum bid, Scoullar would at least gain a preliminary license to harvest timber at the competition's expense.[106] Any penalties to be imposed once the authorities became aware of this subterfuge could, in Scoullar's mind, no doubt be mitigated through his skillful solicitations in the halls of power in Fredericton.

For all its audacity and finesse, the coup orchestrated by William Scoullar did not threaten William Perley's enterprise, nor did it put Scoullar any closer to attaining his ultimate goal of gaining control of a large mill reserve on the shores of South Branch Lake. That this goal might at last be accomplished, Scoullar adopted a wholly different tack. In a petition to the government, in which he explained the hardships he had long endured for the sake of acquiring logs for his mill and expressed his fears that the present run on timber in anticipation of the eventual termination of the colonial Preference would discourage anyone from conducting business with him, Scoullar urged the reservation of the majority of the stands around the Lake as a single block, the timber on which he alone would have the right to cut.[107] Aware that the grant of such a reservation by the Crown would lead to the cancellation of his own berths and thus effectively bar his access to the timber on South Branch Lake, Perley countered Scoullar's claim. After stating that any decision in Scoullar's favour would have the immediate unjust effect of depriving him and his partners of the rightful fruits of their investment, Perley pointed out that Scoullar's dubious financial situation was likely to end in the alienation of Scoullar's mill, which would tend to disqualify him from holding any reserves once granted.[108] Thomas Baillie

---

[106] Petition of George Scoullar, SU/1845, Timber and Saw Mills, 1817-1865, Timber and Saw Mill Records, PANB, RS 663a.

[107] Petition of William Scoullar, SU/1843, Timber and Saw Mills, 1817-1865, Timber and Saw Mill Records, PANB, RS 663a.

[108] Petition of George Hayward, William E. Perley & Duncan W. Perley, SU/1845, Timber and Saw Mills, 1817-1865, Timber and Saw Mill Records, PANB, RS 663a.

himself, on reading the several petitions, was understandably confused by the conflicting arguments, and though he expressed a degree of sympathy for Scoullar's concerns, he was compelled to hold off on judgement until matters could be clarified.

William Perley's immediate reaction to the tabling of the matter by the Surveyor General was to take his case to the people. Pleading amongst the residents of the North West and South Branches, Perley solicited the endorsement of many of his listeners and inspired through his harsh and foreboding words real concern over what was perceived to be nothing less than the lurking spectre of monopoly. Scoullar's objective was, he argued, to lock up for himself the benefits that Perley's initiative had intended to be distributed more evenly throughout the entire Oromocto community. He disparaged Scoullar for pretending to be so concerned with the integrity of his operations when, in fact, he had for years been perfectly content to extract timber from Shin Creek, and that it was only when he saw an opportunity to gain at the expense of others that he began to parade his reputed desperation around the corridors of power in the provincial capital. The result of Perley's agitation was a petition signed by one hundred and twenty-four inhabitants of the river urging the government to ignore Scoullar's claims on the grounds that to do otherwise would unfairly bar the larger body of citizens from acquiring direct access to South Branch timber and, consequently, relegate them to either subletting chances on South Branch Lake from Mr. Scoullar at relatively high rates, or gleaning the occasional twig from less satisfactory berths further upstream.[109]

Despite its apparent testimony to popular sentiment, the petition proved ineffectual in enhancing the merits of Perley's case. And with the advent of the timber season, Perley had little leisure time to devote to any further solicitations. For his own part, William Scoullar had his own concerns to occupy his time, not the least of which was the deprivation of his mills and shipyard by order of the court and their sale to the highest bidder at an auction

---

[109] Petition of Merchants, Farmers and Lumberers of Sunbury County, SU/1845, Timber and Saw Mills, 1817-1865, Timber and Saw Mill Records, PANB, RS 663a.

held at the Burton Court House.[110] The new owners of the two alienated properties, the Central Bank of New Brunswick and Saint John merchant John Robertson, were amenable to Scoullar's desire to lease them; thus Scoullar was able to continue to conduct his business in a manner not significantly different than before. Less auspicious was the discovery of his brother's subterfuge in acquiring Perley's timber berth. Though the government did not levy an extraordinary penalty against him, it did, of course, confiscate his license.[111] The loss of the berth, though nettling to say the least, did not prevent him from fitting out two crews, headed by his brother's agent Charles McCormick and a now fully recuperated George F. Wilmot, for the purpose of harvesting (illegally now) the timber on the expropriated tract.[112] As before, Scoullar's trespass did not go unnoticed.

Having condescended to act as a supplier for Scoullar's mill, Perley was incensed when he learned that Scoullar was not only cutting illegally upon the very berth Scoullar had deprived him title to, but also that the timber so cut was not destined for his mill at all, but for export to the high-priced British market.[113] When confronted with his crimes, Scoullar rationalized them away, arguing that the land onto which his men had ventured was, in fact, contained within the bounds of the larger mill reserve he had every confidence would soon be issued to him.[114] While the government was willing to forgive the offence so long as Scoullar paid the stumpage fee for the timber so far extracted, Perley was not. Thus, when Scoullar renewed his agitation for his reserve in June of 1844, Perley, his uncle and brother resumed their opposition with undiminished zeal. Though they reiterated such points as

[110] Sunbury County Registry Office Records, PANB, RS 95, 18/28, 18/58, 18/177 and 18/191.

[111] Petition of George Hayward, SU/1844, Timber and Saw Mills, 1817-1865, Timber and Saw Mill Records, PANB, RS 663a.

[112] Petition of William E. Perley, SU/1846, Timber and Saw Mills, 1817-1865, Timber and Saw Mill Records, PANB, RS 663a.

[113] Ibid., and Petition of George Hayward, SU/1844, Timber and Saw Mills, 1817-1865, Timber and Saw Mill Records, PANB, RS 663a.

[114] Petition of George Scoullar, SU/1845, Timber and Saw Mills, 1817-1865, Timber and Saw Mill Records, PANB, RS 663a.

Scoullar's ineligibility to merit a reserve, the monopolistic effect the grant would have on the watershed's industry, the primacy of their own claims on the territory and the general popular dissatisfaction with Scoullar's recent course of action, the petitions submitted by Perley and his allies differed from previous ones in the harshness of their tone and the wider approval they curried among the people at large.[115] Yet, as, when a similar statement of the general will came before the Surveyor General, the petitions were shelved pending a more thorough investigation.

Displeased with Perley's repeated attempts to undermine his interests at the Crown Land Office and to turn the entire countryside against him, Scoullar retaliated by informing Thomas Baillie that some timber Perley had recently driven down to Saint John had been illegally extracted from land surrounding South Branch Lake.[116] When the timber was seized on Baillie's order, George Hayward proceeded to Saint John, but his audience there with the deputy in charge of the matter proved less than satisfactory. Though he thoughtfully pondered the written affidavits Hayward presented him and even seems to have acknowledged their authenticity, the deputy could not bring himself to allow the timber to be released without official word from Fredericton. Indignant over the punctiliousness of petty bureaucrats, Hayward stormed off to the provincial capital for a personal interview with the Surveyor General. Realizing the injustice that had been perpetrated, Baillie felt obliged to reveal the source of information that had formed the basis of his directive. Perley and his associates were understandably miffed upon learning that Scoullar's slander had been the cause of their inconvenience, but as the lumber season was again drawing near and the ultimate elimination of the Preference was but a mere year or two away they had not the time to seek redress in the courts. Yet throughout the winter, as they supervised the labours of their workers, they undoubtedly nurtured the hope, even as Scoullar's own crews recommenced their

---

[115] Petition of George Hayward, SU/1844; Petition of the Inhabitants of the Oromocto River, SU/1844, Timber and Saw Mills, 1817-1865, Timber and Saw Mill Records, PANB, RS 663a.

[116] Petition of George Hayward, SU/1845, Timber and Saw Mills, 1817-1865, Timber and Saw Mill Records, PANB, RS 663a.

piratical forays onto the disputed tract, that the government's eventual decision in the matter of Scoullar's mill reserve would be favourable to their interests.

Though Scoullar and his partners undoubtedly benefitted from his undue influence in Fredericton, they could not have been completely pleased with the strength and persistence of popular disapprobation. As politicians, Scoullar and Partelow were likely aware of just how unfavourably the level of popular approval boded for their long-term viability. Scoullar himself was cynical enough to imagine that the scorn of the lumbermen-farmers of the Oromocto could, with the proper alcoholic inducements, be quickly transformed into its opposite. This belief was entertained with confidence only so long as men such as Hayward and the Perleys were his major contenders, but when his old nemesis from the North West Branch, George Morrow, affixed his name to the most recent petition condemning Scoullar's reputed aims, Scoullar could not have felt particularly complacent. Since the onset of the late recovery, Morrow had moved rapidly to expand his influence throughout the watershed. By the summer of 1845 he had won rights to nearly half of the more than two hundred square miles of Crown land offered for lease at the annual auction held in Fredericton.[117] Morrow himself articulated his ultimate objectives to no one, though his accretive habits and begrudging nature were well known; thus when Morrow, with the support of several high placed Frederictonians, requested that the government provide him with greater authority in dealing with trespassers on rented berths, there could have been little doubt that his target was the trespass-prone Scoullar.[118] Faced with a threat more malevolent and dangerous than any represented by William Perley, Scoullar undoubtedly urged greater haste on the part of the Surveyor General in examining his mill-reserve claim. What yelps of joy, then, must have issued forth from his mouth when he learned that the reserve containing a whopping twenty-six square miles

---

[117] *The Royal Gazette*, May 27, 1846.

[118] Petition of William J. Bedell et al., Records of the Legislative Assembly, PANB, RS 24, 1845/pe/file 8/no. 274.

was at last approved.[119]

Prematurity characterized any celebration Scoullar may have held on the occasion of his award. The very economy that had enabled him to resume his pursuit of his ancient ambitions suddenly deprived him of the ebullience he had so ardently hoped might be his to express. In keeping with its earlier arrangement, the British Government finally struck the protective Preference down. Responding to the news, the entire forest industry of New Brunswick slipped into another of its periodic phases of depression.[120] As was the case in 1841, Scoullar was caught overextended and unprepared. Yet for the time being, he was oblivious to the deepening crisis. In the immediate aftermath of his victory he had relinquished the conduct of most of his business affairs to his brother and refocused his attentions on the Assembly, where he proceeded to champion the cause of a railroad to run through Oromocto Village along the St. John River between Fredericton and the Bay of Fundy.[121] Unfortunately, no sooner had Scoullar departed for the capital than did his brother's largest creditor, Saint John merchant John Rhoades, call in a massive £4,000 loan.[122] With most of his property subsequently seized by order of the court, George Scoullar soon found himself engaged in a desperate effort to save his mill dam from destruction by an unusually severe seasonal freshet.[123] So harsh and protracted was the flood that much of his preservative labour proved to be to no avail. When one of his mills became inoperable, Scoullar sluiced his remaining timber and made one last pathetic attempt to salvage his dam. For want of capital he soon abandoned all prospect of continuing his milling operations, vacating the one still operable

---

[119] Petition of William Scoullar, SU/1844; Petition of William Scoullar, SU/1845; Petition of William E. Perley, SU/1846, Timber and Saw Mills, 1817-1865, Timber and Saw Mill Records, PANB, RS 663a.

[120] Wynn, *Timber Colony*, op. cit., at p. 52.

[121] Petition of John M. Wilmot et al., Records of the Legislative Assembly, PANB, RS 24, 1846/pe/file 11/no. 230; and *Journals of the Legislative Assembly* (1846), p. 102.

[122] Sunbury County Registry Office Records, PANB, RS 95, 18/178.

[123] Petition of William E. Perley, SU/1846, Timber and Saw Mills, 1817-1865, Timber and Saw Mill Records, PANB, RS 663a.

frame in favour of the owner's new tenant, who turned out to be none other than George Morrow.[124]

Having long practiced the austere habits that allowed him, yet again, to remain immune to the congenital ailments afflicting the economy, George Morrow had watched with special interest the demise of Scoullar's mill. When Scoullar relinquished part of his lease, Morrow moved quickly to replace him as one of the mill's new occupants. And though he put the establishment to immediate use manufacturing larch sleepers for export to England, there can be no doubt that his real intention was to hold out for the possibility that William Scoullar's vast mill reserve might eventually be annulled and thus become available for bidding on the open market.

The inanition of one portion of the South Branch mill and the alienation of the other portion to George Morrow did not necessarily mean an end to William Scoullar's career as a lumberman. Even in the gloomy spring of 1846 one party of his employees laboured upon his great reserve, while another occupied itself with the minor tribulations of the river drive.[125] Repairs on the mill were no doubt soon effected and its blades put back into operation. Morrow might cling to one of the mills, but so long as Scoullar retained a partial interest in the establishment, no change could be effected in his proprietorship of the largest share of South Branch Lake's timber. Confidence regarding the permanence of his possession, however, was not always absolute. William Perley's foothold on the shores of the Lake was a continual threat, and clearly it boded ill for the longevity of his enterprise. How long the bounty of South Branch Lake would last was uncertain, but clearly the late intensity at which the pace of lumbering there had been prosecuted had greatly depleted the region of an enormous amount of wood. In his own mind Scoullar had no choice but to attempt to expand his reserve. And this could only be accomplished at the long-suffering Mr. Perley's expense. Thus, it was not long before Scoullar was again soliciting the Surveyor General. William Perley's reaction to Scoullar's intrigue was, of course, predictable. After reiterating the entire history of

---

[124] Ibid.

[125] Ibid.

Scoullar's more sordid exploits and pointing out, once again, the loss of his own investment should Scoullar's concession be granted, he demanded that the land in question be kept open to competitive bidding and not released outright as a mill reserve to any one man.[126] Lacking influence in Fredericton to counter Scoullar's own, Perley was truly at the mercy of a biased establishment. Indeed, so familiar were Scoullar's relations with the highest circle of the provincial elite that he found easy access to the exclusive chamber of the Executive Council for the purpose of pleading his case before it passed judgement on the matter.[127]

Thus did William Scoullar, after many years of tireless agitation, and successive triumphs and defeats, at last obtain the monopoly he had so long sought. Embittered by his defeat, William Perley morosely shifted his operations onto several less lucrative berths on South Branch Lake and began a program of acquiring permanent ownership, bit by bit, of territory from which he hoped he would be able to procure an adequate supply of timber. In time, a sense of wistfulness would overcome him whenever he contemplated his loss, and though he still desired some form of compensation for the lost fruits of his labour, an even greater longing for official recognition of the benefits his industry had brought the Province came to occupy the foremost place in his heart.[128] Less inclined to tolerate the degradation of defeat, Perley's brother quit the Oromocto altogether, traveling beyond the borders of the British dominion in North America until he found refuge in the American west and fame as a solicitor in the halls of Yankee justice.[129] Of the three partners only George

---

126 Ibid.

127 Petition of William Scoullar, SU/1846, Timber and Saw Mills, 1817-1865, Timber and Saw Mill Records, PANB, RS 663a.

128 Petition of William F. Perley, Records of the Legislative Assembly, PANB, RS 24, 1847/pe/file 11/no. 386.

129 A notorious figure on the Oromocto, Duncan Perley would win fame in the west as one of the most able, if erratic, lawyers of the age. He was an intimate of famous men, and the flint stone of more than one controversy, including the legendary duel between California Chief Justice David Terry and U.S. Senator David Broderick. By the time of his death in September of 1874, he had made and lost several fortunes, been

Hayward revealed any immediate hankering for retribution. And as the summer waned he made good upon his vengeful urge by carrying his pent-up grievances onto a field whereon Scoullar's own vulnerability would glisten brightly even in the increasingly crepuscular days of autumn.

The field on which Hayward sought to engage Scoullar was the rugged sward of politics. In the legislative elections scheduled for October of 1846, both William Scoullar and Whitehead Barker faced difficulties stemming from a confusion of the economy, the steady elaboration of which, in the minds of the electors, must have appeared to strangely parallel the growing pugnacity of the traditionalists regarding the question of Responsible Government. Scoullar's active involvement in the lumber business and his long-standing patronage of a large number of people living on the Oromocto represented a dangerous weapon with which to smite any prospective opponents, but his recent obsession with the pursuit of his own interests regardless of their negative effect on the community as a whole had undoubtedly given rise to some inquietude among his constituents over his continuing fitness for office. Displeasure with Scoullar's conduct in the Assembly only deepened as the Sheffield Total Abstinence Society stepped up the intensity of its agitation at the Court of General Sessions for a county-wide ban on the sale of alcohol. That Scoullar retained a virtually perpetual license to retail liquor put him squarely at odds with the growing number of teetotallers on either side of the St. John. And his role in depriving central New Brunswick of useful public works and channeling them, instead, downriver, as well as a rather unsubtle public endorsement of a proposal for the transferal of the bureaus of government to Saint John, hardly insulated him from the chilly suspicions emanating from the minds of his constituents that he harboured a secret loyalty to the Province's commercial entrepot that surpassed and countervailed any commitment felt toward the hinterland.[130] Immediately heedless

---

appointed to a judgeship, created a vast estate in the wilds of Nevada and sent the San Francisco Stock Exchange into a frenzy on at least one occasion. His life and exploits, deeds and misdeeds, deserve a full accounting, which this author will one day provide.

[130] *The Reporter and Fredericton Advertizer*, September 25, 1846.

of the divisiveness of his private activity, ignorant of the unpopularity of his public stands and thoroughly oblivious to the growing clamour of support for controls upon the sale and consumption of liquor then building throughout Sunbury County, Scoullar skirted the precipice of total self-possession, busied himself in the agitation for his railroad and contemplated the imminent difficulties posed his business on the river by the thickening shoals at the mouth of the Oromocto.[131]

Aware of Scoullar's inherent and acquired weaknesses, George Hayward showed little reticence in declaring himself early as a candidate for the fall elections. By July he was already engaged at the hustings, doing less preaching of the gospel of reform than reminding his former constituents, with the occasional inducement of ale, of his personal qualities of grace, charm and trustworthiness.[132] His natural affinity with the reformers in 1842 carried over into 1846, yet he did not vigorously (at least at first) campaign with them. His old friend Thomas O. Miles re-emerged as the county reform leader and presently laboured to refashion and consolidate that old clutch of unlikely allies. Whitehead Barker himself was something of a liability. His lacklustre performance in the House of Assembly, as well as Scoullar's own more hearty backing of the agenda of Lemuel Allen Wilmot, blunted the forcefulness of the reformers' critique and muffled the sound of their calls for change in Fredericton. The improbability of their claims regarding the issue of reform were obscured by the larger controversy threatening the viability of the shaky coalition. As in 1842, the ambitions of Calvin Hatheway could not be repressed. Miles himself felt personally obliged to refrain from too heavy-handed a reproof of his friend, apparently hoping that mediation by the caucus could persuade Hatheway to abandon his personal political aspirations for the good of the whole. Such hopes were

---

[131] William Scoullar to Sir William Colebrooke, September 12, 1846, Executive Council Cabinet Series, PANB, RS 9, 12/1846. The letter itself seemed prompted in part by the grounding several weeks before by the steamer *New Brunswick*, which managed with great difficulty to dislodge itself after a day of captivity. See *The Headquarters*, September 1, 1846.

[132] Diary of Thomas O. Miles, PANB, MC 451, July 9, 1846.

dashed when Hatheway, after being confronted at Miles' home with the will of the assembled reformers, refused with a confidence bloated by belligerency to abide by their decision to back Barker and (presumably) Hayward as the two men most likely to foil Scoullar's desire for re-election.[133] Faced with Hatheway's obstinacy and all too conscious of the latter's unpopularity among the all-important Oromocto electorate, the caucus dissolved in a mood of mutual recrimination. To save the coalition, Whitehead Barker offered to withdraw in Hatheway's favour, an act of magnanimity that did much to inspire the distress and protest of his compatriots, who saw in Barker that quality of incumbency that might yet overcome any indifference toward him among the voters.[134] Only Hatheway, who had loudly pronounced that he would yield to no man save Miles (mainly because he understood that Miles was unwilling to run) welcomed Barker's deferment.

Hatheway's victory over Barker and his apparent bending of the reformers to his will proved short-lived, as the desperate members of the coalition scrambled for an alternative in a race that many now presumed to be wide open. One of the reformers, John McNeil Wilmot, surprised his peers with the compelling force of his own objections to their slouching moral and political posture. Seventy-one years of age, with a distinguished career as a merchant and assemblyman already behind him,[135] Wilmot simply could not contain his inborn tendencies for prominence on the public scene. Rejecting the divisiveness of his reformist colleagues, while simultaneously exploiting the subsequent schism to justify the declaration of his own reawakened political aspirations, Wilmot repudiated fellowship with the reform party, quit the serenity of retirement at his Lincoln Parish Belmont estate and ran to Scoullar's side to stand with him for election on an emerging alternative party slate that advocated little more than an ambiguous mixture of personal advancement and provincial self-

---

[133] Id., September 28, 1846.

[134] Ibid.

[135] See T.W. Acheson, "John McNeil Wilmot," *Dictionary of Canadian Biography* (Toronto: University of Toronto Press, 1988), Volume VII, pp. 915-916.

rule.[136] Scoullar and Wilmot were soon joined by provincial aristocrat Andrew Rainsford Wetmore, a young and insufferable lawyer who for the past several years had, with his equally insufferable brother James, cut his teeth at the Burton Court House, defending debtors and vagrants and browbeating judges and juries alike.[137] He was both arrogant and saucy, with a sharpness of tongue that had still to develop that reasoned discipline and mature ferocity that would serve him to greater effect as the Province's first post-Confederation premier and then as its Chief Justice. In these, his youthful days, he displayed a degree of combativeness that could only have stemmed from a sense of insecurity arising from his desire to wreck vengeance on the world for his father's notorious murder at the hands of a political rival.  Justification of his own worth as a member of a family that had produced jurists and assemblymen, as well as an innate craving for distinction, were likely motives behind his candidacy.[138]

Seeing them, perhaps, as a drag on his own prospects, Scoullar remained diffident toward his new political partners, choosing instead to repeat his solitary 1842 whirlwind tour of the Oromocto, the people of which turned out in droves to hear his speech, drink his ale and eat the food his campaign so generously provided. Fearful of the evidence of Scoullar's continuing political vitality and concerned, too, that Wilmot's defection represented the inevitable fragmentation of their coalition, the reformers regrouped in an effort to overthrow the grossly unfavourable Hatheway. Rekindling his antipathy for his old enemy as he watched his progress along the byways around his Blissville home and acting,

---

[136] Wilmot's affinity for Scoullar was naturally enhanced by his interest in the St. John River railroad and his own son George's long-time association with Scoullar's operations. See Petition of John M. Wilmot et al., Records of the Legislative Assembly, PANB, RS 24, 1846/pe/file 11/no. 230.

[137] Diary of Thomas O. Miles, PANB, MC 451, January 5, 1844.

[138] See J.C. & H.C. Graves, Volume 7, p. 83; T.W. Acheson, "Andrew Rainsford Wetmore," *Dictionary of Canadian Biography* (Toronto: University of Toronto Press, 1990), Volume XII, pp. 1096-1098; and James Carnahan, *The Wetmore Family of America* (Albany: Musnell and Rowland, 1861).

no doubt, in conformity with his uncle's preferences, William Perley, accompanied by his uncle's aged father, traveled to the home of Thomas O. Miles and pleaded with him to come forward as a more viable candidate to stand in the way of Scoullar's re-election.[139] In consideration of his loyalty to Hatheway and his own reluctance to again venture into an active political role, Miles approached the request with caution, winning from Perley a commitment to back the reform ticket regardless of who the party candidates would ultimately be, yet not objecting to Perley's resolution to canvass the countryside on his behalf to drum up support for a draft. Saved from the embarrassment of having to answer charges of political opportunism and disloyalty to friends, Miles heeded the prayer of the subsequent requisition. Approaching Hatheway with inspired delicacy, Miles not only reminded him of his earlier pronouncement regarding the conditions of his withdrawal, but succeeded in persuading the vainglorious and haughty man to agree to nominate him as a candidate for the Assembly at a meeting of the electors at the Burton Court House on the 6th of October.[140]

The formal declaration of the candidates ushered in a political season the utter squalidness of which was achieved by the combined efforts of no less than six contestants, the last of whom — an Oromocto trader and lumberman of modest station by the name of James Sutherland — entered the fray simply for the opportunity to hurl inflammatory words at the front and backsides of his more socially exalted competitors.[141] To their credit, Miles and Hayward retained at least a semblance of dignity as they crisscrossed the region in search of support, while Scoullar himself hid his own depravity behind the more obnoxious behaviour of John M. Wilmot. As Wilmot openly declared the home of George Hayward to be "a sink of iniquity from whence all the trickery emanated" and tried (with his son George's assistance), through slanderous machinations and rumour mongering, to weaken the personal and political solidarity of the reformers, Scoullar visited the major settlements of the Oromocto, Sheffield and Maugerville at the

---

[139] Diary of Thomas O. Miles, PANB, MC 451, October 1, 1846.

[140] Id., October 6, 1846.

[141] Ibid.

head of a caravan of wagons filled with provisions to satisfy the baser cravings of his audience,[142] effecting compliance with his request for re-election, if not through his exposition of the role he had played in the elimination of the public debt, the restoration of the Province's credit rating and the substitution of a small export duty in place of the more onerous practice of stumpage,[143] then through the efficacy of strong drink. So shameless an appeal to the remaining pockets of inebriation provoked from Miles the prediction "that all the drinking characters will vote for Scoullar." The strength of temperance, having grown markedly during the first half of the 1840s, ultimately dissipated the potential impact of the County's drunkards upon the final tallies, while criticism of Scoullar's record steadily increased the likelihood that the more responsible portion of the electorate would be out in force come election day. This was true even on the Oromocto, where the growing ranks of teetotalers, displeased with the unseemly resort of drunken Irishmen to Scoullar's table and troubled by the unpleasant dimension of Scoullar's own private conduct, began to turn a ready ear to the words of the gentlemen reformers who, in a less uproarious time a decade before, had served and represented them so commendably.

By election day, the candidates — their energies expired, their loquaciousness overcome by exhaustion and silence — lay scattered throughout the county, each waiting, in quiet anticipation, the outcome at the polls. Only in Burton, the site of the majority of the balloting, did the potential for real trouble breach the already turbulent surface of the pond of democracy. Conscious of his own weakness, Scoullar managed to refrain from personal involvement in skulduggery, but under the aegis of his son Andrew and his trusted adjunct George F. Wilmot, the transient Irish labourers in his shipyard, dependent solely upon Scoullar for work, wages, liquor and purpose, gathered into a modern version of the medieval *busilaria*, prepared themselves for violence under the various encouragements of their leaders and marched, shillelaghs in hand, against all those who dared question the status quo via the ballot box. Unequipped to prevent the massing of Scoullar's

---

[142] Id., October 6, 1846.

[143] *The Headquarters*, September 30, 1846.

men, the local magistrates (the Sheriff included) were resigned to watch the threatening maneuvers unfold just beyond the Court House compound, all the while listening nervously to the shrill barbarity of a host of Gaelic voices rising up with unimpaired vulgarity, taunting them and all other known and suspected partisans of the so-called reformers. Before the polls closed the armed throng disbursed, rumbling with disgruntled hearts through the interval, attracting additional followers and regrouping at the eastern end of Oromocto Bridge— there to meet the most vocal critics to their late exploits and fulfil their promise to exact a painful vengeance. Here they stood, defiantly, antagonistically, reviewing each wagon load of voters as they passed, eyeing furtively each passenger in search of prey on which to vent their collective brutality. When two nephews of George Hayward appeared among the stream of retiring vehicles, undoubtedly chanting in derisive cadence the likely defeat of Scoullar, the thugs provoked the horse drawing their cart to rear, initiating chaos among the surrounding wagons, setting off a pell-mell rush for the western end of the bridge and providing the Scoullarites with the excuse to commence their assault. Some of the travelers remained behind to resist, one man defending his fallen, bleeding brother, shielding him from the remorseless volley of stones until he could convey him to the safety of the river's farther shore.[144]

Yet even as the confrontation on the bridge escalated into a furious exchange, the counting of the vote had been completed. No amount of additional violence could salvage the last hopes of William Scoullar and his dubious faction. As expected, both Maugerville and Sheffield repudiated him. Greater support for his candidacy was found on the South Branch, though a more diffuse dislike for him on the North West Branch diminished his percentage of the final tallies in Blissville. The bitterest fighting of the contest occurred along the lower stretches of the river, where only the community of French Lake escaped polarization. Assured mainly through George Morrow's presence there, French Lake's opposition to Scoullar contrasted sharply with the division that occurred in Geary. Closer to the mouth of the river, the outcome (thanks in part to the efforts of his makeshift militia) was

---

[144] *The Reporter and Fredericton Advertiser*, September 25, 1846.

more favourable to the incumbent, but even here divisions abounded. In the end, Scoullar met his political downfall, as the people of the river solemnized what amounted to (despite the propaganda of the reformers) an exquisitely conservative desire for a return to the good and stable days of the previous decade and rejoiced, finally, in the election of Hayward and Miles.[145] Two days later, the distasteful events of the late campaign forgotten, Hayward and Miles momentarily dropped their aversion to the excesses of alcohol that had so recently garnered them the support of a large segment of the electorate and led a merry assembly of their partisans in near-endless rounds of celebratory toasts.[146]

Hayward's triumph over his old nemeses was soon marred by an impertinence, the logical beneficiary of which was the vanquished Scoullar. Cognizant of his duty to the party to which he had pledged himself, yet angered, too, by his poor showing and thus easily convinced that his repudiation by the electorate had more to do with fraud practiced by the local elite than with any personal unattractiveness as a candidate, Andrew Rainsford Wetmore demanded a scrutiny of the electoral results. Despite Wetmore's clear intention to use the charge of fraud as a means to discredit his successful opponents (particularly Miles) and engineer Scoullar's re-entry into the legislature through the back door, Sheriff Hazen acquiesced in Wetmore's bothersome request, only to suffer the insult of Wetmore's assertion that no fair hearing of his grievance could ever be found in the unsympathetic halls of the very building in which Hazen, according to Wetmore, had perpetrated his unscrupulous manipulation of the ballots. Resolved to take his case to a higher authority in Fredericton, Wetmore prepared himself by examining the pollbooks to discern the incontestable proof of the benefit gained by Thomas O. Miles at Scoullar's expense.[147] Listening to the charges, Miles could not have helped but to recollect that election ten years before, when similar accusations leveled against him by Henry Partelow had cost him his seat in the Assembly; thus it is not surprising that he

---

[145] Pollbooks, Sunbury County Records, PANB, RS 157, J/2/4 (1846).

[146] Diary of Thomas O. Miles, PANB, MC 451, October 12, 1846.

[147] Petition of Andrew Rainsford Wetmore, Records of the Legislative Assembly, PANB, RS 24, 1847/pe/file 4/no. 125.

quickly enlisted the legal services of his friend Lemuel Allen Wilmot as a precaution against a repeat of that earlier yet still galling outcome. Early in the following year, when Wetmore appeared before the House of Assembly and formally asserted that the Sheriff's fraud resulted in a tainted vote, serious consideration resulted, but the ultimate findings of the House could warrant little support for Wetmore's accusations, though its members mercifully conceded that the latter arose for reasons other than frivolity or vexation.[148] Hayward and Miles were secure, while Scoullar, uncontestably repudiated by the people, returned to the pursuit of elusive fortune along the banks of the Oromocto without recourse to the inestimable advantages brought by membership in the legislature.

For all the hopes that may have abounded for a return to the happy days of the 1830s, the election of Hayward and Miles did little to alleviate the dormant condition of the economy. Nor did the state of Scoullar's finances improve with his return to more active stewardship of his personal affairs. His brother's conduct had reduced his business to a shambles, leading not only to the seizure and sale of the family's remaining property,[149] but also the final dashing of all hope of regaining title to the sagging South Branch milling establishment and retaining possession of its attached mill reserve. A new permanent tenant thus replaced the Scoullars and the great mill reserve was carved up into a series of smaller berths, many of which were snapped up by George Morrow. Depressed by diminishing prospects and perhaps somewhat ashamed of his oppressive failures, George Scoullar retired from the Oromocto and returned to his brother's former home in Saint John, where he discovered that life as a police magistrate brought greater rewards and greater public accolades than could have been possible within the ossified bounds of Sunbury County.[150]

---

[148] "Report of the Committee to Take into Consideration the Petition of A.R. Wetmore," Records of the Legislative Assembly, PANB, RS 24, 1847/re/file 1.

[149] Sunbury County Registry Office Records, PANB, RS 95, 18/384.

[150] Scoullar's greatest exploit as Chief of Police was his apprehension of the notorious murderer Breen, whom Scoullar no doubt had known from the days when both had lived on the Oromocto. Coincidentally, the Breen case brought him into contact with Andrew R. Wetmore, who

Stunned by the difficulties facing them, William Scoullar and his remaining partner oversaw the construction of two ships at their rented slip at the river mouth[151] and found some relief from past slights in the small rewards of provincial patronage and local office. Partelow's days were soon consumed with the affairs of the parish schools and the administration of repairs to the great road on either side of Oromocto Bridge— activities that on at least one occasion antagonized the wealthy owners of the interval lands on the river's western bank.[152] Scoullar himself remained optimistic regarding the future, despite his failure at the polls and the ongoing exigencies of his business, and though his initial plans for a railroad to pass through Oromocto Village via the St. John River valley had come to naught, a second proposal for the construction of a line to run parallel to the South Branch Stream offered new possibilities for the venting of his entrepreneurial urges.[153] And for those glories formerly experienced on the provincial stage he was able to find some compensation (as well as consolation) in a seat on the County Court of General Session as a duly constituted Justice of the Peace.[154]

However much pleasure Scoullar found in his modest prominence in County affairs, the opaque shape of the local and provincial economic landscape was taking on an increasingly subterranean aspect. Plagued by unemployment and shortages in relief available to the poor, the people of the Oromocto began to suffer transient visitation by starved, diseased and desperate refugees from Ireland's dread potato famine. In days past Irish emigrants came to the Oromocto with the full blessing and

---

took the case to trial, and with William Perley, who was granted access to the jail for the purpose of visiting with the condemned man following the guilty verdict. When Breen eluded the hangman by committing suicide, Perley bitterly complained to Samuel Leonard Tilley that the constabulary, including apparently George Scoullar, was completely lacking in competence.

[151] Hancox, op. cit., p. 41.

[152] Petition of John M. Wilmot et al., Executive Council Cabinet Series, PANB, RS 9, 1847/9.

[153] *The Headquarters*, November 4 & November 11, 1846.

[154] *The Royal Gazette*, May 19, 1847.

support of provincial officials. Back in June of 1841 a county emigrant society had formed, drawing into its ranks many notable men from Burton and Lincoln Parishes,[155] and, despite the disruptions suffered upon it by the irritable exhortations of Sheriff Hazen,[156] it had worked to some effect to comply with Lieutenant Governor Colebrooke's general call for humanitarian relief. George Hayward, then between terms in the Assembly, had once even arranged to provide employment and lodging for a number of emigrants sent upstream on the steamer *New Brunswick* by his nephew, Emigrant Agent Moses Perley.[157] Hayward's personal sympathies for the hapless Irish represented but a fraction of a greater spirit of Christian charity and common humanity endemic to the people of the Oromocto. So great was this humane spirit that it not only induced a general tolerance for the presence for these and other emigrants, but even managed to push the fractious struggle for control of the river economy into the background while donations were solicited on behalf of the survivors of the tragic fire that destroyed the city of St. John's, Newfoundland in the summer of 1846.[158]

In the impoverished days of 1847, though, hospitality for a now unwelcome set of guests proved wanting, not so much as a result of a sparseness of basic compassion as a scarcity of parish funds. A pervading consciousness of legal obligation and the fervent hopes for provincial reimbursement, however, did help to fuel the capacity for humane concern on the part of the agents of local benevolence. At least six emigrants were saved by hospitalization in

---

[155] Diary of Thomas O. Miles, PANB, MC 451, June 15, 1841.

[156] *New Brunswick Courier*, July 31, 1841.

[157] Moses H. Perley to Captain Wylie, June 7, 1845, Accounts and Assistance, 1840-1849, Records of the Immigration Administration, PANB, RS 555, H/3.

[158] "Resolutions of a Meeting of the Inhabitants of the County of Sunbury, July 7, 1846," Executive Cabinet Series, PANB, RS 9, 1846/11; Diary of Thomas O. Miles, PANB, MC 451; and Rex Grady, "'With Unfeigned Regret': New Brunswick's Response to the Great St. John's Fire of 1846," *Newfoundland Quarterly*, Volume 88 (1994), No. 4, pp. 51-54.

the homes of the generous folk of the river,[159] but as the sickness passed, the ills the convalescent carried with them seemed to descend into the very earth, where they worked a mysterious and frightful magic upon autumn's bounty. When the harvest came, the potato crop was discovered to have been stricken by a ravaging blight that presented the entire countryside bounding the river with the dire threat of starvation.[160] A cry of despair suddenly rose up from the men, women and children in Burton and Blissville parishes. Unable to find sustenance or even refuge in the estimable embrace of employment, the menfolk in particular drifted along with the harsh current of despondency, finding disunctious relief in the bitter taste of spirits that now, following the recent triumph of the local advocates of prohibition, had become wholly illegal.[161] In reaction to the enormity of the crises, the magistrates and great men of the land forgot the differences that divided so many of them and made a united effort to secure aid in the form of provincial grants and a loan from the Central Bank. In this capacity, George Morrow and William Scoullar laboured side-by-side, taking joint initiative in calling for a convocation of local magistrates to determine the most equitable distribution of the fortuitous windfall. Burton, the hardest hit of the several parishes, received the largest portion of assistance; a monetary boon that undoubtedly contributed to the auspicious preservation of the lives of a large portion of its struggling population.[162]

Recovery from famine did not mean the return of a more bearable mode of existence. The local economy remained in its

---

[159] Petition of Archibald McLean, Records of the Legislative Assembly, PANB, RS 24, 1848/pe/file 11/no. 388.

[160] Petition of Jeremiah Smith et al., Records of the Legislative Assembly, PANB, RS 24, 1848/pe/file 12/no. 406; and Petition of William Hoyt et al., Records of the Legislative Assembly, PANB, RS 24, 1848/pe/file 12/no. 422.

[161] Petition of the Total Abstinence Society of Sheffield, General Session, Sunbury County Records, PANB, RS 157, A/2/48. The petition notes the general failure throughout the county, except in Sheffield, of the late county ban on liquor.

[162] General Sessions, Sunbury County Records, PANB, RS 157, A/2/48/b.

retarded condition throughout the rest of the decade. Lumbering endured, but its vitality paled when compared with statistics denoting the performance of earlier days. William Scoullar continued his operations, yet an eagerness for profit did little to facilitate a cure for his ancient habit of indebtedness. Gone to Saint John to ease his timber through the customs establishment, he annoyed one of his creditors, who subsequently complained of Scoullar's capriciousness and convinced the local constabulary to order Scoullar to remain within the city's bounds until the debt was repaid. Scoullar, of course, could not be bothered by such legalities and felt no compunction whatsoever in traveling across the harbour over to Portland as his interests demanded. Becoming apprised of Scoullar's unrestrained and rather indiscrete movements, Scoullar's creditor demanded that the bothersome debtor be declared a bankrupt and made subject to the auditory powers of the Chancery Court.[163] When fire swept through the village of Oromocto, destroying a number of residential buildings before moving greedily into Scoullar's shipyard compound to consume a half-completed vessel still on the stocks, Scoullar's fortunes could not have fallen any lower.[164] Henry Partelow was spared the more excessive chagrins that visited his reckless partner, but his premature death in November of 1849 ended his appreciation of the smaller embarrassments as well. A life insurance policy and the kindness of his brother-in-law, Gerhardus Clowes, helped to provide for his many children,[165] while the several posts he held in the County hierarchy became the inheritance of a small and eager tribe of office seekers. William Perley was one of the more fortunate of these aspirants. His uncle's influence in Fredericton, it seems, proved unusually helpful in his acquisition of Partelow's position as Commissioner of the Nerepis Road — an office the possession of which he did not find in the least compromised by his recent efforts to secure monies for the completion of a competing

---

[163] Case of William Scoullar (1848), Chancery Court Records, PANB, RS 55.

[164] *The Reporter and Fredericton Advertiser*, August 11, 1848.

[165] Estate Papers of Henry Thomas Partelow (1849), Sunbury County Probate Court Records, PANB, RS 72; and the 1851 Census of New Brunswick, Sunbury County.

highway between Fredericton and Saint John intended to pass through Blissville and the Rusagonis.[166]

Pleased with his capture of a small vestige of his late rival's former prestige, Perley continued to allocate much of his time to the affairs of his own modest lumbering business. His industry in this regard returned small profits, but these paled in comparison with those enjoyed by George Morrow. Emerging victorious in the decade-long battle for hegemony on the Oromocto, Morrow made the most of his newly secured pre-eminence. New vistas awaited him on the Musquash in King's County, where partnership in a milling venture with Lincoln-based lumberman John Glasier would give way to new profits and renewed conflicts,[167] but the old familiar ground of the Oromocto remained his primary domain. As the South Branch relinquished its timber, other avenues down which to pursue his industry were eagerly sought. For a brief while Morrow considered plans for the construction of a steam-driven sawmill at the river's mouth in emulation of a similar manufactory built in Fredericton by J.L. Marsh,[168] only to break off this minor flirtation with modern technology in favour of heeding the beckoning call of the exploitable timber lands in

---

[166] Perley had begun lobbying for this highway as early as February of 1847, and would continue to do so into the 1860s, when at last it became a Great Road of the province. See Petition of James Taylor et al., Records of the Legislative Assembly, PANB, RS 24, 1847/pe/file3/no. 87.

[167] Morrow's operations on the Musquash began in 1850, when he and Glasier (a son of Deacon Benjamin and brother of Stephen) went into partnership in a milling enterprise with J.W.M. Irish of Saint John, a Mr. Rourke of Lancaster and a Mr. Peavy of Eastport. Two of his partners proved unreliable-- Irish due to negligence, Peavy due to death-- thus Morrow sought first to obtain a larger share of the mill's reserve in his own name, and later to gain lumbering rights to a large tract of territory on the upper Musquash. He sent his nephew Thomas Wood and North Branch lumberman Benjamin Grey to examine the state of the country. As Wood and Grey found the land broken by clearings and the river itself obstructed by rocks and fallen timber, Morrow successfully petitioned for exemption from normal reserve granting regulations in consideration of the approximately £400 he would be forced to expend in making both land and river profitable.

[168] *The Headquarters*, September 30, 1846.

the rear of his French Lake home. Feeling confident in his strength, he turned a portion of his Geary mill over to William Smith,[169] and pursued the clearing of the uppermost reaches of Brizley Brook.[170] Enjoyment of his success and the further development of his many schemes, however, nearly came to an untimely and tragic end during a trip to Saint John, when the stage he was traveling in fell through the thinly frozen surface of Grand Bay. A farmer named McCoskery heard the urgent cries for help from over a mile and half away; and though he managed to save Morrow and the stage's adolescent driver, the lives of two women, including a sister of Saint John Alderman Thomas Harding, were beyond his power to redeem.[171]

Morrow's escape from an icy burial in the freezing waters of the St. John occasioned great rejoicing on the part of his friends and family. The people of the Oromocto, too, may have held their own private celebrations, and certainly there must have been some relief that the river's greatest patron still walked the earth. General and overt expressions of joy were restrained only by the unfriendly reality that no one man could ever hope to resuscitate the arrested pace of economic life. Even as Morrow recommenced his plans for the expansion of his enterprise, patronage in the form of employment remained minimal. A decade of upheaval, competition and endlessly meandering fortune had left the entire community of the Oromocto fragile and weak. Dependence on timber brought prosperity, but it brought despair, too, and in the painfully bright luminance of such miseries as depression and famine the disconsolateness that so firmly held the imaginations of the people slowly diminished the memory of good and happier days. Out-migration was a real alternative for many on the river, and no doubt some resorted to this option, joining a steady and increasing stream of men and women out of New Brunswick and toward such places as Australia, New Zealand and the American States.[172] Most people in the Province resisted emigration, and

---

[169] Sunbury County Registry Office Records, PANB, RS 95, 19/504.

[170] Petition of George Morrow, SU/1848, Timber and Saw Mills, 1817-1865, Timber and Saw Mill Records, PANB, 663a.

[171] *New Brunswick Courier*, January 29, 1848.

[172] MacNutt, op. cit., p. 283.

certainly aversion to it was strong on the Oromocto. But without the traditional support of timber, a new source of livelihood was necessary if the most vulnerable members of the community were to survive within it.

For years the ideology of agrarianism had rung futilely in the ears of a lumbering populace thought too ignorant and irresponsible to ever appreciate the inherent virtues and stability of a more sedate rural existence, but now, in the agonizing malaise of the late 1840s, the tired old call suddenly struck the collective tympanum of the populace. Deputy Surveyor John Colling expressed supreme confidence in the efficacy of roads as a key to shuffling the new agricultural inclination of the people onto the vacant lands in the rear of Geary.[173] Remembering his rejection by a reputably drunken electorate wholly mesmerized by the discordant caroling of the axe, Calvin Hatheway decried such optimism and pronounced rough judgement on the backward farming practices to be found along Sunbury County's major stream.[174] His harsh opinion was only confirmed by Professor Johnston, who discovered that the settlers between the mouth of the Oromocto and Gagetown were hopelessly given over to those very same deluded and stupid habits that had made the entire Province a veritable laughing stock throughout the British Empire.[175] Removed from the intensity of desperation felt by formerly prosperous lumbermen, men like Hatheway and Johnston failed to appreciate the new resolve that was soon to propel men and women to the limits of the Oromocto watershed, not simply to cut timber, but to permanently settle as farmers. The families of Anderson, Boone, Buckingham, Carr, DeWitt, Frost, Howe, McMinn, Till, Tucker and Wood nearly all partook in the movement in the coming decade, carving out new homes in the wilderness in response to the diminishing rewards of life on the river that had become too much a part of their experience for them to completely renounce.

---

[173] Thomas Baillie, *Report of the Surveyor General of New Brunswick upon the Present State of the Crown Lands* (Fredericton: J. Simpson, 1849), p. 17.

[174] Id., p. 11.

[175] J.F.W. Johnston, *Report on the Agricultural Capabilities of the Province of New Brunswick* (Fredericton: J. Simpson, 1850), p. 4.

# Chapter Three

## THE LIMITS OF DIVERSITY

Having been exhausted by a divisive conflict for control of the timber trade during the 1840s, the Oromocto community experienced a relative boom in the subsequent decade that presented its people with new opportunities. At the outset of the new decade the unseemly implications of the previous era's bitter struggles dissipated. Old staples such as shipbuilding displayed renewed vitality, while new developments, such as the erection of a cotton mill on the Rockwell Stream, seemingly presaged the advent of a new industrial order that would reverse the inevitable decline of the countryside. The South Branch may have relinquished much of its best timber, but a new fascination with previously over-looked tamarack, resulting largely from the expanded prosecution of shipbuilding, extended the longevity of the river's traditional subservience to the whims of the timber baron. The sustained health of the economy also made possible further developments of a social and political nature. New institutions such as the Orange Lodge, the steady spread of the Free Will Baptist creed and temperance, and the rise of a novel yet vague set of political concepts known as liberalism out of the ruins of the reform movement manifest the existence of an intricate web of affiliations and commitments binding the river's people together even more tightly than had been the case in earlier decades.

Yet while the economy remained in a highly animated state and the framework of community grew increasingly elaborate, a new, more ominous series of events marred the progressive character of the 1850s. Most significant of these was the outward movement of a segment of the population into the hinterland. As vibrant as the economy was, it was not advanced enough to provide the sort of opportunities that could completely satisfy the craving for sustenance on the part of the budding populace in the older settlements. New alternatives had to be found if life was to be sustained within the familiar bounds of the watershed. Land settlement was an obvious solution to the vexing demographic problem. As lumbermen moved into the upper limits of the watershed, so too did the settler, anxious not only to establish himself on a freehold as a hedge against privation, but also to cash in on a bonanza of marketable timber. But as land settlement proceeded apace throughout the expansive decade of the 1850s, the outlines of a fateful crisis slowly materialized. Once the boom played itself out and the much-coveted tamarack was largely extracted, the newly cleared lots in the hinterland, located far from the main avenues of civilization and situated on second-rate soil, could hardly long nourish the generation of pioneers, let alone its numerous progeny. Thus, the 1850s were a decade of paradox, extending new complexity and sharper definitions to the old Oromocto community, yet simultaneously compelling a partial migration onto the frontier, where a portion of the old Loyalist-sprung populace would inevitably be faced with the ultimate implications of dwindling resources and diminished options.

≈≈≈

Following the great controversies of the 1840s, the status of the majority of the river's inhabitants had, for the most part, remained unchanged. Benefitting enormously from the general stimulus to the timber trade, yet experiencing inestimable misfortune during the very pronounced and periodic busts, the people had managed to replenish their ranks through natural increase and a process of naturalization. Everywhere within the watershed the population grew.[1] And though jobs were scarcer at the end of the decade than they had been, say, in 1845, the demographic expansion certainly testified to the enduring strength and the as yet unrealized potential of the local economy.

The preservation of the status quo amidst periodic catastrophe and a growing and increasingly competitive population was no more true for the bulk of the river's inhabitants than it was for that

---

[1] Between 1840 and 1851, the combined populations of Blissville, Burton and Lincoln Parishes grew from 2,570 to 3,272. See "Population Returns," *Journals of the Legislative Assembly* (1841), Appendix, xxii and the 1851 Census of New Brunswick, Sunbury County.

familiar and select group of families who had lived so placidly along the river's main course and its several tributaries during the 1830s. At the river's mouth the McMinn family had undergone its share of the general tumult. Retired on his rented lot, free at last from the arduous labours of a lifetime, the patriarch Thomas had broken his traditional allegiance to his one-time employer William Scoullar in the election of 1846 and cast his vote for reform.[2] His son George, who undoubtedly worked in Scoullar's ship yard, could not, however, so easily bring himself to defy the drunken wrath of Scoullar's mob. His unshakable loyalty to his employer, as exhibited in the elections of 1842 and 1846,[3] seems to have heightened his chances for continued employment and may well have helped secure him a relatively lucrative contract to construct a new pound for the parish of Burton.[4] James Frost, whose daughter George would soon marry, likewise expressed his support for the man who paid his wages,[5] and thus, like his son-in-law to be, exhibited before his patron those two virtues, reliability and obedience, that employers have always valued so highly in their hirelings.

Further upstream in Geary Settlement the Boone family, represented by the nuclear units headed by brothers George and John, as well as the Tills, headed by James Till Jr., continued to abide on lots rented from their neighbours. During the early years of the previous decade the three men had been partisans of the cause of William Scoullar, but after the depression of 1846 they defected to the camp of George Hayward and the reformers.[6] While James Till's and the Boones' enthusiasm for Hayward may well have had as much to do with their close kinship with the man as it did with their displeasure with Scoullar, the utter dilapidation of the economy was probably the strongest reason for their rejection of the controversial incumbent. Their own material condition,

---

[2] Pollbooks, Sunbury County Records, PANB, RS 157, J/2/4 (1846).

[3] Id., J/2/3 (1842) and J/2/4 (1846).

[4] Charles Clowes to John S. Brown, July 25, 1844, General Sessions, Sunbury County Records, PANB, RS 157, A/2/45 (1845).

[5] Pollbooks, Sunbury County Records, PANB, RS 157, J/2/4 (1846).

[6] Id., J/2/3 (1842) and J/2/4 (1846).

however, did not measurably improve upon the return of Hayward to the Provincial Assembly; for as the economy remained anemic throughout the rest of the decade, the two families experienced a perilous series of procreative successes. As land within the older community was relatively expensive, as opportunities for labour remained stagnate and the population steadily increased, families like the Tills and Boones would shortly be confronted by important and, perhaps, disconcerting decisions regarding their future in the watershed.

On the South Branch the previous decade's struggles had hardly left the community unscathed. John Anderson Jr., now the head of a large family, continued to occupy the furthest point of settlement on the river. He was a quiet man it seems, and except for a brief venture to the polls to publicly express his support for William Scoullar, the mundane conduct of his life generally helped to guarantee his inconspicuousness. His neighbours, the Buckinghams, were neither so successful nor, perhaps, so fortunate in maintaining a low profile. Solomon Buckingham remained the acknowledged and official chief of the clan, though his position within the household beyond the eyes of the public at large may well have been subordinate to the one occupied by his domineering wife. As patriarch, the duty fell to him to address the needs of his aged mother once she became incapable of fending for herself, as well as those of his elder brother Stephen, who, after the death of his wife and children, had been rendered an emotional and physical invalid.[7] Public assistance from the local Overseers of the Poor,[8] in addition to a war pension granted to his mother in honour of his father's loyal service to the Crown in the previous century, went far in augmenting Solomon's private income, though failure by the Court of General Sessions to apply to Fredericton for the last installment of the pension prior to his mother's death in December of 1843 was particularly injurious. Financial recovery from this blow was achieved once the

---

[7] See Petition of Solomon Buckingham, Records of the Legislative Assembly, PANB, RS 24, 1845/pe/file 8/no. 291 and the 1851 Census of New Brunswick, Sunbury County.

[8] General Sessions, Sunbury County Records, PANB, RS 157, A/2/49/a (1849).

government corrected its mistake and the missing installment was finally remitted. With the resumption of provincial economic health in 1844, Buckingham probably found work with William Scoullar, either at his mill or as a member of the details led by Charles McCormick and George Wilmot. Indeed, so tied were his fortunes to that of his probable patron that he could not fathom abandoning him in the election of 1846.[9]

The magnitude of his own responsibilities and the limitation of his resources prevented Solomon Buckingham from being of more than of cursory assistance to all of his needy kinsmen. The family of his cousin William Tucker, who may have lived on the Buckingham estate throughout the 1840s, is a case in point. When Tucker died in 1849 his wife and five children were scattered throughout the parishes of Blissville and Lincoln, where local officials thrust them upon households whose continuing hospitality was maintained, in part, by periodic disbursements from county coffers.[10] Additional expense on the part of local government was spared by the sincere concern of Tucker's step son, Nathaniel Howe III. Having greater endurance and initiative than either his father or step-father, Howe had managed to purchase a small lot with proceeds from sales of timber to local mill-owners.[11] With confidence in his ability to procure even greater profits and keenly aware of his familial responsibilities, the third Nathaniel Howe soon took it upon himself to cater directly to the needs of his mother and at least two of his half-siblings.[12]

Free of the personal tragedies that plagued the Buckinghams

---

[9] Pollbooks, Sunbury County Records, PANB, RS 157, J/2/4 (1846).

[10] General Sessions, Sunbury County Records, PANB, RS 157, A/2/50/a (1850), and the 1851 Census of New Brunswick, Sunbury County.

[11] See Petition of Nathaniel Howe (1849), Land Petitions, PANB, RS 108 and Sunbury County Registry Office Records, PANB, RS 95, 18/529. Howe sold timber to Richardson Tracy, but seems at times to have accepted promissory notes in lieu of actual payment. When Tracy was unable to honour the promises made, not only to Howe but to a group of other lumbermen, he was forced to sell off his portion of the Tracy establishment.

[12] See 1851 Census of New Brunswick, Sunbury County.

and Tuckers, Charles DeWitt suffered a different sort of discomfort throughout the confusion of the previous decade. Riding the wave of the self-same prosperity that had so magnificently elevated the status of William Scoullar in the late 1830s, DeWitt suddenly found himself at the mercy of the impersonal distemper of the business cycle. When Scoullar began calling in debts to slow his own descent into the abyss of bankruptcy and ruin, the unfortunate DeWitt found himself mired in a monetary disaster from which there could be no easy escape. Tolerance for the fickleness of friends and allies wore thin at such times, allowing the patron to forget his client's past good service as he made his way through the formalities incumbent upon those pursuing legal redress against the actions of delinquent debtors.[13] DeWitt's worsened financial straits following the culmination of Scoullar's successful suit pushed him desperately into the vestibule of George Morrow, to whom he mortgaged a portion of his landed estate.[14] His unwilling and unwanted resort to the conditional friendship of George Morrow hardly contributed to improving relations with Scoullar. Upon gaining his long-sought mill reserve on the shores of South Branch Lake, Scoullar managed to spare both the capital and the malice required to outbid his old client for a berth the latter had long held on the banks of Shin Creek.[15] The enmity between the two men eventually gave way to a mutual remissness that was made all the more oppressive by Scoullar's near total retreat from business along the upper branches of the Oromocto. As the economy resumed its old dynamism, DeWitt returned to his old haunts.[16] Repudiating any plans for the purchase of timber lands in the interior,[17] he quickly established relations with the man who succeeded Scoullar as proprietor of the South Branch

---

[13] Sunbury County Registry Office Records, PANB, RS 95, 16/365.

[14] Id., 16/342.

[15] License no. 905 granted to William Scoullar, Timber Licenses, Timber and Saw Mill Records, PANB, RS 663f, F1/13.

[16] *The Royal Gazette*, June 2, 1852.

[17] Petitions of Charles DeWitt and John L. DeWitt (1843), Land Petitions, PANB, RS 108.

mill.[18]

Yet while families such as Charles DeWitt's may have managed to endure the difficulties of the decade without recourse to desperate measures and were thus able to remain on the land they had settled prior to 1840, others, who had been positioned within the watershed equally as long, had found it necessary to uproot themselves for the purpose of finding a more amenable situation. Attachment to the countryside of their birth and loyalty to the community within which they had been raised and in which most of their friends and relations still continued to live barred a more drastic resort to out-migration, but certainly land settlement on soil within the watershed could be safely undertaken without loss of immediate and comforting attachment to that which was most familiar. Among the first to feel compelled to take to the land was William Carr of Geary, who, in the winter of 1841-42, was discovered by Deputy Surveyor Amasa Flaglor to be occupying a small clearing just to the north of Victoria Settlement.[19] Carr was a lonely figure in these early days of the decade, for while emigrants would subsequently be directed to the region, almost none of them found continued habitation there particularly enticing. Most of them were Irish, while many of the rest were labourers from Saint John who quickly abandoned the land once opportunities for employment back in the city returned with the restoration of the provincial economy.

Though the marked failure of immigrants during the 1840s to establish themselves in Victoria may have deterred others from outside the limits of the watershed from making a similar attempt at settlement there, the success of Carr in the same vicinity proved to many others already living on the Oromocto the efficacy of following his example. Reacting to the very same demographic and economic forces that had prompted Carr to venture into Victoria, Carr's neighbour, Yankee John Howe, planted himself on a lot not far from the tiny branch of Brizley Brook that would later take his

---

[18] Probate File on the Estate of David Kelley (1852), Sunbury County Probate Court Records, PANB, RS 72.

[19] Survey of Victoria Settlement, Sunbury and Queen's County Flat Book (65), no. 6, 6/14, Crown Land Branch Maps and Plans, PANB, RS 656, 17r/203.6.

name.[20] The disappointing nature of the lot's location is undeniable, as it lay far from any extant roads and thus could only be reached after navigating a long and tenuously marked path through Geary's uninhabited woods. Nevertheless, Howe made the best of his situation by clearing and cropping the lot in the winter and spring of 1844. The demands of the timber industry and a boom in employment occurring at that time, however, soon dissuaded him from more vigorous prosecution of his plans for settlement. Frustrated in his efforts to track the claimant down through the maze of lumber paths and deer trails, and after finding the semi-improved parcel seemingly abandoned, Deputy Surveyor James Kerr could only conclude that Howe had relinquished his interest. Unable to spare the time to discuss the legalities of his occupation with the appropriate Crown officials, and too far removed from the amenities of a more civilized existence, Howe did eventually find it more expedient to renounce his intention to further develop the lot, but he ever retained the hope that one day he might perhaps convert his lost labour into some form of personal gain.

Inspired, perhaps, by his cousin's efforts in Victoria and encouraged by the more successful labours of William Carr, a more fitting subject for land settlement, William Howe, soon applied his hand to the arduous enterprise. Victimized by his father's misfortune, Howe had descended into the non-land-owning labouring orders of society, thereby exposing himself to extreme suffering during the first great depression of the 1840s. Following the recovery, Howe made his way with his dependents to South Branch, where he seems to have taken up on a portion of his wife's family's property and made a marginal living as an employee of William Scoullar.[21] But after Scoullar's ruin and the reduction of the South Branch woods, Howe again felt that old discomfort arising from a dearth of real security. It is likely he realized that his continuing dependence on others for both employment and a

---

[20] James Kerr to John McMillan, December 3, 1861, Records of the Surveyor General, PANB, RS 637, 7/j/3/a/5.

[21] Howe's movement from French Lake to South Branch is attested to by school and labour returns for the years 1843 and 1844 in General Sessions, Sunbury County Records, PANB, RS 157, A/2/44-45.

place to live was a contributing factor to his predicament, and certainly he could not have failed to have seen that his lack of resources tended to leave himself and his family exposed to great privation in times of general economic prostration. Thus, in the late 1840s, Howe attempted to rectify the situation. Travelling back downstream, Howe took a detour at French Lake. After passing through Geary he made his way to a parcel of land on the edge of Victoria Settlement, not far from the home of William Carr. His sons, however, did not completely relish the idea of removing with their father into the wilderness. More conditioned to life in closer proximity to French Lake and the more placid and civilized quarter of South Branch, two of them purchased house lots in 1848 carved out of the rear of the old William Smith grant at the foot of Geary Knoll.[22] Howe's son George Henry's enterprise here was particularly unremarkable, as failure to substantiate his initial investment subsequently induced him to make successive failed attempts to clear land in the unsettled portions of Geary and on a parcel abutting a small tributary known as Three Tree Creek that flows into the Oromocto from the back-country of Lincoln Parish.[23]

Like the Howes and William Carr, Daniel James Wood also adopted the aspect of the agriculturalist and transferred himself onto the land. Arriving in the watershed sometime in the early 1840s, Wood and his young family lived at the mouth of the Oromocto, first in Lincoln Parish, but later in the village in Burton, where he undoubtedly spent his days working as a toiler in the shipyards.[24] As opportunities for employment declined, Wood sought a convenient alternative in the form of agricultural labour. One of his McMinn brothers-in-law had already attempted to farm the swampy ground along the Waasis Pond,[25] and though he failed, a like effort, if applied in the context of a more suitable locale, did extend the strong likelihood that a living could in this

---

[22] Sunbury County Registry Office Records, PANB, RS 95, 18/451.

[23] Petition of George Howe, Land Petitions, PANB, RS 108 and Petition of George Howe, Land Petitions, PANB, RS 272, 42/250.

[24] See General Sessions, Sunbury County Records, PANB, RS 157, A/2/47/a (1847) and A/2/49/c (1849).

[25] Petition of Henry McMinn (1840), Land Petitions, PANB, RS 108.

manner be made. However determined he was to adopt a more agricultural habit, Wood was still not so ready as William Carr and the Howes to attempt so arduous an exercise as wilderness settlement. Instead, he secured a lease to a farm property on the Rusagonis that had more than likely already been improved by some previous (though unknown) occupant.[26] Here, in the country of the Free Will Baptists, Wood wavered in his ancestral allegiance to the Church of England, not so much out of any deep commitment to dissent, as from the continuing neglect of the agents of the Society for the Propagation of the Gospel. His own mean station attracted the attention of very few of his neighbours, but a backwardness of thought conditioned by two generations of poverty would incline at least two of his brothers to temporarily leave their moorings along the Washedemoak to partake in the bonanza they perceived their sibling to have discovered.[27]

As strong an incentive for land settlement as may have existed during the 1840s, settlement itself held little fascination for the bulk of the native-born population of the watershed. The lots which offered the best prospects for cultivation had long since been taken up, while those onto which anyone might yet move and on which individuals such as William Carr and William and

[26] The lot in question seems to have been "the Daniel Wood lot," owned by Thomas Treadwell, but eventually sold to Stephen Peabody. In the 1850s, Peabody sold the lot to George Morrow. Morrow's father-in-law, Daniel Wood of French Lake, did own property on the Rusagonis, as did Wood's like-named grandson, so it is possible that the so-called Daniel Wood lot was occupied by one of these two men. Yet as neither of these men are known to have rented or owned property on the Rusagonis, nor to have lived here, at least until after 1851, it seems unlikely that either of them had any connection with the lot in question. Daniel James Wood, however, appears in the records of the General Sessions as a ratepayer in the Rusagonis district in the late 1840s, and is identified as living there in the Census of 1851. That he did not own property here strongly hints that the so-called Daniel Wood lot was the very lot he resided on.

[27] In 1851 Daniel's brother William was living in Lincoln, where he married, while both William and another of Daniel's brothers, Charles, were signers of one of the Sunbury County petitions favouring the Prohibitory Liquor Law in 1854. Both William and Charles returned to Queen's County soon afterward.

John Howe were presently living were not only poor in any nutritive qualities, but also far removed from the heart of the old community with little in the way of roads that might ease the essential dilemma sprung from inaccessibility. To take up the axe, the spade and the plough in so inhospitable a place in a time of economic uncertainty, when proximity to informal and formal agents of benevolence and potential employers was vital to an individual's survival, was a truly reckless action which only the most desperate of men could have entertained.

But as unpopular as land settlement was, it seems more than merely probable that a much wider pursuit of it among the watershed's inhabitants was prevented only by the sudden reinvigoration of the economy occurring at the advent of the new decade. The recognition that provincial trade was not doomed to utter destruction without its traditional preferential shield was only now beginning to dawn upon the people of the Province.[28] As this new revelation worked its way into the collective psyche of the colonial populace, the fortunes of places such as the Oromocto began to revive. Saint John merchants pumped new money into the region, investing in land, timber and a shipbuilding industry dormant since the destruction by fire of the Scoullar shipyard in August of 1848. In the first moments of 1850 there appeared in the village new men with a hankering to fill the expansive crater of economic leadership left by Scoullar's tumultuous fall from the unsteady precipice of inflated ego and overly leveraged free enterprise. Among the first to arrive on the scene was John Wallace Craig, an Irishman who had come to Saint John in 1840 and struck up a partnership with shipbuilder Edward Allison.[29] Impressed by business prospects in the interior, Craig migrated to the Oromocto Village, where he purchased a portion of land fronting the river once occupied by the Scoullars and set to work procuring the capital necessary to prosecute a shipbuilding concern of his own.[30] The presence of his Saint John foreman and fellow Irishman Robert Bryson furnished Craig with the

---

[28] MacNutt, op. cit., p. 330.

[29] 1851 Census of New Brunswick, Saint John County and Esther Clark Wright, *St. John Ships and Their Builders* (Published by Author, 1976).

[30] Sunbury County Registry Office Records, PANB, RS 95, 19/252.

technical expertise necessary to undertake his first commissions,[31] while his former partner, Mr. Allison, provided him with a convenient source of timber following the latter's purchase of a group of lots in Victoria known as the Earls Tract.[32] Craig's initiative, as well as the confidence of the marketplace, soon convinced other, more established (but long dormant) names to attempt to resume their quondam prerogatives in the river's economy. The Dows, led by several of old John Dow's nephews, reconverted a portion of river-front land bounding Craig's compound into a rival shipyard, where they set about the resurrection of that craft which had once been the source of the family's fortune and notoriety.[33]

New investment, new business and the bounding of industrial fancy meant the construction of larger ships and an eager search for skilled labour. To fulfil the needs of new employers, carpenters from as far away as the British Isles and Nova Scotia flocked to the Oromocto,[34] taking up residence in various inns and boarding houses and helping to transform the little village at the river's mouth from a sleepy waystation for postal couriers into a bustling and lively home to an energetic and growing population.[35] With the revival of shipbuilding and the auspicious discovery that the watershed nourished ship's timber of superior quality,[36] a new craze for tamarack swept the entire length of the river system,

---

[31] Hancox, p. 46. According to Sunbury County Registry Office Records, PANB, RS 95, 19/317 and 21/491, Bryson bought the "Treadwell House" at the mouth of the River in 1851.

[32] Sunbury County Registry Office Records, PANB, RS 95, 19/210 and 20/412.

[33] See Hancox; Will of William Dow Jr. (1855), Sunbury County Probate Court Records, PANB, 72a; and the 1851 Census of New Brunswick, Sunbury County.

[34] According to the 1851 Census, there were a total of 51 ship carpenters in Oromocto: 21 from Ireland, 19 native to New Brunswick, 6 from Nova Scotia, 4 from the United States, and 1 each from England and Scotland.

[35] Gesner credited the erection of the Oromocto Bridge and the resulting increase of traffic with enlarging the importance of the village (See Gesner, *New Brunswick: With Notes for Emigrants*, p. 157).

[36] *The New Brunswick Courier*, July 19, 1851.

further helping to restore the prosperity of the decaying local timber trade and returning it to within a quarter of its greatly inflated pre-1846 level.[37] At the forefront of the timber trade's revival was the indomitable George Morrow, who not only possessed the largest number of timber berths, but also held whole or partial interest in two separate milling establishments on Rockwell Stream and the North West Branch. In the course of the previous decade the Tracys' mismanagement of their several mill-frames had led to partial seizure and sale at public auction. Morrow and a kinsman of the Tracys by the name of Hatfield Currie each received a share, though Morrow's solid dominance among the expanded ranks of proprietors tended to nullify any competition among them for control of a very limited number of mill reserves.[38] Morrow himself was inclined to let the Tracys and Currie have, so to speak, the run of the mill, while he tended to more pressing problems closer to the river's mouth. At the nearby Hartt establishment, a similar atomization had occurred, but unlike the fate of Tracy's mills, which had resulted largely from the failings of its proprietors, Hartt's dissolution proceeded according to design. As early as 1840 old Thomas Hartt had granted one of his mills to his son Thomas and son-in-law David Kelley. Feeling now in his old age the nearness of death, Hartt presented half of his remaining mill to two of his daughters and their husbands.[39] While he still lived the possibility of intra-familial strife was remote, though one could harbour little confidence that an accord among competitors, however closely allied by blood, could long be preserved after his passing. Over on the South Branch matters were considerably less complex, as the old Scoullar establishment was now firmly in the possession of David Kelley, who had purchased it from John Robertson in November of 1847.[40] Once the final installment of the purchase price was paid off it would have been reasonable to expect that the mill, despite the large-scale

---

[37] *The Royal Gazette*, June 4, 1851.

[38] See Sunbury County Registry Office, PANB, RS 95, 18/19, 18/529, 19/510 and R.D. Wilmot to George Morrow, May 2, 1853, Timber and Saw Mill Records, PANB, RS 663, e/1/f.

[39] Sunbury County Registry Office Records, PANB, RS 95, 19/550.

[40] Id., 18/367.

diminution of the pine timber in the area, would run a modest profit manufacturing ship's lumber from the still plentiful stands of tamarack.

While the conspiring axes of a thousand lumbermen hacked away at the watershed's remaining forests, the resultant cacophony seemingly resolved into a revelation of the genius of the long-departed Abraham Gesner and his dreams for the river's industrial development. A county branch of the New Brunswick Society for the Encouragement of Agriculture, Home Manufactures and Commerce was soon formed and its officers took upon themselves the task of seeking out prospects for an absurdly diverse agenda for lifting the entire County to economic parity with mother England.[41] That aging agriculturalist Calvin Hatheway, his thoughts shaped by research undertaken a quarter of a century before as a Deputy Surveyor, eagerly wrested control of the society from his agreeable, if less enthusiastic, rivals and took charge of the often inappropriate inquiries. His own bias favouring the advancement of Maugerville over and above that of other districts in the County did little to deter the more fair-minded explorations of John T. Smith and James McAdam as they sought to fulfil the wishes of the Society's main chapter to discover the most advantageous place in the Province at which to encourage the establishment of a cotton mill.[42]

Calvin Hatheway's presumption of stewardship of the local branch of the New Brunswick Society came largely as a result of his own frustrations over past electoral failure and the recent loss of certain emoluments that once had allowed him to entertain the belief that he held precedence atop Sunbury County's social hierarchy. His presumption, too, reflected a larger, more ancient conflict between the two sides of the St. John River, represented on the one hand by Maugerville and Sheffield, and on the other by the Oromocto and its many thriving settlements. An increase

---

[41] *The Headquarters*, April 10, 1850.

[42] New Brunswick Society for the Encouragement of Agriculture, Home Manufactures and Commerce Throughout the Province, *Report of the New Brunswick Society for the Encouragement of Agriculture, Home Manufactures and Commerce Throughout the Province* (Fredericton: James Hogg, 1851).

in St. John River transportation, due in part to the efforts of one of Hatheway's more industrious sons, brought new benefits to the banks of the river below Sunbury's older communities. But the rapidly recovering economy of the Oromocto, with the infusion of capital and the growth of the number of its inhabitants, its new post office and the bridge that bore the main current of overland travel between Fredericton and Saint John gave rise to the refurbishing of that senescent palace of spite first erected immediately following the arrival of the Loyalists. The rivalry worsened when George Hayward, acting on a request from a group of largely emigrant residents of back settlements in Sheffield, attempted to secure the partition of that parish. The anticipated diminution of Sheffield's political integrity was blocked only by Assemblyman Thomas Gilbert of Gagetown, who argued that any such division would result in the creation of a parish too impoverished to care for its own poor and lead, subsequently, to the invasion of Queen's County by a pathetic army of Sunbury beggars.[43] The Christian virtues of Sheffield's inhabitants may well have allowed them to silently tolerate Hayward's foiled scheme, but when Hayward joined forces with his old antagonist, the much reviled William Scoullar, and called for the resignation of Charles Peters Wetmore, Sunbury County's non-resident Clerk of the General Sessions, all tolerance dissolved in a quickening stew of recrimination.[44]

Hayward's and Scoullar's demand seemed rational enough given the ongoing debate within the Executive Council over the question of whether or not a more tangible and sedate tie to the community served should be required of provincial office holders, in addition to the frequent complaints, dating back at least to 1848, by the people of the Oromocto that greater convenience in the conduct of their official affairs might in such a manner be accommodated if travel to Wetmore's Fredericton office could be avoided.[45] Certainly Hayward's and Scoullar's recommendation

---

[43] *The Headquarters*, March 6, 1850.

[44] Charles Peters Wetmore was the uncle of Andrew Rainsford Wetmore.

[45] Petition of William Hoyt et al, Records of Lt. Governor William McBean George Colebrooke, PANB, RS 345, B/5 and Petition of George

for a replacement in the person of the present clerk's nephew seemed an innocuous and reasonable solution to the problem.[46] Yet the people of Sheffield and its kindred community of Maugerville viewed the move through the coloured glass of a generation of mistrust, thus it was only the rumour of Wetmore's imminent resignation that led some of their number to sign a petition in favour of the new candidate.[47]

When Wetmore learned of Hayward's and Scoullar's maneuvering, he denied any intention of retiring, at the same time denouncing, somewhat ironically, the bulk of his opponents as alien petitioners with no stake in Sunbury affairs. That Sunbury County, or, more properly, Oromocto Village, lacked the proper facilities to serve him in his official capacity further contributed to the strength of his objections.[48] Anxious to prevent any additional increase in the prestige of Burton Parish, the people on the north side of the St. John now flocked to Wetmore's cause and declared that the clerk's residency in Fredericton gave rise to no more inconvenience in the conduct of their business with him than would his being stationed along the Oromocto.[49] For the time being Wetmore's argument prevailed, but mindful of his responsibility to advance the career of his young nephew and more or less

---

Grimmer, Records of Warrants, Appointments and Commissions, PANB, RS 538, D/6. The rate payers of the Oromocto, particularly those living on the North West and South Branches, in fact, had opposed the appointment of Charles Wetmore. With respect to these complaints Hayward and Thomas O. Miles had recommended Fredericton attorney George Grimmer, who eagerly expressed his willingness to remove to Burton, to replace Wetmore.

[46] Petition of George Hayward and William Scoullar, Executive Council Cabinet Series, PANB, RS 9, 1850/14.

[47] John Taylor to John R. Partelow, January 17, 1851, Executive Council Cabinet Series, PANB, RS 9, 1851/2.

[48] Charles Wetmore to John R. Partelow, January 6, 1851, Executive Council Cabinet Series, PANB, RS 9, 1851/2.

[49] James Hamilton to Charles Wetmore, January 2, 1851 and the Petition of Justices of the Common Pleas, Magistrates, and other Inhabitants of the County of Sunbury, Executive Council Cabinet Series, PANB, RS 9, 1851/2.

content with the rewards and distinction to be found in his employment as Clerk of the House of Assembly, Wetmore soon withdrew from all involvement with the petulant people of Sunbury County.

While the struggle over reapportionment of the County civil structure and the greater controversy surrounding the County Clerk were indicative of great animosity between the two sections of the County, the animosity itself stemmed from a deeper set of circumstances that are as much ascribable to certain cultural pretensions prevalent in the two regions as they are to basic human jealousies. Of these, religion was undoubtedly the most distinct and perhaps most defining source of contention. In the early days of the County's history, divisions had fallen strictly along lines of Anglican and non-Anglican. Congregated primarily at the mouth of the Oromocto and in Sheffield, the Anglicans had managed to preserve control of one of the two seats in the provincial legislature allocated to Sunbury County, while the dissenters, bridging the several chasms between Methodism, Baptism, and Congregationalism, controlled the other.[50] As the two sections developed distinct economies, the various elements within each sought divergent and often contradictory preferences from the county and provincial establishments, leading, inevitably, to the replacement of the older resentments based on denominational affiliation by a more complex sectional rivalry. Yet strangely, the same process of polarization that had proceeded from the development of divergent economies seems to have occurred, for different reasons altogether, in the sphere of religion. By the 1830s the Baptists and Free Baptists had risen to prominence on the Oromocto, where spiritual neglect by the Society for the Propagation of the Gospel and the transient character of the timber trade had bred the virtue of self-reliance in all matters of body and soul. By 1850 the various Baptist organizations far outnumbered all other denominations in the southern part of the County, and gave the section a predominantly Baptist flavour that distinguished it greatly from Sheffield and Maugerville.

The strength of the Baptists and Free Baptists in the Oromocto watershed was nowhere stronger than on the South Branch.

---

[50] Moore, op. cit., pp. 102-103.

During the 1840s, when the value of timber fell and the politics of the river drove so many of its people into competing camps, it seemed as if any natural sense of hopefulness and community still abiding in the hearts of the South Branch's inhabitants found a safe refuge in the embrace of the walls of the two meeting houses resting snugly upon the stream's narrow interval. The solace of the open communion and the comforting promise of the redeemable nature of even the most reprobate of souls attracted a large proportion of the local populace. In reverent silence they sat, listening each Sunday to the divine message as delivered from the diseased palate of the awkwardly literate, yet commendably diligent Elder Mersereau.[51] On the North West Branch, the small congregation founded at the dawn of the previous decade shook off, with Mersereau's assistance, its depressing mantle of introversion and resolved to draw new fish from the surrounding seas of iniquity.[52] Unable to so easily cast away their more insular habits, the dwindling congregation of the older North West Branch Calvinist Baptist Church met the full force of the renewed evangelism of their more feisty neighbours, only to be driven dejectedly into the shadowy domain of extinction.[53] Mersereau's own prestige only magnified with public scrutiny of such testimonial achievements and so raised him in the esteem of his pastoral peers that when the New Brunswick Free Will Baptist Conference opted to hold its annual gathering at the Rusagonis meeting house in July of 1850, its members selected Mersereau to act as moderator.[54]

---

[51] According to a transcript of a letter written by Mersereau to his wife on September 13, 1852, the condition of his mandible was so troubling that he traveled to Fredericton to seek medical relief. See John A. Wood, "Oromocto Baptists: Stories of the Baptist Church on the Oromocto" (Typescript by author, 1992).

[52] Fredericton Junction Family Histories, Volume 2, Page 96, PANB, MC 1706.

[53] Most of the old Calvinists seem to have become Free Will Baptists. In 1850 and 1852 twelve and thirteen new converts respectively were admitted into the new Free Will congregation.

[54] Free Christian Baptist General Conference, *Extracts from the Rules and Minutes of the Free Christian Baptist General Conference of New Brunswick:*

The choice to hold the conference on the Rusagonis was itself a form of recognition of the maturity of the sect in the Oromocto district, where the appeal of Free Will had spread not only to the banks of the North West Branch, but also further downstream as far as French Lake and Geary Settlement.[55]

Faced with the unrelenting activity of dissenting clergy and laymen, the wardens of St. John's church wavered in the development of an effective strategy to retain the loyalty of the Anglican creed's traditional partisans.[56] While the faithful fell away and began transferring the regular and irregular expression of their devotions to the meeting houses of the Baptists (and, to a smaller extent, to the new hall of the Methodists near the river's mouth), the governors of the old, still rotting church at Burton debated the dubious fertility of the ancient glebe and imagined, perhaps, that the sale of this land and the purchase of a new parcel represented the sole keys to the fastened door behind which thrived the wayward allegiance of the fast diminishing flock.[57] The newly appointed missionary, the Reverend Abraham Wiggins, however, could not be bothered by such concerns and seems to have been more or less agreeable to the new spiritual balance in his district as he happily contracted to board Maugerville's Baptist preacher within the confines of his own home.[58]

The spread of the Free Will Baptists into the middle settlements of the Oromocto was paralleled by that of Orangism. While the Gospel of Jesus arrived through the efforts of nameless preachers from the vicinity of the river's upper reaches, Orangism owed its introduction to the diligence of forever anonymous inhabitants of places more likely than not to be found in and around the city of

---

held at Lincoln, New Brunswick, 6th, 8th and 9th July, 1850 (St. John: George W. Day, 1850).

[55] Ibid.

[56] Between 1846 and 1855, the number of attendants at St. John's Church fell from 150 to 84. See Report of John M. Sterling, E, 1845-6 and Report of Abraham V.G. Wiggins, E, 1854-5 Society for the Propagation of the Gospel in Foreign Parts, PANB, MC 230.

[57] Records of the Legislative Assembly, PANB, RS 24, 1854/bi/file 10/no. 85.

[58] 1851 Census of New Brunswick, Sunbury County.

Saint John. Occasional soldiers, on the move between sea-port and capital, and postal couriers, travelling overland via the Nerepis Road, would inevitably stop for the night in Geary at the home of William Smith, whose many beds and his license to retail liquor were uncontestable proofs of his hospitality. Smith himself, and the local men who gathered at his tavern for refreshment and recreation, may well have heard the tenets of the Orange creed from the mouths of such travelers, and certainly they must have heard tell through conversation and the occasional newspaper of the controversies that raged throughout the Province's major towns in the late 1840s between the adherents of militant Protestantism and supporters of the cause of popery. Geary and the rest of the Oromocto had been kindly spared the more divisive effects of the recent Catholic emigration. Indeed, the amicability of the Catholics who had lately chosen to settle upon the river never provided even the slightest cause for worry or alarm among the river's older, Protestant inhabitants.[59] Lacking the piercing inducements of anxious nativism, the people of the Oromocto nevertheless cherished the potent memories of their fathers' and grandfathers' loyalty. And while the meagreness of their rewards for ancestral steadfastness to a cause not many really completely understood prompted, at times, some consternation, the effects of a common historical experience conditioned a generally favourable response to the hidden mysteries that lay beyond the veil of a rather conventional mix of dissenting religion and imperial politics as found in the Orange creed.

William Smith did not himself resort to the formation of a new lodge. Any predilection he may have had to do so was overwhelmed by the responsibilities entailed by his partnership with George Morrow and the infectious spirits sloshing between the walls of his tavern. Less encumbered than William Smith was Smith's young French Lake cousin, Jeremiah. Young Smith was the son of another man of the same name whose appetite for horses, cattle, timber and coin had brought him a prosperity and prominence that were restrained only by his own inherent lack of pretension. A similar passion for women brought the elder Smith another sort of distinction, as his conquests in the fields of

---

[59] *The Headquarters*, April 10, 1850.

venereal honour made him the father of some twenty-one legitimate children, as well as an unknown number of bastards.[60] The
younger Smith did not express so unbecomingly his father's inor-
dinate drives, but instead seems to have sublimated any inherited
passion into a determination to further the Orange cause. Traveling to the site of some unmentioned and unmentionable meeting
of the initiates, Smith entered into their secret covenant, studied
and learned their ancient precepts, graduated through the different degrees and finally returned home to the shores of French
Lake with a mandate to form the Oromocto's first regular lodge
in an unheated room in the home of James Mills in August of
1849.[61]

Calling itself the King William Lodge in honour of the heroic
victor at the Boyne, the new lodge's first meeting attracted only
fourteen prospective members, drawn exclusively from French
Lake and Geary settlements and almost uniformly made up of
men sharing some blood or marital link with the Lodge's founder.
Exuding a proselytism having roots in his own Free Will Baptist
background, Worshipful Master Smith revealed a slightly greater
degree of discretion than exhibited by the caretakers of his faith.
Discretion was soon mitigated by family sympathy due to the in-
extricable and complicated ties of dependence and kinship that
bound together the local inhabitants. This dilution of discretion
was nowhere more evident than in the enrolment of the Worshipful Master's brother-in-law, George Garrity. Garrity's greatest
and perhaps sole virtue rested on a claim to membership, through
the blood of his mother, in the distinguished Glasier clan of Lincoln Parish. This virtue proved irrelevant upon his ordination as
a Free Will Baptist pastor and was of no consequence whatsoever

---

[60] Allen Boone, a descendant of the elder Smith, recalled many of the
legends surrounding his ancestor's life. The stories he told included ref-
erences to travels to Ontario with aboriginal hirelings to procure and
drive overland a herd of cattle, as well as a reputed philanderous streak.
His pretension, however, was balanced by his position as foreman of the
county grand jury and the rank of captain in the provincial militia. He
never did seek greater office or emolument either from the people of the
county or from the provincial government.

[61] Allen Boone, "History and Records of the King William L.O.L., no.
114, Geary, New Brunswick," Allen Boone Collection.

when, following a scrape with his fellow religious that had less to do with a difference in interpreting dogma than with Garrity's inherently provocative temperament, he was banished from the ranks of the faithful and stripped of his clerical license. Garrity lost no time in realigning himself with the obscure Disciples of Christ, after which he returned to the home of his mother's Baptist kin and opened a questionable practice as a "botanic physician."[62] Garrity's wife's French Lake relations were equally tolerant of his idiosyncrasies, and though they did not particularly appreciate his nettlesome attitude toward their doctrine, his edifying knowledge of the supposed intricacies of papal error all but made up for any reservations concerning the question of his induction into the Orange fraternity.

Garrity's periodic lectures on the faults of popery never seem to have gone so far as to inspire any superabundance of hostility to Catholicism among his listeners, and certainly no member of the King William Lodge is known to have carried his prejudice against the Roman creed to the extremes demonstrated several years before in Fredericton and Saint John. In the midst of the bitter debate in the spring of 1850 over the question of incorporating the Provincial Lodge, George Hayward, citing the good behaviour of Sunbury County's Orangemen, condemned the more irresponsible allegations of one of his colleagues in the House of Assembly and accused him of dragging from the tomb of dead history the one-sided accounts of biased narrators of the bloody excesses of a few Protestant extremists.[63] Hayward's friendly attitude toward the lodge rose in part from his own natural sympathies for its tenets, as well as from the fact that many of his own relations in Geary Settlement, including James Till and several members of the Boone clan, were steadily being drawn into its ranks. Hayward's colleague, Thomas O. Miles, generally echoed Hayward's sentiments in regard to the question of provincial incorporation, though his own secret distrust of a largely foreign-born population who were often prone to violent and intemperate behaviour may well have contributed to his decision to support the granting of official sanction to an organization so dedicated as the Orange

---

[62] *The Reporter and Fredericton Advertizer*, October 15, 1847.

[63] *The Headquarters*, April 10, 1850.

Lodge was to safeguarding the peace and the rights of a Protestant majority.[64]

Thus it was in the fall of 1850 that the people of the Oromocto, grounded in the principles of the Free Baptist creed and the ideals of Orangism and flush with a joy originating in the restoration of the economy, prepared for provincial elections for the first time since 1837 without any overarching concern or brewing controversy. The lack of any real issues of contention seems to have contributed to an absence of the excitement normally preceding the provincial canvass. With no great issues or principles over which to contend, and having had his fill of provincial affairs after a largely undistinguished term, during which he usually rose to speak only in support of comments proffered by his colleague, Thomas O. Miles declined to accept re-nomination. Miles' refusal to entertain thoughts of re-election quickly sparked a contest among the old reformers for his place on the reform ticket. It is not known who Miles favoured as his successor, but surely his confidence could not have been greatly inspired by young Jonathan P. Taylor, an ambitious scion of a distinguished Sheffield line descended from Assemblyman James Taylor, who, transfixed by Masonism, Orangism and the traditions of the Loyalists, was now presuming himself worthy to officially represent the interests of Sunbury County in Fredericton.[65] As an alternative, the reformers had only to look toward Maugerville, where Calvin Hatheway continued to nurture hopes that he might yet find entry into the provincial legislature.[66] The likelihood that Hatheway's presence in the race was a contingency deemed undesirable by the reformers, and that he had opted to enter in spite of being passed over in favour of Taylor is, perhaps, high, but so too is the possibility that they observed an apparent lack of any real controversy that could

---

[64] When the Irish of Fredericton rioted following the 1842-43 elections, Miles commented that "something must be done to keep the Irish down." See Diary of Thomas O. Miles, PANB, MC 451, January 3, 1843.

[65] Jonathan P. Taylor was a grandson of James Taylor, a native of Scotland who lived in Nova Scotia before moving to Maugerville in 1783. The elder Taylor represented Sunbury County in the Assembly from 1809 to 1816 and, again, from 1819 to 1820.

[66] Pollbooks, Sunbury County Records, PANB, RS 157, J/2/5 (1850).

have evoked the kind of exaggerated and uncouth behaviour from the pompous candidate that had so hindered any resonance of his appeal with the voters in the past. Yet as Calvin Hatheway and his reluctant supporters contemplated the relative ease with which it was possible, in this year of 1850, to gain a long-coveted office, so too did another man whose defeat only four years before they had all worked so diligently to effect.

It was a testament to his tenacity that William Scoullar overcame scruple and the shame of past misdeeds and moved decisively to regain that situation of esteem and real authority that he, as a self-professed member of the elite, could not allow to fall prey yet again to his enemies. Hayward's place at the top of the poll was unassailable, but as Sunbury offered two Assembly seats it was not necessary for Scoullar to concern himself with Lincoln Parish's honourable grandee. His old base on the Oromocto might yet be restored, and with Miles out of the way and a political nonentity and a pretender of the grandest and vainest proportions to contend against, victory here seemed within his powers to secure. Stripped of his own past pretensions and humbled by the experience of bankruptcy and vilification, Scoullar had modified his expectations, engaged in a more modest business of harvesting tamarack on several tributaries of the Oromocto and embraced the more sedate life of a country squire. A new appreciation for temperance had lately allowed him to dispose of his liquor business, an act of renunciation that placed him in favourable stead with the growing strength of the teetotalling Free Will Baptists and the looming political might of the Sons of Temperance. With little hope of generating much support on the river's acrimonious northern bank, Scoullar undoubtedly concentrated on winning back the confidence of his old constituency along the Oromocto, managing via this route to overcome both Hatheway and Taylor and thus deny the reform faction a continuation of their monopoly on power.[67]

---

[67] Desperate to finally take what he considered to be his rightful place in the House of Assembly, and no doubt egged on by the electoral success of his son George in York County, Hatheway angrily demanded a scrutiny of the vote so as to determine the precise manner in which deceit conspired to rob him of his political inheritance. His plea for justice ignored and a seat in the legislature denied him, Hatheway became,

Scoullar's fortuitous and skillful combination of the previously incompatible tenets of timbering and abstinence proved a great advantage to him and undoubtedly helped to persuade the two hundred and fifty-two persons who voted for him of his rehabilitation and fitness for elective office. His conversion was a real one, and it was ideally suited to the new climate of intolerance toward the traditional recreational habits of the Oromocto. A county chapter of the Sons of Temperance had already formed, replacing the old Sheffield Total Abstinence Society and attracting members from either side of the St. John. In August of 1850 they revealed the strength of their commitment and sent a potent message to any prospective candidates for office within the bounds of their county as they traipsed through the streets of the provincial capital behind the triumphal orchestrations of a marching band.[68] Mindful of his debt to the sober population that elected him and fully acquiescent in their cause, Scoullar christened his restored career as a legislator with an attempt to convince the House of Assembly of the merits of a moratorium on the tavern-licensing powers of the local Court of General Sessions and the disenfranchisement of those individuals facinorous enough to involve themselves in any aspect of the distasteful traffic in alcohol.[69] But while Scoullar's colleagues apparently disdained this rather blatant example of the intrusion of petty parish affairs into the busy process of provincial law-making, the momentum behind the county agitation for the eradication of intemperance continued to grow, and climaxed in plans to construct a Temperance Hall in the village of Oromocto. Erected on land provided for that

---

instead, the butt of the jokes of the members of his own party. Whenever he met the disgruntled candidate at the meetings of the County Court of the General Sessions, even the more discrete George Hayward could not refrain from addressing him mockingly as "one of Her Majesty's justices of the common pleas." See Calvin Hatheway to Samuel Leonard Tilley, December 16, 1854, Executive Council Cabinet Series, PANB, RS 9, 1855/1.

[68] *The Headquarters*, September 25, 1850.

[69] Petition of the Sheffield Sons of Temperance, # 13, Records of the Legislative Assembly, PANB, RS 24, 1851/pe/file 7/no. 200.

purpose by the stewards of the Methodist chapel,[70] the hall was paid for largely by the voluntary subscriptions of the local inhabitants. When the multi-faith trustees and supporters of the hall contemplated the necessity of a provincial grant to pay off the balance of the costs of construction, Scoullar eagerly presented their case to his peers in the House of Assembly.[71]

Despite the ponderous reluctance of the provincial legislature to authorize a grant of £50 toward the Temperance Hall's construction,[72] the upholding by William Scoullar of the cause of temperance undoubtedly won him the praise of a large number of his constituents. A conduct more righteous than that exhibited during his earlier term augured well for his political future, and it certainly helped to mask the essential self-interest, laying virtually beyond the transforming hand of redemption, that continued to guide so many of his political choices. Indeed, his lumbering activities precluded a total renunciation of self. While he took up a popular cause in which he himself was a fervent believer, he also steadfastly maintained a vigil over the business of the House Committee on Lumbering Interests, watching for any sign of future alteration of the laws that preserved his freedom of access to local tamarack. The still largely uninhabited territory watered by Rockwell Stream and Brizley Brook held the greatest promise for yielding the coveted tree, and though his actions here caused friction with George Morrow, the rewards were too tempting to prevent him from risking conflict with his old rival. The industry of John W. Craig at the shipyards offered additional incentives for Scoullar to continue contending against Morrow, and these only increased as Craig steadily expanded the scope of his operations. Having put his affairs in order and begun construction of the *Wanata*,[73] Craig seems to have invited a former colleague by the name of Thomas Small Hicks from Saint John to join him in his

---

[70] Sunbury County Registry Office Records, PANB, RS 95, 19/386.

[71] Petition of Charles Clowes et al, Records of the Legislative Assembly, PANB, RS 24, 1852/pe/file 10/no. 240.

[72] *Journals of the Legislative Assembly* (1854), p. 339.

[73] The *Wanata* was actually the second ship on the Oromocto the construction of which he was involved in. The first, the *Mohango*, had been built for him by another Saint John merchant, Samuel Smith, in 1850.

venture. The arrival of Hicks, with all his capital, connections and entrepreneurial spirit, could only have meant an immanent increase in production, thus Scoullar rapidly moved to arrange an alliance with the two shipbuilders which was cemented with the engagement of the bachelor Hicks to his niece, Mary Partelow.[74] Despite their willingness to entertain Scoullar's good will, Craig and Hicks were not so naive as to imagine that George Morrow would readily tolerate the emergence of a new consortium. Hicks' involvement in the local Methodist society eased some of the tensions that might otherwise have arisen between the rival interests, and it was here, undoubtedly, in the halls of the chapel built only a few years before, that Hicks and Morrow came to an agreement that possessed the greatest potential for mutual benefit.[75]

Scoullar was but one of several entrepreneurs of the Oromocto who showed interest in the woods about Victoria Settlement. Archibald McLean was another. A native of Kintyre, Scotland, who had married a daughter of a distant cousin following his emigration and initial settlement on the shores of Grand Lake,[76] McLean had come to the Oromocto around 1846. Establishing a small store at the mouth of the river and commencing a small-scale timber operation primarily on the opposite side of the St. John, McLean first rose to local prominence during the emigrant crises of 1848 when, as a County Overseer of the Poor, he distributed assistance to the needy.[77] With the coming of the new decade, the restoration of the economy and the rise in demand for ship's timber McLean anticipated great profits to made from the harvesting of tamarack. The abandoned Scoullar shipyard, owned now by John Robertson, presented additional opportunities, but his own finances were as yet insufficient for him to consider direct

---

[74] Sewell, # C0866.

[75] The two men served as stewards of the Methodist Chapel at Oromocto. Both were acting in that capacity in 1851 when the local Methodist Society granted the Sons of Temperance land for the building of a meeting hall.

[76] McLean Family, New Brunswick Museum Branch Records, Vertical Files, PANB, RS 184.

[77] Petition of Archibald McLean, Records of the Legislative Assembly, PANB, RS 24, 1848/pe/file 11/no. 388.

entry into the shipbuilding industry. Fortunately, the activities of Craig and Hicks were extensive enough to allow him a share of the timber-supply trade. Fueling his enterprise with loans from John Robertson, McLean gathered a force of men around him and began leading them into the Victoria bush. That he had failed to secure berths on which to cut in the watershed's prime tamarack tract was of little concern to him, for McLean was soon to prove that he was not only an aggressive and tenacious businessman, but totally unscrupulous as well.

The brazen criminality of Archibald McLean might have been completely overlooked by his peers had he confined his actions to unclaimed Crown lands. His ravenous search for the best tamarack, however, brought him in direct confrontation with George Morrow. McLean was not so audacious as to invade Morrow's berths, but his activity nearby certainly heightened the sense of imminent danger Morrow felt regarding the integrity of his extensive interests in the Geary hinterland. As early as the winter of 1850, rival gangs of trespassers led by Calvin and George Cogswell and Richard McNeil had in fact been encroaching upon Morrow's licensed berths, stealing his best timber and selling it in Oromocto to the village's newly established shipbuilders.[78] Morrow's personal intervention against the actions of these pirates did little to deter their repeated incursions, despite the fact that two of their number, the Cogswells, shared a bond of kinship with the family of his own wife. Rumours of interest in the settlement and exploitation of land in and around Victoria on the part of many of Geary's residents only inflated Morrow's sense of urgency, thus he allowed the main avenue for the transportation of timber out of the area, the Rockwell Stream, to become trammeled in violation of the County rules governing the maintenance of mill dams. Spurred on by complaints from many quarters that the sluiceway beside Morrow's Rockwell sawmill was so congested that any transit of timber through it was impossible, a meeting of the Court of General Sessions ordered one of the County's mill-dam inspectors, Asa Carr, to examine the situation, report on conditions and present Morrow and his partner, William Smith,

---

[78] Petition of George Morrow, SU/1850, Timber and Sawmills, 1817-1865, Timber and Saw Mill Records, PANB, RS 663a.

with an ultimatum regarding repairs.[79] Happy for the opportunity to preserve the soundness of his own tamarack business, as well as repay his old rival with some measure of the discomfort he himself had once been forced to accept at Morrow's hand, William Scoullar took special interest in the case, and after he returned to Fredericton to partake in the affairs of the House of Assembly he continued to monitor the progress in the rectification of Morrow's rather deliberate indiscretion.[80]

The charging of Asa Carr with the task of enforcing the County regulations against Morrow could not have been more appropriate, for the repairs shortly undertaken at Carr's behest removed the only inhibitions preventing many of his friends, neighbours and relations in Geary from moving into the region to stake claims on land, ostensibly for settlement purposes, but in fact to allow them to operate openly as petty lumbermen on berths held by Morrow with the full sanction and protection of the Province's governing authorities. The ordinances of the Crown Land Office should have been conducive of some degree of peace among the various parties engaged in land settlement at this time, but the conflicts and petty jealousies that were presently brewing among the bureau's deputies spawned a disarray that transformed the already complex and competitive process (however dubious it was) into a state of bedeviling chaos. The ill-defined and overlapping jurisdictions of Deputy Surveyors James Kerr and John Colling represented the primary grievance on which the official conflict centred. Endowed with an enthusiastic, yet aggressive and somewhat extravagant nature, the Irish-born James Kerr was inescapably predisposed to controversy. When he found himself posted in Queen's County alongside Colling after his appointment as a deputy in 1842,[81] he became involved in an excruciatingly petty debate over the question of precedence and the relative size and exact bounds of the districts over which they were individually responsible. An unusually fluid sense of

---

[79] General Sessions, Sunbury County Records, PANB, RS 157, A/2/51/b-c (1851).

[80] Ibid.

[81] Petition of James Kerr, Records of the Surveyor General, PANB, RS 637, 7/j/3/a/1.

geography, as well as an often reckless haste that eventually earned him the reproof of the Surveyor General and the humiliating rejection by the latter of a shamefully inaccurate survey return,[82] only magnified the possibility for strife with his rival. Colling, for his part, maintained a more conservative air, but his demanding ways and his innate sense of primacy over his rival hardly suited him to a more conciliatory posture. His mature years and English birth, as well as his greater seniority in the Crown Land Office, where in the days of the demented Lockwood he had been employed as a clerk,[83] were all the more conducive to any tendency he had toward discordance.

Given the temperaments of the two men, it is not surprising that neither could refrain from asserting claims upon the supervision of the new territory east of the Oromocto River that was suddenly subject to the promise of a more permanent occupation. In the last years of the previous decade the struggle between them in the Victoria wilds had reached its apex, as competing bands of chainmen led by one or another of the emulous deputies helped to create a hopelessly convoluted grid of lots made all the more confused by its superimposition upon the ancient and incompetent survey conducted by Amasa Flaglor in 1841. So heated did their rivalry become that when Colling was forced by illness to retire for the winter to the home of a friend in the city of Saint John, he refused to acknowledge Kerr's desire to act in his place, and, instead, nominated another, less qualified man to temporarily exercise the prerogatives of his momentarily vacated office.[84]

By the time the first inhabitants of Geary ventured into the woods around Victoria, James Kerr had been relieved of most of

---

[82] R.D. Wilmot to James Kerr, February 20, 1854, Primary Letterbooks, 1853-1855, Records of the Surveyor General, PANB, RS 637, 1/a/26, p. 198.

[83] *The Morning News*, August 11, 1859.

[84] James Kerr to R.D. Wilmot, October 27, 1853, Records of the Surveyor General, PANB, RS 637, 7/j/3/a/3; and John Colling to R.D. Wilmot, November 22, 1853, Records of the Surveyor General, PANB, RS 637, 7/j/1/a/5.

his duties there,[85] but his nettling complaints regarding the inappropriateness of Colling's supervision of settlement and statute labour on the county line and his claim that Colling was unable to work amicably with at least one settler along Swan Creek[86] seemed to facilitate a mild tolerance by the Surveyor General of Kerr's continued professional activity between Gagetown and the Oromocto.[87] Kerr's involvement with settlement in Burton Parish slowly receded, however, as the Surveyor General found it more expedient to assign him the thankless prerogatives of a government seizing officer and the more laborious task of searching for cultivatable lands along the swampy, uncleared tributaries of South Branch Stream.[88] In Kerr's place to oversee the advancement of settlement in the vicinity of Victoria the Surveyor General appointed a new man. A reputable soul of venerable Sunbury County stock, sharing the agricultural and temperate biases of his Sheffield neighbours, Stephen Burpee Jr. inherited the troubled, uncoordinated legacy of a handful of earlier Deputy Surveyors. Just how confused the legacy, in fact, was became all too evident when Yankee John Howe re-entered the Victoria woods following a brief period of idleness at his old Geary home and attempted to lay claim to a portion of the ungranted yet improved estate of one Thomas Harper.[89] The indelicacy of Howe's action was eventually rectified once Howe determined it to be more to his advantage to follow the line of road past the tentative shacks of his Howe

---

[85] Andrew Inches to James Kerr, May 19, 1851, Primary Letterbooks, 1850-1853, Records of the Surveyor General, PANB, RS 637, 1/a/23, p. 52.

[86] James Kerr to Andrew Inches, October 6, 1851, Records of the Surveyor General Records, PANB, RS 637, 7/j/3/a/9.

[87] James Kerr to R.D. Wilmot, August 19, 1852, Records of the Surveyor General, PANB, RS 637, 7/j/3/a/3 and R.D. Wilmot to James Kerr, November 5, 1852, Primary Letterbooks, 1850-1853, Records of the Surveyor General, PANB, RS 637, 1/a/23, p. 365.

[88] Petition of Alexander Wooden et al. (1852), Records of the Surveyor General, PANB, RS 637, 7/j/3/a/1.

[89] Petition of John Howe (1852), Land Petitions, PANB, RS 108. Howe applied for lot 42, which already had been occupied to some extent by Thomas Harper.

kinsmen onto the uninhabited prominence known as Geary Knoll.[90]

While the woods east of Geary began at last to experience the heavier footfall of less transient inhabitants, an even greater emprise, threatening the happiness of the river's premier lumberman, George Morrow, proceeded apace. Compelled by the regulative authority of the General Sessions, Morrow's repair of the Rockwell mill-dam not only induced a new influx of settlers into the hinterland, but also fueled the fires of ambition in the hearts of his several competitors. Gratified by an inheritance of the county shrievalty following the death of Sheriff Hazen[91] and guaranteed of a steady supply of ship's timber by the strength of the market to meet the needs of a ship being constructed under his supervision,[92] Thomas Small Hicks retired from the sordid business of open competition in the woods. When a twinge of discomfort over his want of direct access to woodland arose in the winter of 1852, he still managed to refrain from active involvement in the physically dirtier aspects of the timber trade by entrusting his wife's eldest brother with the responsibility of finding him a suitable tract in the ungranted purlieu of Victoria Settlement.[93] Hicks' concession to the traditional practitioners of the trade eased George Morrow's plight only slightly, as bona fide settlers and lumbering charlatans moved onto his Rockwell reserves and undoubtedly began using the thin veil of legitimacy to shroud their secret acts of piracy. The purchase of the Earls tract from Hicks' patron, Edward Allison, reflected Morrow's concern over the problem of legal and illegal competition and the long-term fear that his treasured Rockwell berths would fray at the edges and ultimately disintegrate as the eager blades of axe and ploughshare moved across the face of the land.[94] By the summer

---

[90] Petition of John Howe (1853), Land Petitions, PANB, RS 108.

[91] *The Royal Gazette*, June 11, 1851.

[92] Hancox, op. cit., p. 44.

[93] Petition of William Partelow (1852), Land Petitions, PANB, RS 272. The file includes a letter from Thomas S. Hicks to Andrew Inches dated March 1, 1852.

[94] Sunbury County Registry Office Records, PANB, RS 95, 19/431.

of 1852 he commenced a slow, systematic process of reclaiming the territory from the aspiring clutches of prospective settlers. Relying upon the oft-diluted viscosity of blood, Morrow sent two of his nephews into the Victoria woods to go through the pretext of settlement before relinquishing (on cue no doubt) their chosen parcels following their uncle's placement at auction in Fredericton of a higher bid.[95]

A lesser, but still vexing, cause for concern for George Morrow came from the continuing activity of Oromocto's Scottish community. William Scoullar's legislative duties did not hamper his ability to oversee his timber operations. When the summer sale of timber berths closed, he held legal right to several chances laying on the perimeter of Morrow's Rockwell empire.[96] His obsession with tamarack had indeed continued to grow. As late as the previous fall, men in his employ savagely cut hundreds of trees and desperately tried to ferry them to Saint John before a new export duty would take effect and impinge upon his profits, only to fail in their objective with the abrupt and premature closing of the river due to the early arrival of winter's frost.[97] Archibald McLean was even less restrained. Apprehended once by the agents of the Crown, who seized his illicit cache, McLean offered to erase the penalty imposed upon him through a retroactive bid for the land upon which the timber had been cut.[98] Uncowed by the scrutiny and reproof of the law, McLean subsequently undertook the lawless occupation of lands under cultivation by legitimate settlers. At the head of his crew, McLean cut a horrifying swath through the woods east of the Nerepis Road not far from Mersereau Creek

---

[95] Petition of Daniel Wood (1852) and Petition of George Wood (1852), Land Petitions, RS 272, 28/242 and 28/240; and Daniel Wood, Grant Survey Return Plans, PANB, RS 687b, Q4-46.

[96] *The Royal Gazette*, June 23, 1852.

[97] Petition of William Scoullar, Records of the Legislative Assembly, PANB, RS 24, 1854/pe/file 6/no. 209.

[98] Thomas Baillie to Lt. Governor Edmund Head, September 22, 1851, Primary Letterbooks, 1850-1853, Records of the Surveyor General, PANB, RS 637, 1/a/23, p. 102.

in a search for quality ship's timber.[99] Stirred to action by the complaints of one of the human victims of McLean's devastation, the Surveyor General ordered James Kerr to further investigate the situation. Upon examining the site of McLean's indiscretions, Kerr found it to be in a condition far worse than any of the earlier reports had indicated.[100]

The intensity of McLean's depredations owed in large part to his desperation to rush as much tamarack to the marketplace for export abroad before the aforementioned duty imposed by the legislature took effect. The entire lumbering community of the Oromocto had taken an interest in the issue, and Scoullar, no less responsive to the needs of the people than his own preferences when the two were so easily reconciled, had bitterly fought its passage, but to no avail.[101] Smarting after his failure to prevent the Assembly from imposing the hated duty, William Scoullar organized a popular protest against it. With Hayward's assistance, Scoullar presented a collective grievance and then advocated on its behalf before his legislative colleagues in January of 1852. Taking the tack of defending the indigent of the river, upon whom he claimed the painful effects of the duty trickled down in a scalding torrent of depreciated wages, Scoullar's bid for the duty's annulment met with skepticism and ultimate rejection.[102] In the end, the duty did little to halt the main thrust of trade on the Oromocto. Despite Scoullar's frantic concerns, the most immediate (yet surely limited) emporium for his wares — the local shipyards —

---

[99] R.D. Wilmot to James Kerr, October 24, 1851 and R.D. Wilmot to Samuel Mahood, February 4, 1852, Primary Letterbooks, 1850-1853, Records of the Surveyor General, PANB, RS 637, 1/a/23, p. 109 and p. 178.

[100] James Kerr to R.D. Wilmot, November 12, 1851, Seizing Officers' Records, Timber and Saw Mill Records, PANB, RS 663d, 30/a.

[101] R.D. Wilmot to Archibald McLean, November 22, 1851 and R.D. Wilmot to Archibald McLean, December 3, 1851, Primary Letterbooks, 1850-1853, Records of the Surveyor General, PANB, RS 637, 1/a/23, p. 127 and p. 138.

[102] Petition of William Hoyt, Thomas H. Smith, George Morrow and Fifty Others, Records of the Legislative Assembly, PANB, RS 24, 1852/pe/file 5/no. 121. Scoullar himself avoided the perception of impropriety by refraining from signing the petition.

could only benefit from what amounted to an incentive for domestic consumption.

Any slowdown in the business of the river came less as a result of any meddling by the House of Assembly in the conduct of trade than from the deaths of two of the more significant lumbermen of the watershed. David Kelley's success as a miller had only just begun to rescue him from the more frightful and tenuous implications of past risks when he suddenly expired. Squabbles with his brother-in-law Thomas Hartt Jr. over rights to a reserve the latter construed to be held in common resolved into a contest over possession of assets reposing in winter desolation on the banks of either branch of the Oromocto.[103] To solve the intractable problem of debt to creditors ranging from the Central Bank to mere hired hands still in the midst of the frigid season's operations in the woods, Kelley's executors sold off his vast hoard of boards and raw timber laying indolently in and beside the several millponds awaiting the spring thaw.[104] His widow retained the bulk of the family estate, as well as his portion of the old Hartt milling establishment, while his son, David Jr., purchased title to the still mortgaged South Branch mill and continued on with the slow process of its redemption.[105]

Less untimely, but equally somber, was the death of Thomas Hartt, whose collapse followed closely on that of his son-in-law. His perceptive recognition of his own mortality in the form of a will relieved his heirs of the manifold problems involved in the dissolution of his large estate, but dissolution itself brought dilution of his immediate family's former prestige and presaged a reorganization of the North West Branch's social and economic hierarchy. Happiest of all in this regard was William E. Perley, who not only was able to purchase a portion of the land and

[102] Petition of David Kelley, SU/1850, Timber and Saw Mills, 1817-1865, Timber and Saw Mill Records, PANB, RS 663a.

[104] Probate File on the Estate of David Kelley (1852), Sunbury County Probate Court Records, PANB, RS 72.

[105] Sunbury County Registry Office Records, PANB, RS 95, 20/468.

timber holdings of the late Mr. Kelley,[106] but also became the joyous host of good fortune in the form of eight hundred and fifty acres and a cash endowment from the bank account of his wife's now deceased father.[107] Hartt's son's difficulties in the conduct of his late father's business presented Perley with even greater opportunities for gain, as Perley was soon able to purchase a share of Hartt's mill and initiate a program of economic exploitation along the North West Branch of the Oromocto that would slowly expand his influence and allow for the consideration of possibilities yet undreamt.[108]

Even before an acceptable period of mourning had ended, the river economy unabashedly resumed its healthy course. Thomas Small Hicks launched the Australia-bound *Havana* in the summer of 1852;[109] and though he soon resigned his commission as High Sheriff in favour of his predecessors' nephew and namesake,[110] he lost none of his enthusiasm for the expansion of local trade. Taking heed of the advantages of improved navigation on the St. John River, Hicks gladly lent his name and support to the County elite's call for a recommencement of work on the stalled excavation of the canal at Grimrose Neck.[111] His subsequent removal to Fredericton did little to inhibit the Oromocto's thriving state, as his partner, John W. Craig, completed work on a ship so large that the draw in the twelve-year-old bridge spanning the river had to be removed to allow it clear passage to the Bay of Fundy.[112]

---

[106] Probate file on the Estate of David Kelley (1852), Sunbury County Probate Court Records, PANB, RS 72 and Sunbury County Registry, PANB, RS 95, 20/388.

[107] Will of Thomas Hartt (1852), Sunbury County Probate Court Records, PANB, RS 72.

[108] Petition of William E. Perley, SU/1853, Timber and Saw Mills, 1817-1865, Timber and Saw Mill Records, PANB, RS 663a.

[109] Hancox, op. cit., p. 44.

[110] Minutes and Orders in Council, 1852-57, PANB, RS 6, p. 59.

[111] Petition of Thomas O. Miles et al., Records of the Legislative Assembly, PANB, RS 24, 1853/pe/file 6/no. 211.

[112] Petition of Charles H. Clowes et al., Records of the Legislative Assembly, PANB, RS 24, 1854/pe/file 16/no. 490. The ship in question could only have been the 1227-ton *Matoaka*.

Craig's enterprise generally thrived, though the expense of doing business so far from the provincial hub was beginning to show in the number of loans he was forced to negotiate. Repeated mortgage of his shipyard finally led to partial bankruptcy, and after paying off the large sum of £1,500 he abandoned the river for his old Saint John home.[113] The shipyard he retained, as he did his shipbuilding enterprise, but he left all practical aspects of its prosecution to his trusted foreman, Robert Bryson, who shortly became the most prominent shipbuilder in the village. Hardly spelling the decline of local shipbuilding, Craig's difficulties seem only to have encouraged the interest of others. Convinced of the enduring profits to be found in the trade, George Morrow purchased the old (and currently derelict) Scoullar yard from John Robertson for £1,000 and began to organize matters so as to usher in a new phase of his astoundingly successful mercantile career.[114]

The growing community and the demands of petty merchants and innkeepers, of tavern owners and shipbuilders, meant not only an increase of overland traffic to and from Oromocto Village, but also the steady rise in the number of riverboats dropping off and picking up passengers and supplies. The confused and hazardous loading and unloading to and from the quayless south bank of the St. John caused concern and shame among the eminent people of the area.[115] Aware of Sheffield's precociousness in this regard, Archibald McLean and several other interested parties inquired into the prospect of provincial aid for the construction of a wharf. When a vague promise by the Executive Council for compensation for funds raised through private subscription came,[116] a wharf site was purchased from old Sheriff Hazen's widow for the nominal sum of £15.[117] Such improvement in the quality of life and business of the Oromocto did not come without stirring the anxiety of the poor, who now clamoured for

---

[113] Sunbury County Registry Office Records, PANB, RS 95, 20/222, 20/397, 20/412, 20/427, 20/447, 20/489 and 20/521.

[114] Id., 20/146.

[115] Petition of Charles H. Clowes et al., Records of the Legislative of Assembly, PANB, RS 24, 1853/pe/file 7/no. 247.

[116] Minutes and Orders in Council, PANB, RS 6, p. 198.

[117] Sunbury County Registry Office Records, PANB, RS 95, 20/127.

more secure title to their properties and a stripping of mineral rights from the concession-granting discretion of government.[118] Fears that a new wave of industrialization would disturb the quiet fields and forests watered by the Oromocto may have been exaggerated given the inaccuracies of Gesner's geological discoveries in the watershed, but renewed plans on the part of unnamed entrepreneurs for the construction of a steam-driven sawmill not far from the river's mouth certainly contributed to a climate of worry that permeated the prosperity of the moment.[119]

Less enthusiastic over the progress occurring in and around Oromocto Village, if equally less worried over the perturbing implications of a new industrial order, the people of the North West and South branches harboured a jealousy that sprung, it seems, from a knowledge of the twofold advent of communal maturity and perceived neglect. A road from Saint John running through the Douglas Valley and past the settlements on either branch of the Oromocto en route to the capital had given the upper basin a new sense of vitality that was reflected in the opening of a postal way-office and an outcropping of hotels for travelers. Denied a request that the new thoroughfare be granted the status of Great Road through the concerted opposition of the inhabitants of Oromocto Village, the people of the branches drew the funds required to pay for its continued improvement from the provincial allocations for by-roads. Sacrifices of this order hastened the enhancement of the rude path through the Nerepis Hills that had traditionally served to link the upper Oromocto with the main road to Saint John. The resulting perception of disavowal by the government and its favouritism toward supposedly more deserving settlements closer to the river's mouth soon enough occasioned the nurturing of an envy that at last manifested itself in a popular attempt to oust the Deputy Post-Master at Oromocto from his long-held sinecure and replace him with James Stewart White. A native of Amherst, Nova Scotia, who had forged strong business and family connections with the Hazen clan following

---

[118] Petition of Thomas O. Miles et al., Records of the Legislative Assembly, PANB, RS 24, 1853/pe/file 7/no. 245.

[119] Petition of Charles H. Clowes et al., Records of the Legislative Assembly, PANB, RS 24, 1854/pe/file 16/no. 490.

his migration to the river in 1851,[120] White had, for the past several years, made his living as a courier of the mails to the settlements on the river's branches. Too preoccupied with the duties of office to protest the assault upon his privileged position, Deputy Post-Master James McPherson experienced a happy windfall stemming directly from his decade of diligence as processor of local correspondence. Grateful for McPherson's honourable and useful service, a group of merchants from the river's mouth defeated the mischievous ploy orchestrated by White's Hazen kinsmen and given legitimacy by disgruntled peoples of Blissville and Hartt's Mills, who, according to the wording of the subsequent petition advancing McPherson's cause, had no justifiable complaint against the present officeholder. Indeed, except for the infrequent purchase of a newspaper, most of them had never had any reason to call upon him at all.[121]

In seeming ignorance of the great changes rapidly transforming the river community, paradoxically creating both solidarity and strife, the members of the recently formed Prince William Lodge basked in the enchanted light of a mysterious secret known to all, but quietly guarded from the impure scrutiny of the uninitiated. Secure in his post as Worshipful Master, Jeremiah Smith Jr. led the advancing neophytes through the secret catechism of complex signs and gestures, exhorting the humble assembly of brothers with the weightiness of their oath and its pre-eminence above all other species of vow if only for the reason of its voluntary nature.[122] Matching the indefatigable spread of temperance and the tenets of the Free Will Baptist creed, the appeal of Orangeism extended further into Geary until nearly every family in the settlement had sent at least one representative to the regular meetings still held at the French Lake home of James Mills. The conversion of Geary occasioned a need for greater diffusion of

---

[120] J.C. and H.B. Graves, Volume 8, p. 55. White may have been a member of the White family of Simonds, Hazen and White fame, thus a cousin of the Hazens.

[121] Petition of Charles F. Street et al., Executive Council Cabinet Series, PANB, RS 9, 1852/14.

[122] Boone, "History and Records of the King William L.O.L. #114, Geary, New Brunswick."

lodge activities throughout an expanding Orange realm; thus, the homes of William Smith (whose repudiation of the dull spirit of drunkenness transformed his old den into a place for more sober recreation) and of the immigrant John Perry became the joyous retreats of festive Orangemen. The celebration of the high holy days of the Orange calendar enlivened the entire countryside, as sharpshooters and the very fleet of foot vied with each other for victory in gay and boisterous contests.

This modest streak of self-indulgence on the part of the local Lodge, however, deterred the development of a wider commitment to the Orange cause, inuring the Lodge's members to the efforts expended by Burton Parish Justice of the Peace Nathaniel Hubbard and the Orangemen of Sheffield and Maugerville for provincial incorporation,[123] at the same time putting an end to any transhumance between the river and Fredericton on the anniversary of the Boyne. In place of distant celebrations and wider Orange fraternity, exultant parades were inaugurated, complete with facsimiles of the colourful banners of King William hoisted atop caravans of wagons that quickened their pace "through the old land of Geary" as the inspired participants, clinging to the swaying carriages, chanted in loud strains the hallowed words of "God Save The Queen." The momentary defection of the Worshipful Master's brother John for the chimeric allure of gold on three continents represented the only great loss of esteem for the local Order's holy obligations,[124] though the troublesome presence of the Reverend Garrity was hardly conducive of either the Lodge's prestige or amity among its members. Carrying out an ill-conceived vendetta against the Free Will Baptist sect that had excommunicated him from the ranks of its priesthood, Garrity chastised the majority of his brethren by presenting at one of the Lodge's meetings a circular published by the Free Will Baptist Conference denouncing Lodge activity. Tolerant of Garrity's excruciatingly poor manners, the members of the Lodge found fortunate compensation for his outbursts in his more edifying

---

[123] Petition of Nathaniel Hubbard et al., Records of the Legislative Assembly, PANB, RS 24, 1851/pe/file 7/no. 154.

[124] John Smith to Jeremiah Smith, September 16, 1852, Allen Boone Collection.

addresses on the virtues of King William and the great achievement effected by that grand monarch through the efficacious employment of Protestant arms.[125]

The blissful revelries of the King William Lodge proceeded according to a schedule that knew little variation from year to year. But even while the happy Orangemen celebrated in their immutable way, change of an oddly industrial order was busy transforming the countryside around them. The previously fruitless inquiries begun by Calvin Hatheway and continued by his colleagues in the New Brunswick Society for the Advancement of Agriculture, Home Manufactures and Commerce now produced an unlikely site for the construction of the Province's first mechanized manufactory of cotton cloth. A solution to the problem of just where to erect the cotton mill came in the person of George Kingston, a scion of a dynasty of brewers, whose emigration from England in the summer of 1843 had belatedly attended a socially mismatched marriage to a woman of reputed noble breeding.[126] Joined by several other kinsmen, one of whom eventually boarded with George Morrow,[127] Kingston settled along Back Creek in Blissville Parish, where he quickly assimilated into the Protestant Irish community that had grown up there in the course of the previous two decades. His brother Joseph remained behind in England, where his dexterity in the ways of cotton and a spirit of enterprise yet untapped very likely came to the attention of the genteel members of the Society as a result of conversations with his less artful siblings. Though no correspondence exists to confirm the connection between the emigration of Joseph Kingston with the exchange of any words between his brother and the peers and colleagues of Calvin Hatheway, it is certainly feasible that representatives of the Society, acting on intelligence provided by one brother, contacted the second in 1851 when visiting England on the occasion of the London Exhibition and suggested to him

---

[125] Boone, "History and Records of the King William L.O.L., #114, Geary, New Brunswick."

[126] Allen Boone, a descendant of George Kingston, related the story to the author. The story is in general accord with the account found in *The John C. Tracy Book*, PANB, MC 80/601.

[127] 1851 Census of New Brunswick, Sunbury County.

the possibility of establishing a cotton mill in the colonies.[128] The support of well-placed men in the provincial elite and administrative establishment undoubtedly persuaded Kingston of the correctness of any decision to emigrate, while the existing presence of kinsmen on the Oromocto and the favour of George Morrow, who soon publicly expressed his support for the prospective enterprise,[129] inclined him to settle down in the watershed. In fact, so sympathetic to the initiative was Morrow that he and William Smith turned over to the would-be industrialist a small portion of land adjoining their sawmill on the Rockwell Stream on which Kingston could construct the necessary facilities.

Kingston's auspicious procurement of the capital required for the undertaking of so prodigious an engagement in the middle of the colonial woods, far removed from the main centres of provincial trade, allowed him to put his establishment into operation by February of 1854. Employing the labour of women from the surrounding countryside,[130] Kingston's ambition to "manufacture cotton and woolen cloths and homespun in a superior style suitable to the wants of the country"[131] soon collided with the inevitability of short-term deficits. Peddling specimens of his work around Geary and the branches of the Oromocto, he not only convinced the humble settlers of the watershed of the efficacy of his enterprise, but also impressed the anxious members of the New Brunswick Society of the indubitable importance and

---

[128] That a New Brunswick Society delegation was sent to London seems evident from a letter addressed by John A. Beckwith to one R. Pennefather. See John A. Beckwith to R. Pennefather, May 30, 1850, Records of Lt. Governor Sir Edmund Head, PANB, RS 346, A/5/b.

[129] Petition of Charles H. Clowes et al., Records of the Legislative Assembly, PANB, RS 24, 1854/pe/file 7/no. 253.

[130] The labour of women at the mill is hinted at in the account of the operations of Kingston's successor, Thomas Smith, written by Smith's daughter, Mrs. Lena Phillips, in 1953. F.A. McGrand, on page 127 of *Backward Glances at Sunbury and Queen's*, also indicates the presence of female labour.

[131] Petition of Charles H. Clowes et al., Records of the Legislative Assembly, PANB, RS 24, 1854/pe/file 7/no. 253.

viability of his industry, inducing them to press the legislature for a just disposal to him of public subsidies until the threat of financial ruin had passed. Not insensible to the greater benefits posed his constituents by the diversification of the economy, William Scoullar presented the case in support of the Kingston mill to the House of Assembly, after which he was duly awarded the task of investigating the premises of the manufactory and reporting upon its prospects for the future.[132] Traveling to Geary with five of his legislative colleagues at the close of winter, Scoullar was treated to the thriving spectacle of twelve looms of differing specification and purpose, all in the process of warping, weaving, carding and winding. Proud of his achievement and eager to impress these impressionable envoys of patronage, Kingston boasted of his plans to steadily expand his operations with the introduction of devices for the manufacture of fustians and homespuns. Comically ascribing any delay in acquiring the necessary machinery to the retardation of either ocean travel or the Customs establishment, Kingston declared his confidence in his mill's eventual output of five hundred yards of finished cloth per day.[133]

Scoullar's successful solicitation for aid on behalf of Joseph Kingston and his fledgling cotton mill came just as preparations for provincial elections were being made. Anxiety over the yet unknown implications of the recently enacted Reciprocity Treaty vied for the attention of the people, yet no issue pressed so feverishly upon the popular imagination as the question of Prohibition. Scoullar's own advocacy of that cause in the session of 1852 had contributed to the passage of a prohibitory law much applauded along the Oromocto's banks, yet the resulting regulatory act proved so arbitrary when it finally took effect, so ill-defined and essentially unenforceable, that its stipulations were easily violated, not only in Sunbury County, but throughout the entire province.[134] At Oromocto Village and the lower portions of the river several miles above the great Baptist stronghold of French Lake, liquor retailer Archibald McLean rallied the most passionate of his customers in formal opposition to the criminalization of

---

[132] *Journals of the Legislative Assembly* (1854), p. 87.

[133] Id., p. 344.

[134] MacNutt, op. cit., p. 351.

a once accepted and still very popular form of recreation.[135] Claiming the law to be an improper interference in the affairs of conscience and corrosive to the health of a provincial budget formerly balanced with the assistance of taxes collected on imported spirits, McLean and his allies soon met a fierce and committed resistance that consisted of William Scoullar, the majority of the County elite, the bulk of the male settlers of the Oromocto's hinterland and the collective fury of over four hundred women unwilling to fathom a return to the dark days of the ale-induced stupor, barbarism and lethargy of their menfolk.[136] In the steamy halls of the legislature, Scoullar acceded to the expressed will of the majority of his constituents and defended the constitutionality of the liquor ban, but his passion and coherence faded as his colleagues could neither ignore the law's profound inconsistencies nor let its advocate forget his own disreputable past as a chandler of the very substance he now sought to banish from provincial shores.[137]

Stung by the taunts of his peers and ultimately unsuccessful in resurrecting the decrepit Prohibitory Liquor Law, Scoullar did not necessarily lose the confidence and support of the people of the Oromocto. Despite the late reversal of fortune, the people of the river still believed in the cause of temperance with a passion undiminished by recent failures. But while Scoullar still maintained his attachment to the virtue of sobriety, he exhibited other, more ominous signs of the dereliction of duty and conflict of interest that once before had led to popular re-examination of his future as a member of the Assembly. His wood-hauling business remained a major preoccupation. And while he relentlessly pursued the remission by the government of the duty money he believed unjustly levied upon him for exported tamarack,[138] his speeches

---

[135] Petition of Charles F. Street et al., Records of the Legislative Assembly, PANB, RS 24, 1854/pe/file 16/no. 491.

[136] Petition of Thomas Wetmore Bliss et al. and Petition of Sheriff John Hazen et al., Records of the Legislative Assembly, PANB, RS 24, 1854/pe/file 12/no. 394-5.

[137] *The Headquarters*, May 3, 1854.

[138] Petitions of William Scoullar, Records of the Legislative Assembly, PANB, RS 24, 1853/pe/file 7/no. 244 and 1854/pe/file 6/no. 209.

in the House of Assembly, wrought with wit and provoking much laughter, also brought ridicule so widespread that even the provincial press picked up upon it and began portraying the balding Scoullar as a caricature of the expedient politician.[139] Exempted from criticism only for reason of its present fashionableness and great utility, Scoullar's almost equally intense obsession with railroads was beginning to push even his concern for "hacmatac knees" into the more neglected corners of his imagination. When the provincial government offered monetary incentives toward the construction of new lines, Scoullar leaped at the chance to seize that prospective bonanza and began to formulate a list of likely investors willing to throw in their lot with him and pursue the creation of a new avenue of communication and trade to be known as the Grand Falls Railway. Fronting a third of the initial capital himself, Scoullar gathered such enormous support for the venture that when he managed to have the scheme brought before the Assembly in the spring of 1854 there was little chance of rejection, either of his plea for incorporation, or of his more prodigious request for land concessions and a £3,000 subsidy.[140]

His personal interests expanding beyond the confines of a tiny county in a minor colony on the periphery of a very large empire, and his aspirations for the kind of success attained a generation before by his countryman Hugh Johnston finally coming to the point of fruition, Scoullar began to view himself less a citizen of the Oromocto than a dweller of the rugged coast at the mouth of the St. John River. As early as December of 1853, when he expended over £600 on the purchase of a building in downtown Saint John, it must have become evident to the people of the Oromocto that their old patron's loyalties lay not with them but with the dreams of wealth and social status to be found in that distant city.[141] Insensible to the popular climate of disapproval, Scoullar weathered a physical assault upon his person by none less than a former parish constable and presented himself before the people,

---

[139] *The Provincial Patriot*, September 23, 1853.

[140] *Journals of the Legislative Assembly* (1863), p. 139-140 and the Petition of William Scoullar, Grand Falls Railway Company, Railway Administration Records, PANB, RS 22, 68/b.

[141] St. John County Registry Office Records, PANB, RS 94, B/5/298.

in June of 1854, for re-nomination to the privilege of representing them in the provincial House of Assembly.[142] He would not, however, do so unopposed. Destined to be fought amidst the tumult of the temperance struggle, the concerns over the future of provincial and local trade, the seemingly uncontrolled changes taking place on the county scene and the growing perception of the distracted state of William Scoullar, the coming election promised all of the divisions and controversies traditionally associated with the Sunbury hustings.

Fortunately for Scoullar, the very faction most capable of engineering his defeat was in a state of partial disarray. Of unassailable record and possessing an esteem all the more exalted since taking a seat on the Executive Council, where he had subsequently basked in the applause of the entire populace of the inland districts of the Province for his reputed steadfastness in the protection of their interests,[143] George Hayward approached the electors sporting the armour of political invincibility. Yet he was no leader of parties, nor a builder of coalitions. He relied on his own inimitable prestige to sway voters, and thus was unreliable to the faction to which he nominally adhered. Of late, too, he had displayed a marked empathy for the once again reviled Scoullar and had even joined with him on a number of initiatives of local and provincial scope. New leadership and new commitment were required if the reformers were to make a viable challenge, but since the retirement of Thomas O. Miles no one came forth to give the party more concrete form and instill in its members a solid sense of purpose. The amorphousness of the reform apparatus contributed to so uncertain a climate within the party and so strained the mutual affinities of the members that internecine antagonism naturally arose. With no effective or universally accepted leaders to curtail the effects of internal jealousies and direct collective focus on clear-cut objectives, antagonism exploded into schism and produced no less than five additional alternative reform candidates: Solomon Smith, a Free Baptist preacher and temperance advocate of the Rusagonis; a defeated but not yet

---

[142] Petition of Andrew Murray, Executive Council Cabinet Series, PANB, RS 9, 1853/25.

[143] *The Reporter and Fredericton Advertiser*, September 24, 1852.

conquered Jonathan P. Taylor; David Tapley and Charles Sidney Burpee, both of prominent Sheffield families; and, finally, Enoch Barker, a brother of the man who had won on the reform platform in 1842 and the candidate in whom George Hayward presently expressed the greatest confidence as a potential partner in Fredericton.[144]

The splintering of the County's only real political organization instilled little confidence among those less committed to reform principles than to the defeat of William Scoullar. Unable to summon too serious a regard for Smith, or Taylor, or Tapley, or Burpee, or Barker, the people of the Oromocto entertained their own favourite in the person of Enoch Lunt, a major entrepreneur whose interests lay mainly on the opposite side of the St. John. Lunt's attractiveness as an alternative to Scoullar was attested to by his knowledge of the intricacies of timber and farming and his cordial relations with the Oromocto's greatest of patrons, George Morrow.[145] His hopes for assuaging an 1844 electoral defeat in Queen's County ascending and his ego stirred by the sycophantic praise of the masses, Lunt declared himself at the people's service, embellishing his declaration almost to the point of nausea with an overly dramatic avowal of personal sacrifice and hardship such service would undoubtedly entail.

More than a month of campaigning throughout the County culminated in the election held on June 27. The diverse field presented the electors with a variety of choices only slightly tempered by the inevitable idiosyncrasies of the candidates themselves. The lesser known reformers generated only scant interest in their various pet projects involving agricultural development, steamboat navigation, temperance and any number of semi-secret fraternal organizations. Their presence in the race, however, did manage to utterly marginalize any remaining support for Scoullar. His reputation shattered, his self-indulgent interests increasingly incomprehensible to the lumbermen-farmers of the Oromocto, the hapless Scoullar met only rebuke in his effort to

---

[144] Hayward nominated Barker for candidacy at the formal meeting of the electors at the Burton Courthouse. See Pollbooks, Sunbury County Records, PANB, RS 157, J/2/5 (1854).

[145] *The Headquarters*, June 14, 1854.

recapture the enthusiasm for a candidacy once fueled by the wild possibilities for a prosperity now all too ambiguous to properly ascribe to the ledgers of success. Only in Blissville did even the slightest echo of his past glories resound, while in Maugerville and Sheffield his already questionable popularity evaporated to the point of virtual nonexistence. At French Lake, Geary and the surrounding countryside his old core of support defected, as the Carrs, Howes, Boones, Tills and McMinns resorted to varying ballot combinations involving George Hayward, Enoch Lunt and temperance crusader Solomon Smith. In the end Hayward and Lunt were pronounced victorious. And though the former did not afterward resume his high position in the government, his venerableness in the Assembly helped to immunize both him and his constituents against the often-unpleasant consequences of demotion.

Failure in the election was not necessarily a cause for woe, particularly among the reformers. Possibly dissatisfied with Hayward's preference for so obscure a man as Barker, as well as with Hayward's failure to take a firmer role within the reform faction after Miles' retirement, the most successful of the vanquished reformers, Charles S. Burpee, became convinced of the need for real leadership and thus dedicated himself to the tasks of redefining the faction's mission and devising a formula for gaining greater currency among the voters. Despite his victory, Hayward was likely viewed by a majority of the river's people as yesterday's man, committed less to the principles of reform, temperance and true responsibility in government than to an older order governed by the contours of personality and the heady promise and venal depths of patronage. Charles S. Burpee recognized this, and though he may have harboured some loyalty to Hayward simply on the grounds that the latter was of near relation to his wife, he began in earnest to forge a new coalition of individuals of like interest and common vision that, with the blessing of the Smasher hierarchy in Fredericton, would shortly declare itself to be nothing less than the Sunbury branch of the nascent Liberal Party.[146]

---

[146] Cover page to the Charles Burpee Papers, York/Sunbury Historical Society Collection, PANB, MC 300, ms. 5. In her article "'Smashers' and 'Rummies': Voters and the Rise of Parties in Charlotte County, New

Only William Scoullar remained outside the several consolations of defeat. Convinced of his unfitness for continued existence on the Oromocto and driven by the increasingly onerous demands of his railroad company, Scoullar departed the red soil of the lower river and returned with his family to his old abode at Saint John. A brief foray into electoral politics in 1855 ended in a defeat worse than the one suffered in Sunbury County; and though he presented the most comprehensive agenda, his words caused only slight amusement and even greater confusion among the gritty urban electorate.[147] Riven by the stupidity of his partners and the fallibility of his own speculative faculties, Scoullar's dreams of railroad riches eventually dissipated in a cloud of ruin.[148] Forced to beg for relief in the very halls once graced by his rambling oratory, he inspired the pity of his friend and former colleague Samuel Leonard Tilley, who, through the influence of the office of the Provincial Secretary, helped gain him appointment to the post of Police Magistrate for the European and North American Railway.[149] He died in March of 1868, surrounded by

---

Brunswick, 1846-1857," Dr. Gail Campbell indicates that the Liberal Party, in Charlotte County in any case, came into being during the temperance battle of the mid-1850s. The same seems to hold true for Sunbury County, but with some qualifications. In Sunbury the Liberals of the 1850s could clearly trace their lineage to the older reformers of the 1840s and 1830s. And as strong a commitment Sunbury's Liberals had to temperance, the men who ran on what would become the Conservative slate were equally committed to the temperance cause. As a determinant of party in Sunbury County, temperance seems to have been somewhat irrelevant. In the place of lofty ideals, semi-feudal personal relationships seem to have dictated party affiliations more than anything else.

[147] *The New Brunswick Courier*, September 22, 1855 and September 29, 1855.

[148] Petition of William Scoullar, Grand Falls Railway Company, Railroad Administration Records, PANB, RS 22, 68/b and the *Journals of the Legislative Assembly* (1863), p. 139-140.

[149] Commission of William Scoullar, Records of Warrants, Appointments and Commissions, PANB, RS 538, F/11 and Samuel Leonard Tilley to William Scoullar, October 30, 1857, Letterbooks, 1857-1860, Provincial Secretary Correspondence, PANB, RS 13, volume 9, page 2.

his family at his country estate at Apohaqui in King's County.[150] Not unmoved by the passing of the once great man, and having forgiven him his many trespasses, Charles DeWitt celebrated the birth of a new grandson not long after the former assemblyman's mortal demise. In commemoration of the by-gone age and its most defining spirit, the newborn infant was bestowed, as a Christian title, the controverted name of Scoullar.[151]

Aside from the two victorious candidates, by far the greatest winner in the election of 1854 was George Morrow. Long suffering the presence of his old rival in the House of Assembly, Morrow now prepared to reclaim the debt owed him by Lunt for support given during the late contest. Their interests similar, the geographic sweep of their common business generally demarcated by the width of the St. John River, Morrow and Lunt rested easy against the threat posed by the kinds of conflicts revolving around turf that had spoiled the former's relations with so many of his rivals. With disputes over territory out of the question, Morrow confidently resolved to collect his due at the opening of the 1855 session of the legislature. A momentary downturn in the local economy following the implementation of the Reciprocity Treaty made access to the legislature all the more vital. With timber in the doldrums and all progress in the local shipyards essentially halted, Morrow could not generate the revenues he needed to pay for the improvement of his industry. Recent renovation of his mill on the North West Branch drained him substantially. As a quick return on that investment was now doubtful, he and his partner, Jeremiah Tracy Jr., relied on Lunt to proffer an unusual request to the Assembly for special exemptions from the regulations governing mill reserves.[152]

Likewise, the state of his operations on the Rockwell Stream induced a solicitous mood, especially with the rise of new attractions for settlement in the interior following the construction of the Kingston cotton manufactory. Having suffered heavy diminution along the stream by the seasonal invasions of Morrow's

[150] *The Morning Telegraph*, March 10, 1868.

[151] 1871 Census of New Brunswick, Sunbury County.

[152] Petition of George Morrow and Jeremiah Tracy Jr., Records of the Legislative Assembly, PANB, RS 24, 1855/pe/file 7/no. 270.

lumber crews, the potential value of the forest in this locale was already negligible. Yet as ravaged as the Rockwell's banks had become, a sizeable amount of the marketable pine and tamarack so essential to Morrow's enterprise remained intact. For this reason, the spilling over of both transient and more permanent settlers from Geary was a great irritation to him. Unable to halt the steady torrent of claims, Morrow watched helplessly as the berths east of French Lake rapidly lost the kind of long-term viability that would otherwise help to suppress the mandate of the staff of the Crown Land Office to further the cause of provincial land settlement. Equally concerned in the matter, though perhaps somewhat more sympathetic to the efforts of the interior settlers (many of whom were his kinsmen and brothers in the Lodge), William Smith assented to his partner's legislative solution and thus agreed to entrust the case to the beholden hands of Mr. Lunt.[153]

The assistance rendered George Morrow by Enoch Lunt did not exclude the possibility that others might also benefit from the latter's legislative influence. But while Lunt's efforts for Morrow generally met with success, his assistance on behalf of men such as Joseph Kingston did not end so satisfactorily. With the downturn in the economy, Kingston's normally high overhead rose to unforeseen levels. The mortgage of a portion of his property to Asa Carr solved some of his immediate pecuniary obligations,[154] but his plans for the introduction of a steam engine to relieve his manufactory of its dependence on the more primitive animus of nature abiding in Rockwell Stream could only be redeemed from the lonely domain of oblivion through the assistance of the Provincial Treasurer. The limits of the Assembly's generosity toward the cotton manufactory, however, had already been exceeded in the previous year, and though most of its members undoubtedly looked favourably upon Kingston's initiative, no sympathy for what may well have been viewed as his profligacy could be found among their ranks.[155] His operations endured in spite of this

---

[153] Petition of George Morrow and William Smith, Records of the Legislative Assembly, PANB, RS 24, 1855/pe/file 7/no. 271 and the Journals of the Legislative Assembly (1855), p. 106.

[154] Sunbury County Registry Office Records, PANB, RS 95, 20/362.

[155] *Journals of the Legislative Assembly* (1855), p. 111 and p. 149.

failure, but only just barely. And while his relations with Morrow were amicable, it is likely he felt the prickly lumberman's silent and growing exasperation over the continuing rush of settlers past the struggling textile plant into the woods beyond.

This rush itself seemed only to quicken with the onset of the present economic disturbance, as if the distress of industry were now delivering in secret communications to the Oromocto's un-propertied class of residents the message that land ownership represented a hedge against the claims of the creditor and the growing penury of wage labour. The arrival of foreign migrants during the late boom had only heightened the level of competition in the more settled parts of the river community, and as the economy worsened, new, more extreme, options batted around the troubled minds of those not fortunate enough to possess title to a freehold and a special claim to either private or public patronage. Cash shortages in such uninviting times precluded outright purchase of land, thus eyes turned to the hinterland for relief, only to find that even here the restless, exiled hands of emigrant Irish were wresting the ancient legacy of the Loyalists from the neglectful grasp of their rightful heirs. The ancient tracts of Victoria Settlement now received the first of its more permanent inhabitants, as Irish Protestants, belonging primarily to the Church of England, ambled through the woods along the lumber paths cut by men in the employ of George Morrow and staked claims upon parcels surveyed an eternity before.

The unambiguous favour bestowed by Lunt on his backers was in itself not particularly vile given the political traditions of colonial New Brunswick, yet in the context of growing liberal sentiments it was becoming less tolerable to the people at large. The victory of the Smashers in the very election that had brought Lunt to Fredericton had been secured largely through appeal to the will of the people. Municipal incorporation, direct selection of parish and county officials, even prohibition, had all captured the imagination of the provincial populace, and this was no less true in Sunbury County. Appealing to the rhetoric of the provincial liberals, the people of Maugerville had engineered the overthrow of Nathaniel Hubbard from his position as supervisor of the road running along the north bank of the St. John and replaced him with one of their own. More auspiciously, at the mouth of the

Oromocto, serious talk was underway regarding the formation of a county municipal government. At the forefront of this debate stood Charles Hatfield Clowes. A member of a distinguished Burton family, Clowes, since the early days of the decade, had steadily emerged as a substantial player in community affairs and taken a leading role in nearly every major development.[156] It was undoubtedly at Clowes' urging that Sheriff Hazen convened a meeting for the purpose of drawing up a county charter, but so careless in following correct procedure were the various interested parties that their efforts to democratize county affairs were disqualified by provincial officials.[157] Clowes himself was undaunted. Working tirelessly to secure the desired charter and lay the groundwork for its implementation once it was granted, Clowes soon achieved his end, and when the first elections were held for the new municipal council, he was duly chosen to be the representative for Burton Parish. Not surprisingly, his fellow councillors went on to elevate him to the position of County Warden, thus allowing him to guide the nascent polity through it first uncertain days of autonomy. In spirit, as well as in practice, the trappings of the old order were banished from the scene. Patronage, at least that which had been granted by the non-elected members of the Court of General Sessions, was abolished and a new ideal, government by the people, became ascendant.

Oblivious to the implications of the ongoing revolution in county affairs, Lunt proceeded to commit even more outrageous acts in total opposition to the prevailing spirit of the times. Whenever a post became vacant, Lunt used his influence to secure the appointment for one of his friends– an old custom, admittedly, but one that was, in the new era of democracy, wholly inappropriate. Thus, even when Lunt acted in a way that was in accord with popular sentiments, such as when he lent his support to the

---

[156] Specifically, Clowes had been prominent in the push to construct the Burton Wharf, the defense of the Nerepis Road against the pretensions of the Branches and the effort to obtain subsidies for the Kingston Manufactory.

[157] Samuel Leonard Tilley to John Hazen, January 22, 1856, Provincial Secretary Correspondence, PANB, RS 13, 8/268.

successful effort to pass a more effective prohibitory liquor law,[158] the people found it difficult, if not impossible, to applaud him. One good deed was erased by a bad one. Indeed, in the case of the prohibitory law, he almost immediately soiled the high principle on which he had stood by packing the local prohibitocracy with a host of booze-sellers and die-hard liquorites. Long-time liquor trafficker Morrow took a seat on the Court of General Sessions and the committee to oversee enforcement of the new law, while young John McLean, a son of the staunchly intemperate Archibald, became the County's sole retailer of non-proscribed intoxicants and liquor inspector for the entire Oromocto.[159]

Manifestly displeased by this performance, the people of the river suddenly found themselves with the opportunity to voice their disapproval when the Lieutenant Governor dissolved the House of Assembly over the insoluble problems caused by prohibition.[160] The fortuitousness of this occasion could hardly have been contested by the majority of Sunbury's enfranchised inhabitants, but with the absence of the traditional electoral alternatives, a degree of uncertainty surely engulfed the electorate as the contest scheduled for June of 1856 approached. Throwing off the stigma of past rejection and making a highly public embrace of the tenets of liberalism and temperance, Charles S. Burpee prepared to test the viability throughout Sunbury of the Liberal cause. To lead the Liberal ticket, he selected his former competitor, David Tapley. A son and grandson of Oromocto shipbuilders, Tapley himself had spent much of his early life in Sheffield, though of late he had been residing in Saint John.[161] Ongoing efforts to improve and increase steamboat traffic on the St.

---

[158] *Journals of the Legislative Assembly* (1855), p. 260.

[159] Enoch Lunt to Samuel Leonard Tilley, April 4, 1855, Executive Council Cabinet Series, PANB, RS 9, 1855/7 and General Sessions, Sunbury County Records, PANB, RS 157, A/2/56 (1856).

[160] MacNutt, op. cit., pp. 359-360.

[161] See J.C. and H.B. Graves, Volume 8, p. 50; Harriet Silvester Tapley, *Genealogy of the Tapley Family* (Danvers, Mass: The Endecott Press, 1900), PANB, MC 80/no. 596; and *The Canadian Dictionary and Portrait Gallery of Eminent and Self Made Men* (Toronto: American Biographical Publishing Company, 1881), PANB, MC 80, no. 407.

John River hardly hindered his appeal in the County.[162] Nor did distant ties to the ancient Maugerville Tapleys and a goodly number of the inhabitants of the Oromocto dampen his prospects for overcoming the traditional ill will expressed by the people of Burton, Lincoln and Blissville toward would-be representatives from the northern parishes.[163]

Charles Burpee would not send David Tapley out to stand alone on the Liberal platform. To join Tapley in the Liberals' challenge to the two incumbents, Burpee chose his kinsman, William E. Perley.[164] Unwearied by his hoary struggles against the once indomitable William Scoullar, and having now achieved the kind of success as a lumberman the dream of which had originally launched him onto his fateful exploration of South Branch Lake, Perley emerged from the relatively quiet confines of upper Blissville to accept Burpee's offer. His ancient Reform credentials, his support for temperance, his Free Will Baptist background and his role as a dispenser of patronage both in the context of his business and as supervisor of the Nerepis Road highly recommended his candidacy and foretold its favourable conclusion. The recent implementation of a new provincial election law only broadened his appeal among the electors, as the poorer, largely wage-earning and subsistence fringe of the populace flocked to his banner in near total disregard of the arrogant pronouncements of Enoch

---

[162] In 1853 Tapley and his partner, Hugh Morris, built the steamer *Magnet*. Difficulties in procuring a boiler led to a delay in putting it into operation along the St. John River. In the fall of the same year he acted as commissioner to superintend the erection of a steamboat wharf in Maugerville. He gained some renown in 1855 when, after the wharf had been destroyed in an unusually high freshet, he undertook to rebuild it at his own expense. See Petition of David Tapley and Hugh Morris, Records of the Legislative Assembly, PANB, RS 24, 1854/pe/file 6/no. 221 and Petition of David Tapley, Records of the Legislative Assembly, PANB, RS 24, 1856/pe/file 3/no 96.

[163] David Tapley was a second cousin, twice removed, of early Maugerville settler Alexander Tapley. See Harriet Silvester Tapley, *Genealogy of the Tapley Family*.

[164] Burpee's wife at the time was the daughter of Thomas Perley, who was a son of old Israel's brother Oliver. Mrs. Burpee and William Edward Perley, thus, were second cousins.

Lunt. Unfortunately, the provisions of the new law were not well understood by the men entrusted with implementing them, thus it was not surprising that a large number of individuals not meeting the new minimum requirements for claiming the franchise managed to push themselves onto the revised list of voters.[165] Unmindful of the legalities involved, Sheriff Hazen opened the polls. The results were outright stupendous. Unable to muster his old supporters and completely alienated from the interests and aspirations of the younger reformers of the Liberal Party, George Hayward slipped into an enforced retirement resulting from electoral defeat, while Enoch Lunt, virtually ignored in the Oromocto frontier, experienced the momentary disappearance of his hopes for a more enduring political career.[166]

Lunt did not long remain content to accept the dubious verdict of an enlarged roster of electors. His ally George Morrow remained at his side, and together, with additional support from a number of Sheffield partisans, they angrily demanded a scrutiny of the two victorious candidates' tallies.[167] Unable to suppress their bitter candour over this unveiled accusation of electoral fraud, Perley and Tapley retaliated with their own demands for a scrutiny of Lunt. Hazen dutifully set the date for the examination of the ballots, but on the assigned day all save Lunt appeared on the court house steps. Detained by urgent personal business, Lunt was not so derelict of courtesy as to totally neglect the gathering throng of his friends and enemies, and in his absence, sent his lawyer to retract his complaint against the discretion of the people and announce, instead, his intention of presenting the case to the members of the House of Assembly for what he imagined would be less prejudicial consideration. Consumed by the dire necessity to resolve the problem of temperance, the members of the House who met at the July session tabled the complaints of Lunt and his allies, thus extending the late assemblyman's successors a certain degree of relief as they battled, alas unsuccessfully, for a more

---

[165] "Questions to and Answers from the Clerk of the Peace, County of Sunbury," *Journals of the Legislative Assembly* (1857), Appendix cccxviii-cccxx.

[166] Pollbooks, Sunbury County Records, PANB, RS 157, J/2/7 (1856).

[167] Ibid.

acceptable alternative to the failed provisions of the prohibitory liquor law.[168]

When the second session of the new legislature opened in February of the following year, both Lunt and Morrow were on hand to submit their several grievances. An elaborate hearing ended abruptly with the dismissal of the complaints, as the documented improprieties evidenced in the late contest were apparently found to be ascribable less to the incompetence of Sheriff Hazen and the dishonesty of the victorious candidates than to the inherent difficulties and ambiguities to be found in the text of the new election law.[169] The pleas of Charles S. Burpee and the Liberals of Sheffield undoubtedly helped convince the Assembly of the justness of its decision,[170] as did those of Warden Clowes.[171] In the end, Lunt's only hope for an imminent resurrection of his legislative career lay in the instability of the present government, and when the shaky coalition headed by Edmund Baron Chandler collapsed,[172] both he and his former colleague announced their candidacies. Greater regard for meticulousness when administering the balloting prevented the recurrence of charges of tampering, yet when the much reduced tallies were counted, Lunt had no choice but to accept defeat and retire to the ennui of his Sheffield home.[173] More schooled in the graces incumbent upon civilized men to practice when in the company of their fellow mortals, George Hayward retained his dignity throughout the confusion, and though he may well have missed his old duties in the Assembly, he never begrudged his nephew, nor his nephew's new colleague, their accession to the honour of representing the people.

---

[168] *Journals of the Legislative Assembly* (1856-1857), p. 17-18.

[169] *Journals of the Legislative Assembly* (1857), pp. 26/31/91-92.

[170] Petition of Charles Burpee et al., Records of the Legislative Assembly, PANB, RS 24, 1857/pe/file 3/no. 98.

[171] Petition of Charles Clowes et al., Records of the Legislative Assembly, PANB, RS 24, 1857/pe/file 3/no. 97.

[172] MacNutt, op. cit., p. 362-3

[173] Pollbooks, Sunbury County Records, PANB, RS 157, J/2/5 (1857). Lunt eventually retired from Sunbury County. He settled in Saint John, where for several years before his death in 1872 he was heavily involved in the steam navigation business of the river.

Though belied by the results of the polls, it is interesting to note that William E. Perley's acclaim did not universally resound throughout the land, nor even throughout the entire upper district of the Oromocto. Inspiring deference from the supplicant souls of the wage-earning populace of the river, his status as a business-man also had given rise to a reputation for occasional breaches of ethical conduct. Too busy with his own affairs to adhere to the regulations governing the purchase of Crown lands, he had re-peatedly sought ways around the tiring requirement to travel all the way to St. Andrew's to formalize his applications for land along the shores of South Branch Lake that happened to lay within the jurisdiction of Charlotte County.[174] When pressured by credi-tors, he felt little compunction in seeking refuge in the protective sheath of the provincial bankruptcy law, while in his administra-tion of the Nerepis Road he was known to have somewhat blatantly stooped to rewarding friends and clients with contracts for labour and supplies.[175] Yet any misgivings about the man him-self following his election generally retreated behind the banner of local pride. As William E. Perley confidently marched back and forth between the capital and his home on the South Branch, he carried with him the collective aspirations of the people of that long-ignored tributary. Attending to the recommendation of his new ally, Charles Clowes, to the post of County Surrogate for the Supreme Court[176] and the strange matter of the dismissal of a sus-pected atheist from the post of County Supervisor of Schools occupied only a fraction of his time.[177] With these matters dis-posed of, he turned his attention to the long-stalled progress of

---

[174] Petition of William E. Perley, Land Petitions, PANB, RS 108 and Pe-tition of William E. Perley, Land Petitions, PANB, RS 272, 42/138.

[175] Petition of Thomas Smith, Executive Council Cabinet Series, PANB, RS 9, 1852/14.

[176] William Perley and David Tapley to R.D. Wilmot, August 28, 1856, Executive Council Cabinet Series, PANB, RS 9, 1856/9.

[177] Ibid. The suspected atheist, George Taylor, had first met resistance to his occupation of the post several years before when Reverend Wig-gins stirred popular concern over Taylor's teaching and professing "openly a denial in the authority of scripture." See Executive Council Cabinet Series, PANB, RS 9, 1854/2.

the Douglas Valley Road. The entire population of the country-side from Nerepis to Rusagonis clamoured more loudly than ever for the elevation of the well-traveled highway to the status of Great Road,[178] and though Perley could not easily effect the desired result, his advocacy for the needs of the maturing population of the upper regions of the Oromocto secured the monies necessary for the construction of a durable new bridge over the South Branch Stream that some postulated would stand for at least half a century.[179] The only great defeat for the people of Blissville during this period of Perley's political novitiate came with the rejection of Perley's stepbrother, Justice of the Peace Benjamin S. Bailey, for the office of High Sheriff following the sudden death of the younger John Hazen.[180] The bulk of any resentment arising from this affront was constrained by the appointment of that old favourite of the South Branch, James Stewart White, to the shrievalty and the selection of Bailey to fill a vacancy on the county Inferior Court of Common Pleas.[181]

In Oromocto Village and the country immediately surrounding it, hostility to the ambitions of the ungainly settlements of the interior no longer inspired the kind of jealousy that formerly provoked visceral opposition to any sort of change in the status quo. With the establishment of the municipality, all roads in the county led to the mouth of the Oromocto. Unlike during the sleepy days of Sessional rule, no inhabitant of the County, let alone the wilderness districts of the river's hinterland, could now so easily ignore the political precedence of Burton Parish. With the assistance of the other elected representatives of the parishes, Charles Clowes rapidly consolidated his supremacy in county affairs,

---

[178] Petition of James Slip et al., Records of the Legislative Assembly, PANB, RS 24/pe/file 1/no. 25; Petition of Thomas Leonard et al., Records of the Legislative Assembly, PANB, RS 24/pe/file 1/no. 30; and Petition of William Sinkler et al., Records of the Legislative Assembly, PANB, RS 24/pe/file 1/no. 32.

[179] *Journals of the Legislative Assembly* (1857), p. 34 and *Journals of the Legislative Assembly* (1859), Appendix dlxxx.

[180] Petition of William Hoyt et al., Executive Council Cabinet Series, PANB, RS 9, 1857/10.

[181] *The Royal Gazette*, January 12, 1859.

liberalizing the stipulations governing use of the local gaol, drafting a county constitution and seizing from the local Justices of the Peace control of provincial grants for county roads.[182] Only the people of Lincoln Parish expressed any dissatisfaction over the new state of affairs, but with the rescheduling of local elections from December to October and the moving of the site of parish meetings from the extreme north to a more central location at a schoolhouse on the Waasis Stream, the bulk of any disgruntlement vanished.[183]

A more auspicious development came under the direction of Burton Justice of the Common Pleas Nathaniel Hubbard. Smarting from his recent removal from the post of Road Supervisor,[184] Hubbard undertook the raising of interest and subscriptions for the purpose of emulating the arrogant people of Maugerville in the construction of a new church.[185] More advanced than Hubbard's plans for building a second Anglican church in Burton Parish, those for the reconstruction of the bridge spanning the Oromocto now came to fruition as well. No longer able to ignore the complaints regarding its growing instability, provincial authorities awarded the contract to build a new bridge to Archibald McLean,[186] evidence of whose industry as a builder presently emerged in the local shipyards in the form of the ninety-three ton

---

[182] Draft Minutes, 1857-1881, Sunbury County Records, PANB, RS 157, A/1/9; By-Laws, Sunbury County Records, PANB, RS 157, H/1/1-I/4/1; and Petition of the Municipality of Sunbury, Records of the Legislative Assembly, PANB, RS 24, 1857/pe/file 3/no. 70.

[183] Petition of Thomas H. Smith et al., Records of the Legislative Assembly, PANB, RS 24/1859/pe/file 5/no. 93.

[184] Petition of John Brown et al., Executive Council Cabinet Series, PANB, RS 9, 1855/4.

[185] See R.P. Gorham, "Notes on the History of the Church of England in the Parish of Maugerville, Sunbury County, N.B." (1937), Archives of the Diocese of Fredericton, PANB, MC 223, M3-16; and "A Brief History of the Associated Parishes of Maugerville and Burton, by a Senior Church Warden," Archives of the Diocese of Fredericton, PANB, MC 223, M3-16B.

[186] *Journals of the Legislative Assembly* (1858), Appendix dxii-dxiii.

woodboat, *Oromocto*.[187] By September of 1857 the glistening new avenue spanning the river's two hundred and twenty feet, with a draw in the middle, four bays on each side and approaches framed by compactly laid boulders to stifle the erosive powers of wind and water, was opened to traffic. Solid craftsmanship, however, could not overcome the ancillary effects of the momentary incompetence of the captain of the steamboat *Transit*, as it made its way downstream from the Oromocto's uppermost point of navigation. The *Transit's* full-speed collision with the north draw pier damaged the piles in November. Though the damage was repairable, the lateness of the season and delays in procuring the proper materials demanded a makeshift remedy in the form of wooden planks laid so as to reconnect the sundered passage.[188]

The tumultuous history of the Oromocto bridge, enlivened with incidents of setback and accomplishment, mirrored the greater history of the community strung out along the river over which the conjoining structure loomed. It was in fact the tale of two bridges, the first built at the beginning of the previous decade, the second at the end of the present one. And just as the present bridge differed in its design and function from that of its predecessor, so too did the last days of the present decade radically contrast with the initial moments of the first. Gone was the old government of the General Sessions, with its elitist verdure and oligarchic tang. Gone were the old leaders like William Scoullar and George Hayward, and a number of the older entrepreneurs according to whose whims and discretion the people of the river pursued the rigours of their livelihood. The old ideas of patronage, too, no longer sat so firmly on the ridge of acceptance, as democratic institutions arose and a new language of political morality sidled its way into the popular consciousness through the influence of the Sons of Temperance, the Free Will Baptist movement, the nascent Liberal Party and the ever-resolute cries of the expanding ranks of the Orange Order. Such institutions and the ideas they fostered had spread so widely along the Oromocto by the end of the decade that few were the individuals and families ignorant of or unconvinced by the forceful earnestness of their

---

[187] Hancox, op. cit., p. 46.

[188] *Journals of the Legislative Assembly* (1858), Appendix dxii-dxiii.

appeal. Surrounding the budding growth of a new mentality, the traditional staple of life, the forest industry, continued to hold sway over the destiny of the river's people. By the end of the decade the slowdown occasioned by Reciprocity ended and shipbuilding and the quest for tamarack resumed their formerly healthy pace. Through all of this, George Morrow remained the dominate personality. In the last years of the 1850s, having finally put the affairs of his shipyard in order, Morrow actuated his desire to diversify his interests and constructed his first sailing vessel on the banks of the Oromocto.[189] For the poorer segments of the population, particularly in the Geary area, an equally ambitious resort to the plough and spade was still in the beginning stages, but as the decade ended the success of this more popular form of diversification remained questionable.

Agriculture and land settlement had never been a completely serious venture, and none of the settlers of the area near Victoria, many of whom worked and continued to work for George Morrow, ever really seem to have aspired to a way of life completely free of the familiar ordeals characteristic of a primarily lumbering vocation. Nathaniel Hubbard knew as much when he reported on the lack of progress made by the County Agricultural Society in the vicinity of his Burton home in spreading the religion of agronomy among the restless lumbermen of the region.[190]   When the provincial government, inspired perhaps by the success in finally generating interest in land settlement in the region around Victoria, attempted to undertake a similar experiment not far from Great Oromocto Lake at a place called Peltoma,[191] none of the old families of the river paid much heed. With no timber to harvest, and no capital in the form of wages paid by entrepreneurs for labour on licensed berths, no man would forsake better known, more thickly settled latitudes for an uncertain, isolated existence in an essentially desolate wilderness. In the 1860s James Kerr

---

[189] Hancox, op. cit., p. 48.

[190] "Summary of Answers to Circulares issued by the Agricultural Commission, 1857," *Journals of the Legislative Assembly* (1858), Appendix dcx-.

[191] "Regulations For Facilitating the Sale of Crown Lands to Actual Settlers, 1856-7," as found in Executive Council Records, PANB, RS 7.

would have greater success in populating the region around South Branch Lake, but the settlers who followed him would be Saint John mechanics and poor emigrants attracted by the perceived stability of the farming life, not the old lumbering kindreds of the Oromocto.[192] For families such as the Frosts and McMinns of the village, the Boones, Carrs, Howes, Tills and Woods in Geary and Victoria, and the Andersons, Buckinghams, DeWitts and Tuckers of the South Branch, the life of the woods lost none of its timeless enchantment, but while they continued on according to the patterns of their ancient habits, the steadily vanishing stands held out the imminent prospect of a crises. Once exhausted to the most marginal level, the traditional forest economy could no longer support them, and as their land was poorer than the interval lands of the main stream, and as their own meagre prosperity had already forced them to migrate into the interior, the only direction left to move when the fateful day of reckoning came would be away from the formerly life-sustaining waters of the Oromocto. The disavowal of lumbering and the wholehearted embrace of husbandry could not save them from the inevitable fate of the unfortunate settler of the periphery. No interest existed in such a transition, and even if it did, the land itself on which a new agricultural foundation could be laid exhibited so sparse a bounty that no amount of precipitation, fertilizers or nutritive freshets could instill lasting life into its acidic strata.

---

[192] See Chapter Five.

# Chapter Four

## NORTH LAKE INTERLUDE

When the migration from the Oromocto to North Lake commenced, the individuals who participated in it did not do so in total ignorance of the place to which they were moving. Nor was North Lake an uninhabited, untamed locale, bereft of history and dependent upon the native sons of the Oromocto for its initiation into the ken of civilization. In the late 1860s, when a select group of Oromocto inhabitants began to make their way to the upper St. Croix, the region had already undergone three formative decades of sustained human activity, during which the objectives of government, entrepreneur and settler tended to mutually reinforce one another and create a matrix of settlement that allowed for the development of a series of related communities that one day would form the parish of North Lake. The rise of these communities over a thirty-year period was likewise assisted by the outbreak of the American Civil War. While the competing American factions engaged in their damnable slaughter, new opportunities arose throughout the North Lake district, attracting investment and additional labour, sparking the local economy and expanding the region's demographic potential. It was this boom, resulting in part from the War Between the States, that made it possible for the people of the Oromocto to consider relocation to North Lake a viable alternative to continued residence in Sunbury County. Their decision to move, however, required a more intimate stimulus. Arriving in the 1850s, Oromocto native Hugh McMinn represented the necessary link between North Lake and the older Oromocto community, providing the people of his former abode with tangible evidence of their own probable compatibility with their prospective new home. Without McMinn's presence, North Lake would likely have been unappealing as a destination and the movement of Oromocto natives into the district would never have occurred. In order to fully understand the eventual movement of Oromocto peoples into North Lake, it is, thus, necessary to examine North Lake's history, the economic and social trends at work within it, and, finally, the appearance there of Hugh McMinn, whose own prosperity would ultimately persuade many of his kinsmen and former neighbours of the advantages to be gained by transferring themselves to the St. Croix.

≈≈≈

Throughout the period during which the community of the Oromocto emerged from the doldrums of rural quietude, another community had begun to develop at a more relaxed pace. The North Lake district lay far from the Oromocto's deep waters, and there is little doubt that prior to 1850 anyone living in Burton, or Lincoln, or Blissville would ever have heard of, let alone visited, so obscure and remote a countryside. Marked by a series of rough and wildly undulating hills, the boundaries of the North Lake district clearly distinguished it as laying on the eastern side of the very upper extreme of the St. Croix watershed. As late as 1830 the great advancement in human affairs that had already made the towns of St. Andrew's, St. Stephen and Calais minor hubs of international trade had yet to penetrate the interior of a country that, while laying outside the immediate political jurisdiction of the aforementioned places, exhibited a peculiar geography that naturally inclined to link North Lake's fortune with that of the river below. In 1830 this natural inclination proved less real than theoretical, as a series of rapid and treacherous falls, cedar swamps and a confusing labyrinth of deceptive channels and inlets confounded any speculative impulses exciting the imaginations of St. Croix entrepreneurs and prevented them from venturing much further than the forks between the east and west branches of the river, a mere twenty miles from the main centres of civilization to the south. Beyond the transforming ambience of industry, then, lay a wilderness wherein human beings were not, with any certainty, known to have lived, and where shiner and togue, eagle, wolf, bear and caribou roamed with little fear of violent destruction by man. Only the indigenous peoples of the continent moved with any confidence or regularity through the district, travelling across paths well worn by centuries of use in search for ofttimes elusive game. Their's was a tranquil, ageless existence, little changed since that time, before the European reconnaissance, when the New World was still old. Cut off from the main haunts of the white man and as yet beyond the limits of the latter's confidence to easily subjugate, the North Lake district, from its lower limits at the Palfrey Brooke, to its upper reaches at the source of the Monument Stream, represented a strange and anachronistic relic of an earlier day, but one which could not, if only for the reason of its still inaccessible stands of timber, forever remain outside the influence of a certain covetousness inspired by an awkward alliance of curiosity and need.

The first intrusion of the white man into the blissful country around North Lake came in the early 1830s. Obsessed by an indefatigable quest for profit, a coterie of Woodstock lumbermen led by the Connell clan began to ascend Eel River and delve into North Lake's northeastern quarter. Assemblyman Jeremiah Connell erected a camp on the western shore of First Eel River Lake, thereby granting nocturnal haven to his employees, who, by day, toiled to extract what could only have been, for reason of mere remoteness from the marketplace, a meagre and inconsequential harvest.[1] On the American side of the St. Croix, small groups of settlers congregated to take advantage of the bounty of a luxuriant yet still largely unknown fishery, wherein a host of rare and mysterious species, unadapted by the peculiarities of natural selection to the hungry wiles of man, became inevitably ensnared in nets strung across the narrow portions of the waterway.[2] Less concerned with the niceties of international law than with the more immediate demand for sustenance (as well as the not so imminent promise of trade abroad), these settlers, Americans all, crossed the border with impunity — a violation that offended no one, save, of course, the fish themselves, who, though born perhaps in New

---

[1] Playford's Survey of Blocks Between Deadwater Brook and Eel River, and East of Monument Brook, Survey Plans, PANB, RS 656/IL, York County, Volume 12/No. 7, 1835.

[2] Abraham Gesner, *Fourth Report on the Geological Survey of the Province of New Brunswick*, p. 37.

Brunswick waters, were as yet unable to lay claim to the privileges and protections entailed by British citizenship.

Of greater consequence for the development of the North Lake district was the interest shown in the region by a tight-knit, incestuous group of St. Stephen businessmen, the most significant of whom were the assorted members of the Hill family. Of English origin, with a brief sojourn in Nova Scotia behind him, the emigrant patriarch of the family, Japeth Hill, had settled at Machias, Maine, around 1770. Marrying there and raising a substantial brood, Hill became a prominent partisan of the Revolutionary movement.[3] His son, Abner, proved somewhat more ambivalent toward the legacy of independence, and when the occasion arose, he crossed Passamaquoddy Bay to the vicinity of the emerging Loyalist parish of St. Stephen in a rather opportune search for land. Disappointed in his inquiries, Abner Hill returned to the American side, to Calais. He was, however, eventually able to muster the capital required to purchase interest in a St. Stephen sawmill. For five years he lived a disjointed life, boarding in Calais and working in St. Stephen. But in 1797, when the needs of business became too pressing and purchasable land became more available, he transferred his domestic quarters, complete with his growing menagerie of children, over to British soil.[4]

Success as a sawmill proprietor naturally led Abner Hill into other related endeavours, not to mention an esteemed position in the local social hierarchy, which he enjoyed despite a failure on his part to submit to the swearing of the customary oath of allegiance to the Crown. Uninitiated into the higher arcana of the liberal arts, Hill was nevertheless determined to introduce his children into the distinguished culture of academia. He sent his eldest son first to a preparatory school in Massachusetts, and later to Dartmouth College.[5] This eldest of sons, George Stillman Hill, put his father's investment to good application. Upon returning

---

[3] Memo of A.M. Hill, undated, Hill Manuscripts, PANB, MC 1001, Ms 6/1.

[4] Memo of George Stillman Hill, Hill Manuscripts, PANB, MC 1001, Ms. 6/5.

[5] George Stillman Hill to Thomas Hill (editor of the *Loyalist*), July 22, 1845, Hill Manuscripts, PANB, MC 1001, Ms. 6/5.

home from New Hampshire, George S. Hill almost immediately came under the tutelage of the Honourable Ward Chipman as a student of the then still high and respected calling of law. A man of deep religious sentiments of the Wesleyan variety, though a somewhat late convert to the principles of alcoholic abstinence, George S. Hill harboured a profound sense of public duty, so much so that even his natural modesty could not, when elected to the House of Assembly in 1830, restrain him from taking the side of reform in opposition to the reviled "compact party."[6] His stand against the rule of privilege little interfered with his own private obligations to his father, nor did it deter him from taking a brotherly interest in the advancement of his younger siblings when they began entering into a family business that was being increasingly drawn toward the upper reaches of the St. Croix.

In the same year that George S. Hill gained election to the House of Assembly, his brothers Abner and Stephen stumbled upon the so-called Narrows between Grand and Spednick Lakes, whereon a clearing was made for the purpose of growing and harvesting wild grass.[7] Though the thought of actual movement into that wilderness may never have been particularly inspiring, the utility of possessing land in this locale could not be denied, especially as the stands downstream were steadily receding. Assisted by the presence of brother George in Fredericton, the Hills, by 1833, had acquired nearly six thousand acres of land in the North Lake district.[8] The hostility of Thomas Baillie, whom George Hill admired no more than he did the other members of the privileged elite,[9] never hindered the Hills' procurements, though a lost receipt did initially present the imperious Commissioner with the

---

[6] Hill's correspondence with his wife gives ample evidence of his own political persuasion.

[7] Petition of Abner and Stephen Hill (1832), Land Petitions, PANB, RS 272, 16/4.

[8] Evidence of Horatio's role appears in several letters George Hill wrote to his wife dated February 12, February 18 and February 21, 1833, in the Hill Manuscripts, PANB, MC 1001, Ms. 6/8.

[9] George Stillman Hill to Sarah Hill, March 8, 1833, Hill Manuscripts, PANB, MC 1001, Ms. 6/8.

grounds to disqualify the release of at least one parcel abutting the Narrows.[10] Once the affair was sorted out, Abner and Stephen Hill discretely constructed a crude dam at the entrance to Grand Lake to facilitate the conveyance of timber, which they hoped to begin cutting in earnest.[11]

The scarcity of labour in North Lake and the district's absolute seclusion from the more settled state of mankind barred the immediate prospect that the Hills, and others like them, could soon overcome the impositions of nature and transform the country into a substantial producer of a much demanded resource. The Hill brothers' vague intimations of the potential the region had for permanent settlement did manage to persuade the responsible agents in the government to refrain from disposing of lands thought most fit for cultivation, though a certain ignorance of the rocky terrain of the district led to the apparent creation of settlement reserves much more suited to the prerogatives of the quarryman than to the steady application of the plough. The Hills' activity also attracted the attention of Moses Henry Perley, who shortly began to contemplate a foray of his own into the shadowy world of large-scale land speculation. A native of Maugerville who was currently residing in Saint John, the young barrister had found it to his advantage to hover about the corridors of power in pursuit of the fruits of his own exorbitant ambition.[12] Fully condoning the unpopular Baillie's determination to favour the holders of large sums of capital with the sale of blocks of land of unprecedented size, Perley submitted an application for an enormous tract of country beginning at the Digdeguash Stream and extending northward along the eastern shore of the St. Croix watershed.[13] Admitting the obstacle to his own plans for developing

---

[10] George Stillman Hill to Sarah Hill, February 12, 1833, Hill Manuscripts, PANB, MC 1001, Ms. 6/8.

[11] The dam was present by 1841 when Gesner explored the region. It is not clear when it was constructed.

[12] The ever-insightful George Stillman Hill referred to Perley as "a regular government hanger-on and ready to serve any master who will give him bread."

[13] Petition of Moses Henry Perley (1835), Land Petitions, PANB, RS 108.

the region represented by the existence of several large parcels previously alienated to others (including, apparently, the Hills), Perley proposed the transfer of the intervening territories to himself, thus allowing him to subsume a contiguous eighty thousand acre piece of country dubbed "the Barony of St. Croix." The ultimate concern of Lieutenant Governor Campbell that so large an alienation of Crown land could only serve to fuel the growing popular discontent with the privilege of the executive and lead to charges of aiding and abetting the agents of monopoly disposed the responsible functionaries in the government to reject Perley's scheme.[14] Pleading breach of faith, as well as of law, and professing his personal discontent and imminent financial ruin if the nullification of the application was allowed to stand, Perley presumed the privilege of a personal interview with the Colonial Secretary,[15] but was saved from the humiliation of repudiation from this quarter by the generous grant of a more modest parcel in the vicinity of Saint John.[16]

Perley's bid to assume control of a vast block of New Brunswick wilderness may have failed, but it apparently had the unintended effect of convincing the Hill family of the expeditiousness of a more concerted and serious consideration of the means by which the upper St. Croix in the vicinity of North Lake could become a secure and accessible component of their enterprise. Cognizant of the utter futility of any attempt to open the country without sustained occupation thereon, the Hills conceived the notion of establishing settlers at the Narrows as a way around the otherwise insoluble problem of the transportation and purveyance of labour. Solicitations among the people of St. Stephen produced an adequate number of individuals who were more than willing to accept all the tribulations incumbent upon wilderness settlement in return for both tenant lots on the presently idle Hill estate and employment at the saw and grist mills the Hills

---

[14] Thomas Baillie to Moses Henry Perley, July 17, 1835, Records of the Surveyor General, PANB, RS 637, 2/d/35.

[15] Moses Henry Perley to Lieutenant Governor Campbell, July 16, 1835, Records of the Surveyor General, PANB, RS 637, 2/d/35.

[16] MacNutt, op. cit., p. 244.

aspired to erect. So enthusiastic for the plan did the brothers become that little could be done to restrain their imaginative faculties. Two of the youngest of the siblings, Daniel and Horatio, even envisioned the day, not long in coming, when the entire circumference of the upper lakes would be populated by a myriad of industrious settlers. Not so satisfied, apparently, with this flowery prognosis for success, a more sanguine George S. Hill applied himself to the cares of state and the administration of the St. Stephen Bank. Indeed, George Hill said nothing of the matter in his usually loquacious letters to his wife when Horatio, on one of his frequent trips to Fredericton, petitioned the provincial government for an interest-free loan for the purpose of forwarding the family's plans.[17] Less convinced of the utility of reclaiming the as of yet undeveloped provincial lands than of the political expediency of investing Crown revenues in those regions where the electorate abounded, the House of Assembly rejected the petition, choosing instead to grant the prayer of the people of the Rusagonis for assistance in the novel construction of a windmill.[18]

Though the Hills experienced the most daunting of barriers to the fulfillment of their hopes to found a great city in the woods, their positive assessment of the practicality of opening the upper St. Croix for business and settlement was soon confirmed by a man of reputed expertise in such matters. Employed since 1837 as Provincial Geologist, Dr. Abraham Gesner had, by the end of 1840, explored much of New Brunswick in an effort to thoroughly map its terrain and assess its prospects for future development. Gesner's edifying lectures to the public, free of charge to the members of the House of Assembly, attracted the attentive interest of none other than George S. Hill.[19] Blessed with a piercing intuition into the motives and character of others, Hill took an immediate liking to Gesner, whose knowledge and integrity he admired. When Gesner announced his intention to survey the St. Croix following the legislative session of 1841, Hill undoubtedly greeted

---

[17] Petition of Daniel and Horatio Hill, Records of the Legislative Assembly, PANB, RS 24, 1839/pe/file 2/no. 35.

[18] *Journals of the Legislative Assembly* (1839), PANB, p. 294.

[19] George S. Hill to Sarah Hill, February 4 and February 12, 1841, Hill Manuscripts, PANB, MC 1001, Ms. 6/10.

the news with pleasure, as it offered him not only the opportunity to entertain the good doctor, but also to ascertain the veracity of his brothers' own somewhat wild pronouncements on the possibilities for more thoroughly developing the district of North Lake.

Hiring three expert Indian guides for the purpose, Gesner, his son Henry, his friend and assistant Charles Ketchem, and all their provisions and equipment were ferried by canoe through the various cataracts of the lower river. Entering the transparent waters of Grand Lake after much confusion in navigating the Spednick and the periodic encroachment upon their various camps by wild animals, the exploratory party succumbed to the eerie beauty of the untamed country, where they found only the occasional traces of Indian trails to remind them of the existence of a greater body of humanity. Forested hills loomed majestically above them, while large granite boulders, the remnants of the era when glaciers moved freely across the face of the earth, encrusted the shore, much to the delight of Dr. Gesner, whose only occasion for sorrow during this happy interlude came with the discovery that a particularly rough passage further downstream had resulted in irreparable damage to several of his scientific instruments. At the so-called Deadwater, connecting Grand Lake with North Lake, the way was blocked by the nets of the aforementioned Americans. Despite the discovery of their depredations on British territory by an agent of the Crown, the Yankee fishermen offered Gesner and his party hospitality and directed them to nearby Baskegan Settlement where a new supply of provisions could be procured. The hum of activity at the rising town, soon to be re-named Danforth, did not go unnoticed by the perceptive doctor, who, when back on the waters of the St. Croix, could only re-experience, in his own particularly vivid and somewhat wistful way, the very vision of rural advancement that had so recently animated the aspirations of the Hills. After nearly getting lost on the portage to the St. John watershed, a situation from which he and his party were rescued only by the timely discovery of some ancient Algonquin hieroglyphics depicting the proper direction of travel, Gesner had little difficulty transferring his new vision to the more fertile banks of Eel River. A softness for scenic wonders and a peculiar romantic temperament allowed him to overlook several of the more awkward characteristics of the country, most notable of which were the lack of any means of easy communication with nearby outposts of civilization and the steep, uneven terrain that made the construction of even the most simple of paths an exercise worthy of the most gifted of engineers.[20]

Upon his return to Saint John, Gesner, by the incalculable workings of invisible Providence, suddenly found himself with the means to test his assessment of the settlement potential of the North Lake district. Desperate to ameliorate the effects of the depression wracking the entire province, Lieutenant Governor Colebrooke turned to Gesner to help implement his recently devised Association System of land settlement. Having already proven his public-spiritedness through involvement in the St. John Agricultural Society, Gesner was asked by Colebrooke to assume a position as a volunteer land agent, upon the acceptance of which he was instructed to seek out persons amenable to immediate wilderness settlement. Transforming his own private quarters into a smaller replica of the Crown Land Office, Gesner received a deluge of inquiries from distressed residents of the city, all anxious to try their luck at farming as a means of escaping the most extreme ravages of the present financial panic. By December of 1841 Gesner convened a public meeting, during the course of which two dozen reputably sober and industrious heads of households agreed to form an association and repay any monetary assistance they would henceforth receive from the government for the purpose of forwarding their objectives.[21] As most of the associates were emigrant Irish Protestants, native mainly of the Irish counties of Derry and Coleraine, and had lately been residents of the fire-scorched parish of Portland, the problem of fostering a spirit of community did not present itself. The prospect of settlement in the midst of the notorious New Brunswick winter, however, did pose something of a dilemma.

Moved as much by the previous example of winter settlement performed by a group of Irish settlers at Cork as by an utter lack

---

[20] Abraham Gesner, *Fourth Report on the Geological Survey of the Province of New Brunswick*, pp. 28-38.

[21] Abraham Gesner to John Hay, May 1, 1844, Executive Council Records, PANB, RS 7, Volume 22/file 2/p. 2610.

of any viable alternative available in Saint John, Gesner led the twenty men to their appointed destination. Avoiding the several surveyed tracts already prepared by the government to accommodate associate settlers, Gesner proceeded instead directly to North Lake, the very district where his aesthetic fancy had of late been so decisively entertained. As the upper St. Croix lay too far from the reassuring proximity of roads and humanity, Gesner opted to plant his people on the western bank of Eel River, the interval of which offered a better opportunity for rapid cultivation upon the arrival of spring. Despite Gesner's own glowing reports of the virtues of the country, the initial reaction of the settlers once they discovered the true nature of their new home was one of dismay and disaffection. Less impressed by the land's scenic qualities than by the threat of early frosts and the wolves who prowled with incessant ferocity about the outskirts of their camp, the settlers asserted their reservations, only to accede to the will of their benefactor after he presented them with provisions and made promises of additional aid in the near future.[22] Gesner's continued advocacy for the Eel River settlers secured the deliverance of the promised aid,[23] though the good doctor's growing preoccupation with the demands of increasing numbers of prospective settlers still residing in Saint John somewhat diluted the full force of his subsequent solicitations. Allocations for supplementary monetary disbursements for the fledgling community at Eel River completely stalled as the House of Assembly refused to surrender the power of the exchequer to more responsible hands, thus compelling the Lieutenant Governor to refuse to accede to the spending of any provincial funds for public improvements.[24] An emergency compromise allowed several thousand pounds to proceed to the most devastated regions of the province,[25] while two smaller benefices were confirmed for the purposes of employing the Eel River

---

[22] Abraham Gesner, *New Brunswick: With Notes for Emigrants*, p. 170.

[23] William Odell to Abraham Gesner, February 16, 1842, as found in the *Journals of the Legislative Assembly* (1842), PANB, p. 115.

[24] MacNutt, op. cit., p. 284.

[25] William Colebrooke to Lord Stanley, October 28, 1842; reproduced in *The Royal Gazette*, November 26, 1842.

settlers in the construction of a much needed road to the St. John[26] and supplying them with additional provisions.[27] Following an old and barely passable bridle path, Deputy Surveyor Henry Garden laid out the line of the proposed highway, after which he began work on a more ambitious series of surveys for proposed settlements dubbed Maxwell and Monument near the ultimate source of the St. Croix.[28]

The early success achieved by Gesner in nurturing the Eel River settlement eventually gave way to a more distressing situation once Gesner resumed his prosecution of the geological survey. Replacing Gesner as Eel River commissioner was Walter Hay,[29] a Woodstock gentleman who had been carrying on in the lumber business along the lower reaches of Eel River since 1837.[30] Upon making his way to the spot some fifteen miles above Meductic where Gesner, only a few short months before, had deposited his people, Hay was shocked by what he found there. Having been apprised (no doubt by Gesner) of the great triumphs of the noble settlers of the bush, Hay discovered a scene of pathetic destitution. In a vacuum of effective supervision, proper rationing of provisions had quickly succumbed to gluttonous consumption, following which a number of the associates simply abandoned the collective enterprise in search of employment elsewhere. Those who remained managed to convince the compliant Hay to accede to a revised and extremely loose set of terms for the repayment of the sums expended upon them by the government. Touched by the real instances of penury, but unable to identify the truly profligate, Hay listened to the settlers' professions of willingness to continue on in their present endeavour and then

---

[26] *Journals of the Legislative Assembly* (1842), PANB, p. 253.

[27] Id., pp. 290 and 293.

[28] Garden's Survey of Canterbury Parish, York County and Woodstock Parish, Carlton County, Carlton County Flat Book, RS 656/17e, Volume 28/no. 5, 1842; and John Saunders to William Colebrooke, January 23, 1842, Records of the Surveyor General, PANB, RS 637, 2/g/3.

[29] William Odell to Walter Hay, April 9, 1842, Letterbooks, Provincial Secretary Correspondence, PANB, RS 13, 3/1, pp. 237-238.

[30] Petition of Walter Hay, YO-1838, Timber and Saw Mills, 1817-1865, Timber and Saw Mill Records, PANB, RS 663a.

hastily handed over to them a new store of provisions.[31] When Colebrooke learned of the manipulations suffered upon his agent by the shifty settlers of Eel River, he expressed deep annoyance, demanding of Hay a fuller account of his activities, even accusing him of gross mismanagement and improper and tardy response to his several requests for further information.[32] Amidst Hay's protests that the remaining settlers were, in fact, presently engaged in fulfilling their obligations as well as awaiting the harvest of their "considerable crop,"[33] the Lieutenant Governor's own reprimand of the besieged Hay ended with an unfavourable comparison to Lemuel Allen Wilmot and the triumphs achieved by settlers at Cork under the latter's more strict supervision.[34] For his own part, after professing his own good intentions, Hay presumably returned to Eel River to press for the full repayment of the government grants and the completion of the road whose construction the settlers, overcoming their sloth, had already begun to undertake.

Upon his return from the conduct of his latest round of surveys, Abraham Gesner recommenced his operations as a land agent for the association settlements. The continuing stalemate between Colebrooke and the Assembly prevented the allocation of his salary in spite of his completion in January of 1843 of his latest geological report.[35] Desperation moved him to mill about the halls of government in an earnest attempt to interest the great men of the land in his plight. His lobbying proved to be a profitless exercise, earning him nothing more than the unwanted distinction of membership in the so-called Poor Knights of Windsor— an

---

[31] Walter Hay to William Odell, May 21, 1842, Executive Council Records, PANB, RS 7, Volume 22/File 2/pp. 2567-2573.

[32] William Odell to Walter Hay, July 15, 1842, Letterbooks, Provincial Secretary Correspondence, PANB, RS 13, 3/1.

[33] Walter Hay to William Odell, July 21, 1842, Executive Council Records, PANB, RS 7, Volume 22/File 2/pp. 2574-2576.

[34] William Odell to Walter Hay, July 29, 1842, Letterbooks, Provincial Secretary Correspondence, PANB, RS 13, 3/1.

[35] William Colebrooke to William Gladstone, Dispatch No. 7, February 12, 1846, C.O. 188, PANB, MC 416, F1522.

unsympathetic group of supplicants in search of official preferment and patronage.[36] The kindness of George S. Hill, whose own
family's interests had been furthered by Gesner's high estimation
of the value of the lands watered by the upper St. Croix, gave
some consolation to him, though it was not enough to salvage
Gesner from the ominous threat of personal financial ruin following the Assembly's unannounced termination of his official
position.[37] A victim of the political wrangles over the question of
Responsible Government, Gesner did not easily forgive the dis-
honourable conduct of New Brunswick's legislature, and upon
his return to his original home in Nova Scotia he dedicated his
efforts to the final remission of his long-overdue salary. His distinguished and, in large part, successful efforts as a land agent had
fostered six new settlements throughout the Province, though his
sterling reputation in this regard soon came into question when
two of the Eel River associates, Thomas and James Clark, accused
the doctor of pocketing money they had asked him to forward to
the Crown Land Office as payment for their chosen lots. Gesner
denied the charge, insisting that he had been advised by the Lieutenant Governor to keep the money in lieu of direct compensation
for the personal sums expended in the provisioning of the Eel
River association. A great investigation nevertheless commenced,
culminating in Gesner's indignant return to Fredericton in 1844,
where he continued his ongoing struggle with the Assembly over
his disputed salary and attempted to dismiss the slights his once-
reputable character had suffered through the improvident and
ungrateful utterances of the Clarks.[38]

Despite Gesner's own troubles and the sometimes disgraceful
behaviour of the Eel River settlers, Gesner's leadership had succeeded in planting the first settlement in the North Lake district.
Unable to stomach the first, difficult days of foundation, a number

---

[36] George Stillman Hill to Sarah Hill, March 25, 1842, Hill Manuscripts,
PANB, MC 1001, Ms. 6/10. Another letter dated approximately 1843 and
found in Ms. 6/8 also refers to Gesner's lobbying efforts.

[37] Abraham Gesner to George Stillman Hill, August 7, 1844, Hill Manuscripts, PANB, MC 1001, Ms. 6/5.

[38] Abraham Gesner to John Hall, May 1, 1844, Executive Council Records, PANB, RS 7, Volume 22/File 2/p. 2610.

of the original party had, as Hay discovered, fled in search of a more amenable situation, while others, eager to return home to jobs made viable again by the resumption of economic normalcy, sold their improvements to later comers directed to the region by Gesner and the officials employed at the Crown Land Office. Of those who abandoned the settlement, some eventually returned,[39] while those who never wavered in their commitment began sending word to friends and relatives in Ireland and Saint John to join them in their heroic enterprise of building a new home in the North Lake woods.[40] Within the first several years of the Eel River Settlement's existence, its residents managed to clear modest farms whereon they grew Indian corn and a variety of grains and garden vegetables.[41] Following in the wake of Gesner's party, Patrick Dinnin, a Catholic Irishman most likely from County Cork, managed to make his way to the banks of the Eel, where he took up upon one of the original lots in the Garden Survey and built a small saw and grist mill.[42] This auspicious construction only hastened the arrival of additional individuals and families eager to occupy many of the remaining parcels in the vicinity, including those surveyed at the remote extremity of the Monument Stream.

Somewhat less enthusiastic over the prospect of these new developments were the Hills, whose own designs upon the region had undoubtedly been aided by Gesner's evaluation, but who, in a state of paralyzing ambivalence, did little to act in a way that might harness the new influx of settlers to the yoke of Hill enterprise. The men of Eel River may have been too far from the centre of the Hills' still unripened North Lake operations, but only the slightest of encouragements were needed to bring additional

---

[39] Walter Hay to William Odell, July 21, 1842, Executive Council Records, PANB, RS 7, Volume 22/File 2/p. 2574.

[40] Abraham Gesner to William Colebrooke, February 16, 1842, as found in the *Journals of the Legislative Assembly* (1842), PANB, pp. 114-115.

[41] Abraham Gesner, *New Brunswick: With Notes for Emigrants*, p. 171.

[42] When Dinnen built his mill is uncertain, though its existence was attested to by Deputy Surveyor Alfred Whitehead in a Survey Return dated June 22, 1860. See John McIntyre et al., Y6-40, Grant Survey Return Plans, PANB, RS 687b.

settlers to the Hills' upper St. Croix domain. Already, by 1844, several men had mysteriously begun to clear farms near the so-called Deadwater, but their presence likely struck more fear than hope in the breasts of the Hills, as two of the newcomers, James A. Huson and William Russell, had no apparent connection with them, and certainly were not living as tenants on their estate.[43] Fear of trespass upon their unprotected lands soon began to inform the business decisions of the brothers, and when lumberman James Murchie approached them with a request to haul timber from their North Lake holdings, the Hills required him, in addition to abiding by set limits on the number of men and beasts to be used in his operation, to actively guard against the wiles of any clandestine wielders of the axe.[44]

As great as the fear of trespass may have been, the practice of this particular brand of criminality remained minimal. As the demands of the marketplace further downstream were met by the still lush stands lying on tributaries situated at latitudes of lower inclination, the extent of timber operations so far within the interior, both legal and illegal, was minor. At these more southerly locales, and still further downstream in the various towns strung out along the tidewaters of the St. Croix, a great boom now overcame and banished the lethargy so recently holding sway over the entire region.[45] The magnitude of this new prosperity removed even the most innocent necessity for competition, giving rise to cooperative ventures among the already mutually congenial timber magnates of St. Stephen.[46] The Hills, in particular, prospered under these conditions, and none more so than the fortune seeking Daniel and Horatio. Expanding their operations onto the American side of the river, the two brothers translated a $25,000 investment into a voracious set of sawmills known as *True Blue* and the more aptly named *Blood Thirsty* that together accounted

---

[43] Petition of Richard Cropley, Land Petitions, PANB, RS 272, 37/384 and Petition of Nathaniel Jones, Land Petitions, PANB, RS 272, 43/103.

[44] James Murchie's Permit granted by Abner and George S. Hill, December 19, 1843, Hill Manuscripts, PANB, MC 1001, Ms. 3/7.

[45] Harold A. Davis, *An International Community on the Saint Croix: 1604-1930* (Orono: University of Maine Press, 1950), p. 146.

[46] Id., p. 152-3.

for over three million board feet of lumber annually.[47]

In the throws of optimism, the Hills' waning concern over the immediate fate of North Lake produced little anxiety amoung their ranks. However, toward the end of the decade, when a new group of settlers appeared beneath the prominence known as Lake End Mountain at a place soon named Fosterville, distress of mind surely found more fertile ground in which to germinate. These new settlers were a generally homogeneous lot drawn from the Parish of Wickham in Queen's County, where a growing population occasioned constraints on opportunities available to many of its native-born sons and daughters. Led to North Lake by Josiah and David Foster, the settlers set about the slow process of land clearance, preparing the way for others waiting hopefully back home as the initial trials of homesteading were endured and overcome. For the sake of their early initiative, as well as for the fact that the settlement was soon graced with the presence of the families of three more of their siblings, Josiah and David Foster seem to have accepted the honour of eponymous founders. But the nascent little community named for them soon divided, as several of the newcomers found it more advantageous to establish themselves on the summit of the aforementioned mountain. In respect to the lushness of its vegetation, the rise, following the completion of a survey by Deputy Surveyor James Davidson in 1854, was appropriately rechristened Green Mountain. Not surprisingly, the scattered cabins perched atop it in blustery isolation were soon dubbed Green Mountain Settlement.[48]

Awakened to the new threat to the integrity of their business, the lumbermen of St. Stephen conceived of a new scheme to safeguard their interests. The threat did not stem solely from the new settlers in Fosterville. Even before the Wickhamites could turn away from the immediate demands of settlement and

---

[47] Id., p. 147.

[48] The story of the settlement of Fosterville can only be pieced together through meticulous examination of land petitions, parish registers and census data, a full account of which would occasion too great a diversion from the main narrative. In the future, however, the author hopes to present a complete prosopography of first settlers of the entire parish.

contemplate outrageous acts of piracy in the surrounding woods, groups of Americans had begun crossing the border and making off with timber from the large granted parcels held by the Hills and their various St. Stephen cronies.[49] To protect themselves, as well as bring some semblance of order to one of the district's more extensive tributaries, William Porter, the Hills and several other St. Stephen entrepreneurs proposed the formation of the Pirate Brook River Driving Company.[50] The company would collect tolls upon the use of the stream to convey timber into the Chiputneticook Lakes. The construction of dams and other appropriate measures could then be paid for out of the general fund into which the tolls would be deposited. Convinced of the efficacy of the measure, and perhaps spurred on by the advocacy of Executive Councillor George S. Hill, both houses of the legislature assented to the company's proposal to incorporate under the sanction of law.[51] A series of apparent misunderstandings between the members of the company's board and difficulties in summoning adequate capital prevented the fulfillment of the specifications of the act and occasioned the dissolution of the venture. Without the power to properly coordinate and control lumbering on the upper St. Croix, the major operators had no choice but to continue to struggle to meet the ever-growing menace of illegal and legal competition. Successful settlement had set in motion a chain reaction, as new settlers and new entrepreneurs, attracted by the emerging prospects for profits in the region, entered into the hunt for the remaining tracts of ungranted land.

Stimulated by the demands of the market, land prices in the vicinity rose,[52] and the Hills and their allies, fearful of losing the opportunity to expand their dominion, fell prostrate at the feet of their powerful kinsman, George, whose own elevated status as an Executive Councillor and the constant vigilance of the Smashers

---

[49] William Porter to George Stillman Hill, March 6, 1850, Hill Manuscripts, PANB, MC 1001, Ms. 3/10.

[50] Bill to Incorporate the Pirate Brook River Driving Company, Records of the Legislative Assembly, PANB, RS 24, 1850/bi/file 7/ no. 26.

[51] *Journals of the Legislative Council* (1850), PANB, p. 827.

[52] N.D. Shaw to George Stillman Hill, October 19, 1850, Hill Manuscripts, PANB, MC 1001, Ms. 3/9.

for any sign of internal corruption now made intervention on behalf of his relations a matter of the highest indelicacy. The continuing health of his siblings' enterprise closer to St. Stephen and his own growing obsession with the uncertain fate of the St. Andrew's and Quebec Railway mitigated any guilt the great man may have felt upon not being able to more directly facilitate their designs. But certainly George Stillman Hill, a man praised in some quarters as possessing the ponderous demure of a true philosopher,[53] was not unaware of the need for greater attentiveness to the problems facing his family in the northern most range of their industry. The greater improvement of the region along lines first conceived by his brothers required sustained investment of a degree still not forthcoming from even the most enterprising and wealthy of St. Croix magnates. Recognizing his own responsibility, not only to his family, but to the Province as a whole, Hill sent a clarion message to the possessors of idle capital in the American States, pointing out to them the still untapped resources of the upper reaches of the river and the prospects thereon of constructing vast manufactories and mills at the most trifling of expense, without heed to tariffs and duties, as most had lapsed with the onset of Reciprocity.[54]

Within two years of making his appeal for greater foreign investment, George S. Hill was dead. Deprived of their patriarch, as well as their voice in the secret chambers of government, his family pondered the alternatives laying before them. The steady pace of settlement of the North Lake district had inspired great confidence at the Crown Land Office for the progressive expansion of agriculture. In 1852, the Surveyor General authorized John Davidson to survey several tracts on either side of the Eel River Lakes, in addition to a line of road connecting Fosterville with the

---

[53] M. Hill to David Upton, December 22, 1846, Hill Manuscripts, PANB, MC 1001, Ms. 6/1.

[54] Draft of Letter of George Stillman Hill to the Editor of *The Boston Anglo-Saxon*, February 8, 1856, Hill Manuscripts, PANB, MC 1001, Ms. 3/27.

so-called Howard Settlement in the heart of Canterbury Parish.[55] Previous to Davidson's commission, all travel to and from the various settlements to the east had been accomplished either by following ill-marked and ofttimes perilous trails through the New Brunswick forest, or by embarking upon long circuitous journeys through American territory. The occasional resort to river navigation brought some North Lake settlers to the older settlements of the lower St. Croix, where the vital work of purchasing provisions and securing patronage could be properly conducted. As trespass continued and American lumbermen threatened to extend their own sway over the district, the magnates of St. Stephen sought new means of exerting more firm control over the upper portion of the St. Croix watershed. It soon became clear that only the thorough annexation of the region to Charlotte County could accomplish that design, and those occasional visits by North Lake settlers to the heart of old Charlotte County seem to have presented the very grounds on which such a move could be justified.[56]

The proposition to annex a very sizeable portion of the County of York could never have been acceptable to the political leaders of the York municipality, who naturally registered their protest with the legislature when William Porter, the Hills and their colleagues presented a bill to expedite the matter.[57] Ironically, it was the Reverend Thomas Hartin, a man who had once curried the favour of George S. Hill, who provided the most stubborn opposition. A native of County Derry, Ireland, Hartin had attended King's College in Fredericton, and after teaching for some time in the school houses of the lower Oromocto, received ordination as an Anglican minister. Assigned to the Parish of Canterbury, Hartin rose, through Hill's influence,[58] to the position of Justice of the

---

[55] John Davidson's Survey of Lots East and West of Eel River Lakes, Survey Plans, PANB, RS 656, IL, York County, Volume 12/No. 14, 1852.

[56] Petition of William Porter et al., Records of the Legislative Assembly, PANB, RS 24, 1860/pe/file 1/no. 19.

[57] Petition of the Municipality of the County of York, Records of the Legislative Assembly, PANB, RS 24, 1860/pe/file 5/no. 90.

[58] Thomas Hartin to George Stillman Hill, March 15, 1849, Hill Manuscripts, PANB, MC 1001, Ms. 3/10.

Peace and became, as a result, the natural object of his neighbours respect and admiration. Now, as his old benefactor's kinsmen sought to carve out a portion of his mission and disrupt the lives of numerous people living in settlements that the proposed boundary between the two counties would sunder in half, Hartin raised a fateful protest that gained the support of people through-out all of Canterbury.[59]

As happy an occasion the defeat of the annexation measure proved to be for the greater number of the inhabitants of Canter-bury Parish and York County, the laurels thus achieved through the agitation of the Reverend Hartin did little to solve the more immediate problems of North Lake's residents. Still cut off from the more expansive centres of civilization to the south and east, the people of North Lake cultivated a brand of self-reliance famil-iar to wilderness settlements. Their virtuous autonomy was only slightly modified by the success achieved by the lumbermen of St. Stephen following the defeat of the annexation bill in winning a second approval for the incorporation of the Pirate Brook River Driving Company.[60] Stream drivers in the employ of the new cor-poration now appeared in the locale and an orderly series of dams and sluices were rapidly constructed to permit the free flow of timber past the shallow places of the tributary. Labour presuma-bly was plentiful, despite the obstacle posed by Green Mountain to ready access by the district's settlers to the site of the company's operations. Other opportunities arose elsewhere in the district, as the St. Andrew's and Quebec Railway, thanks in part to the efforts of the late George S. Hill, acquired a monstrous reserve on the east side of Eel River. Many North Lake men flocked to cut timber here for the purpose of supplying the railroad, though others came simply for the opportunity to steal the occasional haul, which they then dragged with much effort to the waters of the St. Croix for transport to the Fundy shore.

---

[59] Petition of Thomas Hartin et al., Records of the Legislative Assem-bly, PANB, RS 24, 1860/pe/file 6/no. 94.

[60] Bill to Incorporate the Pirate Brook River Driving Company, Records of the Legislative Assembly, PANB, RS 24, 1860/bi/file 7/ no. 51; and *Journals of the Legislative Assembly* (1860), p. 228.

Concerned with the long-term integrity of the Company's reserve and the theft of resources vital to the development of the railway, the Surveyor General pointed out to his deputies the special need for added vigilance in guarding against trespass, and advised them to ignore the pretensions of the Railway's agent and to fine anyone cutting timber without a legitimate license.[61] Deputies Patrick Curran and Alfred Whitehead divided the official chore between themselves, though the severity of their exactions was rather dubious to say the least. While Curran found it difficult to carry out the full force of his instructions against men whose poverty compelled them into the ken of illegality,[62] Whitehead went so far as to join the people of North Lake in a plea for the government's consideration of their isolation and the allowance for the appointment of a resident magistrate.[63] Convinced of the honesty of the settlers' request, and recognizing the sizeable number of settlers now inhabiting the district, the Executive Council agreed to the selection of Nova Scotia emigrant Patrick Selvage to be North Lake's first Justice of the Peace. Even before the appointment of Selvage, the impact of the American Civil War had begun to be felt throughout the entire St. Croix watershed. Seizing the opportunity to meet the seemingly endless requirements of the belligerents, the proprietors of the various manufactories of St. Stephen intensified the pace of their operations. Meanwhile, a horde of American citizens, finding the peace in New England disturbed by a conflict of distasteful origin and loathsome expression, took shelter in border towns and wilderness hideaways, waiting for the day when the spirit of accord might allow their inconspicuous return home.[64] An accident of political geography made North Lake a convenient terminus for this new and expedient American emigration. Once here, some of the emigrees purchased improvements from older settlers for the purpose of

---

[61] John McMillan to Patrick Curran, January 15, 1863, Letterbooks, Records of the Surveyor General, PANB, RS 637, 1/a/30, p. 80-81.

[62] Report on Logs seized in the Spring of 1861, Patrick Curran, Deputy, Executive Council Cabinet Series, PANB, RS 9, 1861/3.

[63] Petition of Thomas Hartin et al., Executive Council Cabinet Series, PANB, RS 9, 1862/8.

[64] Davis, op. cit., p. 191.

temporary occupation,[65] while the vast majority squatted on seemingly ungranted lands a few miles north of the Narrows. Hardly offended by the arrival of uninvited guests so close to their own properties, the surviving Hill brothers contemplated the new vistas the unfortunate struggle of their American neighbours now presented. Demand for leather goods, in particular, had risen on account of the war, and recent innovations involving the bark of hemlock in the curing of hides made the establishment of tanneries close to the source of the vital resource economically prudent.[66] North Lake, with its ample supply of hemlock and accessibility by water to the major entrepots downstream, represented an ideal place for such an establishment. As the labour needed to construct the required facilities and to see to the tannery's various functions was already present, Daniel and Horatio Nelson Hill decided to finally fulfil their long-dormant dream for a great settlement in the woods.

Having purchased their elder brothers' North Lake properties, in addition to a vast contiguous tract on the American side of the watershed, the Hills led a party of men to the designated site of their establishment in July of 1863. Upon clearing trees on either side of the Narrows, the Hills employed Deputy Surveyor Curran to conduct a private survey of a town site on British soil, while a similar series of surveys were completed on the American side for the placement of the tannery itself. Almost immediately a sawmill was built not far from the old dam. Once completed, the mill was employed in the manufacture of the lumber needed for the construction of the sheds and various apartments to house the men and machinery required for the tannery's proper operation. At the cost of $25,000 the Hills created a company town, complete with a store, three boarding houses, a blacksmith shop, a school for the edification of the young and no less than two bridges to allow for easy transit from one side of the border to the other. Within a year of the time when construction had commenced, the Hill brothers' tannery was turning out its first finished hides. An energetic

---

[65] Samuel McIntyre Jr. to Bliss Botsford, September 27, 1865, Records of the Surveyor General, PANB, RS 637, 2/p/13.

[66] Davis, op. cit., p. 217.

population quickly appeared, and the subsequent shouts of joy and frolic emanating from the periodic balls held by one Jackson Calkin soon rose above the sylvan wilderness where only a short time before nothing was ever heard, save the occasional howl of the wolf and the quiet patter of moccasined feet.[67] So delighted was Horatio Hill with the products of family enterprise that he abandoned his comfortable home on the lower St. Croix and re-treated to his new town, which, in recognition of its distinctly arboreal setting, he soon named Forest City

The immediate expectations the Hills had for a return on their investment were not disappointed by the temperamental work-ings of the invisible hand of fate. The modesty of the tannery's production at the end of its first full year of operation was more than amply offset by the contribution of the Forest City sawmill to the Hills production of six million feet of sawn lumber.[68] And as the residents of the entire district were quickly enlisted in the hunt for hemlock, Horatio Hill sent samples of the fruits of his industry to Fredericton as evidence of his intention to make a more complete showing of his wares at the annual provincial ex-hibition.[69] The outbreak of fire temporarily stalled operations,[70] but in the end this setback did little to hamper the exuberance of a settlement praised by a wandering correspondent of *The Re-porter and Fredericton Advertizer* as owing its existence solely to the business energies of the pertinacious brothers.[71] On nearby Pem-berton Ridge, the fortunes of the expatriate Americans likewise flourished, as their thrifty habits helped inaugurate a dozen cleared fields, each subject to regular cultivation, in addition to a completed line of road stretching northward over Green Moun-tain into the heart of Fosterville. In the northern portion of the district, where hay was becoming a major agricultural staple, the formerly proposed line of road to Canterbury had finally been prosecuted, though the inexplicable destruction by fire of a costly

[67] *The Reporter and Fredericton Advertizer*, August 26, 1864.

[68] *The Saint Croix Courier*, December 23, 1865.

[69] *The Reporter and Fredericton Advertizer*, September 23, 1864.

[70] *The Saint Croix Courier*, July 28, 1866.

[71] *The Reporter and Fredericton Advertizer*, August 26, 1864.

new bridge spanning a small stream along the way briefly hindered more voluminous communication abroad.[72]

Long deprived of adequate facilities for the reception of the mails, the link now established between North Lake and the main settlements of Canterbury Parish justified the establishment of a local postal wayoffice.[73] But while the people of North Lake suddenly found themselves no longer dependent upon the services of the town clerk of the nearby American settlement at Orient for the processing of their correspondence, the obligations of the local Crown magistrate to so diffuse a population occasioned an increasing degree of local dissatisfaction.[74] When a son of the eponymous David Foster was appointed to join Patrick Selvage in the promotion of the local peace, the convenience of the people was markedly improved,[75] though a scarcity of polling places, even in the more settled parts of the parish, continued to offer them little opportunity to formally express their political inclinations. Proximity to the American border and the activity of lumbermen such as Ephraim Gates, who relished the present ease by which his Calais-based business gained access to the rich timber lands of New Brunswick, made local enthusiasm for the shocking novelty of the recently proposed British North American Union somewhat ambiguous. The antipathy of the Hills, who relied to a nearly fatal degree on American capital, and the gratuitous largesse of American operatives eager to sway the loyalties of the people, soon killed any local support for Confederation. When word of widespread disdain for Union in the vicinity of North Lake spread to the capital, the anti-Confederationists took heart. Soon enough, York County Assemblyman

---

[72] Ibid.

[73] "The Ninth Annual Report of the Post Office Department of New Brunswick Being for the Fiscal Year 1864," p. 22, *Journals of the Legislative Assembly* (1865), PANB, Appendix IV.

[74] The dependence of the locals on the services of the Orient Post Office is hinted at in a letter of Thomas Bubar to the Surveyor General, April 6, 1863. See Records of the Surveyor General, PANB, RS 637, 2/n/17.

[75] Petition of Elias Foster et al., Executive Council Cabinet Series, PANB, RS 9, 1865/6.

John Allen was stumping throughout the region in an effort to bolster the confidence of all those apprehensive of the fearful continentalist enchantment that had subverted the parochial sensibilities of the Honourable Mr. Tilley and his cohorts.[76] When the opponents of Confederation gained control of the House of Assembly in 1865, they quickly established a polling place in North Lake, thus ending the inconvenience that may presumably have prevented so many of the district's eligible and largely anti-Union voters from travelling to Canterbury to cast their ballots.[77]

Amidst the furor of local development, hastened in large part by the establishment of the tannery at Forest City, the quiet, unassuming progress of individual settlers proceeded on course. Among the ranks of these largely inconspicuous men and women was Hugh McMinn. Born on the Oromocto river in 1822, McMinn suffered at an early age bodily possession by a wayward and restless spirit. In keeping with the dictates of the commoving spectre within him, McMinn left the haunts of his childhood sometime after 1839 and set out on a series of aimless and secret wanderings that finally, in the middle years of the 1850s, brought him onto the very northern edge of the St. Croix watershed. A certain sense of design had in the intervening years given him a degree of control over the seemingly purposeless compulsions of his inner demon, and thus it was with some relief that he was able to make contact with a family undoubtedly known to him many years before during his more complacent days near the mouth of the Oromocto. This family was called Winship. Of New England origin, the Winships had settled at the Oromocto's mouth in Lincoln Parish around 1810, having been drawn there apparently by the twin booms in timber and ship building. For unknown reasons the two nuclear units of the clan headed by brothers Thomas and Benjamin[78] moved back to New England and settled in Amity, Maine.[79]

McMinn's marriage to one of Benjamin Winship's daughters

---

[76] *The Headquarters*, March 1, 1865.

[77] Bill to Establish New Polling Places in York County, Records of the Legislative Assembly, PANB, RS 24, 1866/bi/file 1/no. 7.

[78] The presence of the Winships on the Oromocto is attested by the marriage there of the brothers Benjamin and Thomas in 1819 and 1822.

[79] The brothers first appear in Amity, Maine, in 1830.

seems to have finally exorcized his roving inclinations and inspired within him a resolution to return to New Brunswick. But
rather than moving himself back to the place of his birth, where
good land and opportunities were increasingly scarce, McMinn
established himself on the south side of the Deadwater Brook on
a parcel owned by a St. Stephen lumberman by the name of William E. McAllister. McAllister's enthusiasm for proprietorship did
not long withstand the difficulties posed to his collection of rents,
thus it was not long before McMinn was deeded the property.[80]
The opening of the tannery gave added encouragement to any
lumbering McMinn previously engaged in, while the periodic
trips he seems to have made home to the Oromocto for the purpose of visiting family allowed him to spread tales of the
prospects open to the industrious man on the frontier. His
younger brother Andrew became particularly enthralled by his
stories. Consequently, Andrew left the banks of the Oromocto in
1864 to seek his own fortune on the shores of the Chiputneticook
Lakes.[81] Sadly, the lingering inhospitable character of the land, despite the evidence of human advancement occurring all around
him, dissuaded the younger McMinn from persevering in his
newly chosen vocation as pioneer. A reported disaffection on the
part of his present wife for his child from a previous marriage,
however, inclined him to leave his well-intentioned brother a
parting gift.[82] Unable to have children of their own, Hugh and his
wife gladly accepted charge of Andrew's daughter Almeda, and
in time could not help but think of her as the natural reward of
their own mutually endearing affection.

Hugh McMinn's brother's disinclination to abide permanently
in North Lake did little to deter Hugh's own strivings. The tannery's operations created new avenues for his private fortune,
and, as he accumulated the profits of his labour, he invested in
local real estate. The purchase of an improved lot on Green

---

[80] There is no records of McAllister's sale of the land to McMinn,
though McMinn's possession of it is indicative of just such a transaction.

[81] Petition of Andrew McMinn (1864), Land Petitions, PANB, RS 108.

[82] The legend of the friction within Andrew's family was related to the
author by Allen Boone.

Mountain was soon followed by the expansion of his homestead through the acquisition of the farm of one of his neighbours.[83] His new affluence likewise allowed a more competitive stance in the harvesting of hemlock. When the annual auction of timber reserves was held in Fredericton in the summer of 1866, McMinn was able to outfox the conniving Gates and win possession of a two and a half square mile chance at the head of North Lake that Gates had held throughout the previous year.[84] Gates' annoyance was all the greater due to the inability of his crew to clear the berth of all the timber they had cut during his tenure. When McMinn apparently attempted to bar Gates' access to the tract for the purpose of removing his logs, so embittered an antagonism arose between the two men that only the intervention of the Surveyor General could avert the escalation of hostilities.[85] With the integrity of the still uncut ground guaranteed by the promises of the Crown Land Office,[86] McMinn cagily ignored the invisible bounds marking Gates' remaining reserves, and when Deputy Surveyor Curran came to examine the progress of the various operations in the vicinity, the presence of timber laying at the mouth of Hay Brook clearly cut on Gates' property became subject to immediate seizure. McMinn's efforts to win release of the impounded timber soon became complicated by the competing claims of one Washington Weatherbe. Confused by the disputations of the two men, Curran appealed to the wisdom of the Surveyor General to solve the matter before retreating down the St. Croix to the familiar hearth of his Milltown home.[87]

---

[83] York County Registry Office Records, PANB, RS 98, 46/493 and 47/771.

[84] "The Seventh Annual Report of the Crown Land Department of the Province of New Brunswick for the Year Which Ended 31st October 1867," p. 11, *Journals of the Legislative Assembly* (1868), PANB, Appendix II.

[85] Robert Gowan to E.C. Gates, January 12, 1867, Letterbooks, Records of the Surveyor General, PANB, RS 637, 1/a/33/p. 34.

[86] Robert Gowan to Hugh McMinn, January 12, 1867, Letterbooks, Records of the Surveyor General, PANB, RS 637, 1/a/33/p. 36.

[87] Patrick Curran to Charles Connell, March 21, 1867, Records of the Surveyor General, PANB, RS 637, 7/d/4/a/5.

Provoked by a strange mingling of personal animus and the perception of ever larger profits to be gained on the emerging frontier of North Lake, Hugh McMinn's aggressive and sometimes unscrupulous practice of business would only grow in proportion to the success it helped secure. At the dawn of Confederation, McMinn was one (and a minor one at that) of a number of lumbermen competing with one another throughout North Lake for the preference of Crown and market. And, to be sure, it had been an unusual set of circumstances that had introduced the North Lake district to the peculiar economic habits of men such as these. Alternatively entertained by the extremes of optimism and nagging anxiety over the future of their business, yet convinced of the utility to themselves of sponsoring the introduction of more widespread human activity into a then uninhabited region, the Hill family of St. Stephen and their allies provided the first impetus for North Lake's development. Dr. Abraham Gesner, expressing without hesitation the potential the region had for advancement and empowered with the authority to see to the fulfillment of his own optimistic pronouncements, managed to do what the Hills, with all their access to capital, had yet failed to do by forming the district's first settlement. And though Gesner's community at Eel River proved vexatious not only to himself personally, but also to the entire provincial establishment, it formed the basis for all later settlement in North Lake. The Hills' own undying ambition to subdue North Lake and place it firmly within the constellation of their commercial dominion eventually allowed for the greatest encouragement of all to local aggrandizement, the tannery, and with it the means by which a man of limited resources and constrained opportunity could conceive of rising from the anonymous mass of the rural proletariat and assert himself as an individual of financial acumen able to attain a certain degree of prosperity. For his friends and relations back on the Oromocto, the success achieved by McMinn occasioned a pause for consideration of what the frontier district of North Lake might have to offer them. As many of them possessed either no land of their own or lived on marginal lots cleared during the period of expansion in the 1850s, and as the prospects for other employment on the Oromocto were progressively shrinking, the attractiveness of McMinn's new home and the reputed opportunities to be found there grew all the more attractive. But, still, their own peculiar fate within the Oromocto community had yet to unfold to its ultimate conclusion, the shared experience of a final generation inhabiting the Oromocto's various settlements had yet to fully bind them as one, and the compulsions pushing them toward the final, mutual decision to migrate were not yet fully matured. By the end of the decade of the 1860s, in the immediate wake of the real and imagined convulsions spawned by economic and political transformations, all these things would come to pass, and the transference of the old community to the new, and the survival of the old in an entirely new setting, would at last emerge as a distinct reality.

# Chapter Five

## ALIENATION & ADIEU

Long before the advent of the 1860s, the Oromocto had developed into a distinct community, unified by geography, defined by
a broad set of social values, its people engaged in a single local
political dynamic and employed by several major patrons. A kind
of tribal mentality had arisen as a result, reaffirming already profound attachments and loyalties and cementing the community
into a seemingly indissoluble whole. As early as the 1830s, however, the basis for the community's material existence had begun
to erode, heralding dire consequences for its various members.
While a moderate diversification of the economy and the discovery of new stands of timber during the 1840s and 1850s may have
ameliorated many of the untoward consequences of the inevitable
economic decline, these developments and the opportunities inherent within them had proved, by the 1860s, to be little more than
a temporary patina. Many members of the Oromocto community
did indeed prosper during the 1860s, but for marginal souls who
had depended upon the hopeful implications of the economic expansion of previous decades to extend their tenure on the river,
the ensuing stricture on wages, labour and resources became increasingly more difficult to bear. Reacting to the stimulus of
relative economic decay, the very structure of society began to
change. In earlier days the river patron had stood at the heart of
the community, but, as the economy deteriorated, his central role
deteriorated as well. And as his status diminished, outsiders, possessing larger stores of capital to invest in local industry, usurped
the patron's traditional position, thus depriving the river's people
of the kind of intimacy with the dispensers of patronage they had
been accustomed to since the community's foundation.

Though not related to the travails of the economy, the rise of
new institutions likewise altered the traditional structure of the
community. The elaboration of the new municipal form of government, first established in the late 1850s, may have provided the

people with more immediate control over their own affairs, but the emergence of party machines, both Liberal and Conservative, contributed to the denigration of a traditional network of allegiances characterized by a very complex series of intimacies defined by family, economic dependence and religious affiliation. An increasingly antagonistic relationship between the parties compounded the problems arising from shifts in communal loyalties by dividing the people of the river into two largely uncompromising camps, giving rise to two strongly articulated factions within a formerly united community.

As unsettling as the events of the 1860s would prove to be for many members of the Oromocto community, the community itself would survive. Yet toward the end of the decade the alternatives available to those people living on the community's fringe were generally unattractive. With continued residence within the watershed all but ruled out by the steady downturn of the local and regional economies, the only other reasonable choice facing them was outmigration. As the changes prompting resort to this rather radical solution to the problem of shrinking opportunities affected the entire community, it was a solution favourably entertained by settlers the entire length of the river. For those individuals who possessed a bond of kinship, common heritage and common livelihood, and who shared membership in the Free Will Baptist Church, the Loyal Orange Lodge and even, perhaps, the same political party, the choice to move proved less an expression of individual resolve than an incidence of collective action. So intimate was the communal link between people in the watershed that when outmigration ultimately occurred, it took the form of a mass transferal of the old community to a place where the economic foundation for sustained existence was much more promising.

The selection of North Lake as the site for this transference of a portion of the old community to a new setting highlights the communal factors informing the migration. The presence at North Lake of Hugh McMinn, a former resident of the Oromocto, provided the migrants with an intimate link with an otherwise totally unfamiliar locale and undoubtedly induced among them a sense of relative calm as they endured the trauma of uprooting themselves and their families and undertook together the task of building a new home far away from the place of their common nativity.

≈≈≈

At the dawn of the seventh decade of the Nineteenth Century, the venerable timber staple enjoyed the inestimable favour of distant consumption and demand. For the people of the Oromocto, the munificence of the marketplace extended the longevity of the prosperity commenced in the 1850s and held forth the promise of comfortable subsistence despite a gradual expansion of the local population. During the winter of 1859-60 nearly 150 square miles of Crown land situated on the Oromocto's tributaries were subject to the industry of individual operators.[1] When the subsequent sale of timber berths was held in the summer of 1860, the amount of land remaining under license changed only marginally.[2] Perpetuating his hegemony over the watershed into yet another decade, George Morrow retained one-fifth of all Crown timber lands. And though he waxed indifferent to the ways of business in direct proportion to his annual advance in age, the energy of his sons, particularly the eldest, George Daniel Morrow, more than made up for any decline in wealth and family prestige that may otherwise have occurred. For the Morrows, the Oromocto River, with the rapid destruction of its few remaining virgin stands and the steady eradication of the finest of its marketable timber over the span of previous decades, represented only a minor avenue for possible profit. While Assemblyman William Edward Perley and the owners of the anatomized remnants of the old Tracy and Hartt milling establishments eked out moderate livings, the Morrows reoriented themselves for exploitation of the pristine upper reaches of the St. John. The markedly decreased importance of the Oromocto, at least from the Morrows' perspective, held true even in regard to the ground in the vicinity of Victoria Settlement, where the mill operated by Morrow's partner, William Smith, underwent a crisis inexplicable in these times of plenty, and passed,

---

[1]  *The Royal Gazette*, July 4, 1860.

[2]  Id., July 3, 1861.

sadly, into the partial control of a local businessman by the name of John Currier.[3] Smith's own problems mirrored in smaller scale those of his neighbour Joseph Kingston, whose skill in management could match neither the reality of the local market nor the greater competitiveness of the industrialists of Saint John. By 1857 Kingston's seventeen looms could, if properly manned, produce a thousand yards of cloth per week, but high overhead prevented him from hiring the labour required to keep the looms in operation, thus he was unable to generate the capital gains that might have saved his enterprise.[4] Broken by debt and proved wrong in his vision for a profitable manufactory in the New Brunswick woods, Kingston sold the bulk of his machinery to his urban entrepreneurial counterparts. Bequeathing the remaining carding facilities to William Smith, Kingston settled down to a more unassuming and inconspicuous life within sight of the ambiguous scene of his greatest triumph and defeat.[5]

The continuing vitality of the timber economy did not completely mitigate the various difficulties still facing the Oromocto's inhabitants, particularly those whose scanty incomes had already necessitated their somewhat involuntary, yet unavoidable, transportation into the desolate purlieu of want. Decades of timbering and population growth pulled the fortunes of the vast majority of the watershed's people from two ill-omened directions, presenting everyone with the grim possibility that declining employment and increased competition would rip their community asunder. Thus, despite the ongoing health of the economy, those who had moved into the interior during the 1850s could not consider a return to their old homes closer to the banks of the main stream. This was particularly true for those who had moved into the country in the rear of Geary, in the vicinity of Victoria Settlement. Here, John Boone had led his family in 1855.[6] He was by this time an old man, so it is likely that he acted in a supervisory role while his sons made the necessary improvements. Boone's son-in-law,

---

[3] Sunbury County Registry Office Records, PANB, RS 95a, 20/510.

[4] Petition of Joseph Kingston, Records of Lt. Governor John Henry Thomas Manners-Sutton, PANB, RS 347, C/4.

[5] McGrand, op. cit., p. 128.

[6] Petition of John Boone (1855), Land Petitions, PANB, RS 108.

Yankee John Howe, had also come here around this time, likewise bringing his family and, as has been noted already, establishing himself on a lot atop Geary knoll.[7] With Howe came another kinsman, James Till Jr., who laid claim to and began clearing a parcel adjoining Howe's.[8] Further in the interior many of their friends and relations had made claims as well, though almost none of them actually carried out their stated intentions to settle. Timber harvesting, however dubious, remained the prime activity of most of these pseudo-settlers.

One of their number, Daniel James Wood, did manage to satisfactorily demonstrate the sincerity of his profession to homestead by breaking the soil for the purpose of permanent settlement and farming. That Daniel James Wood had come here at all is somewhat surprising, considering the fact that he had obtained a lease to land on the Rusagonis on the opposite side of the Oromocto. The wake drawing settlers from Geary, however, proved especially powerful, and when one of Wood's Lincoln Parish neighbours, Robert Touchburn, opted to try his hand at land settlement in the eastern portion of the watershed, Wood became inspired by the prospect of improving his social, if not economic, status through possession of a freehold.[9] Touchburn himself had been a veteran of the Victoria woods, having been directed there by the government as early as 1845 immediately after his emigration from Ireland.[10] The miseries of land settlement in this early period, when Victoria was completely uninhabited, proved too great even for this hearty immigrant; thus he moved to the mouth of the river in search of patronage, wage labour and a home. Given shelter by George Hayward and able to make his living through the adhibition of the loom,[11] Touchburn regrouped his energies and rejuvenated his pioneer spirit until he was able to

---

[7] Petition of John Howe (1853), Land Petitions, PANB, RS 108.

[8] Petition of James Till (1853), Land Petitions, PANB, RS 272, 47/215.

[9] Return of Survey for Daniel Wood et al., Grant Survey Return Plans, PANB, RS 687b, S3-57.

[10] Petition of Robert Thorburn [sic] (1845), Land Petitions, RS 108.

[11] 1851 Census of New Brunswick, Sunbury County.

return to the site of his former endeavours, bolstered this time by the comradeship and commitment of friend Wood.

Despite the enduring problem of diminishing resources and a growing population, the migration outward of poor settlers into the periphery of the watershed, so commonplace throughout the previous decade, presently underwent a degree of abbreviation. Regular employment in the woods, stemming from the relative vibrance of the economy, eliminated the nagging stimulus behind the agricultural impulse. Land clearance in the hinterland continued, but the manic energy that had once inspired the activities of pioneers from Geary, French Lake and a number of older settlements along the Oromocto now abated. Those few who continued to clear farmland in the interior did so only as a clever ruse to disguise their real intentions to steal, under the opaque veil of legitimacy, the increasingly difficult to find sticks of marketable timber. So long as timber remained, timber would be cut, and the improvement of the land itself would be neglected. In truth, only the Irish settlers conducted themselves with any real diligence toward the cultivation and steady improvements of their granted tracts— though their dependence on the poor man's crops of buckwheat and rye and the only marginal superiority of their harvests over those of their Loyalist-sprung neighbours hardly yet distinguished them as successful yeoman farmers.[12]

The dilapidation of fortune in this blighted locale did nothing to dissuade the ugly genie of discord from creeping unseen between competing expectations. Fifteen years of inefficiency in surveying and supervision by agents of the government only heightened the intensity of the ensuing local conflicts among individuals whose presence in so inferior a countryside supremely attests to the high level of their desperation. The turnover and confusion among the various deputies entrusted with land settlement here created opportunities for land to be granted to more than one party— an occurrence the vexatiousness of which could not have been any more acute when the blood heirs of an earlier claimant for a Victoria lot appeared on the doorstep of a settler by the name of William Wilson and presented that simple,

---

[12] Based on analyses of agricultural data in 1861 Census of New Brunswick, Sunbury County.

industrious soul with reputed proof of his illegal occupation.[13] The claims of these descendants of unheard of and undeserving transient inhabitants on land improved through Wilson's labour understandably confused and angered the man and gave a harsher edge to his all too justifiable castigation of a government that had sanctioned his settlement. Less legitimate than Wilson's case was that of Yankee John Howe, who, upon learning of the imminent transference of his original but long-abandoned Victoria lot to a recent arrival by the name of John Forbes, claimed priority and made the ridiculous assertion that the overgrown and barely perceptible improvements conducted almost two decades before should rightfully entitle him to some form of compensation.[14]

The modest standard of life on the main branches of the Oromocto differed little from that to be found closer to the river's mouth. While land settlement at such places as Back Creek now reached a climax, the progressive breeding of Durhams and Ayrshires had succeeded in creating a competing quadrupedal population far outnumbering that of man.[15] On the South Branch, Charles DeWitt still dabbled in the timber business, occasionally working berths purchased at the annual auctions in Fredericton. Further upstream, the Buckinghams pathetically tended their meagre fields. The patriarch Solomon, however, was no more. Having left home one morning in the fall of 1852 to procure hay, Buckingham did indeed find what he was looking for, but in the process of loading it onto a friend's wagon for transport back home he was struck down in so mysterious and immediate a

---

[13] William Wilson to Andrew Inches, September 6, 1860, Records of the Surveyor General, PANB, RS 637, 6/a/22.

[14] James Kerr to John McMillan, November 22, 1861, Records of the Surveyor General, PANB, RS 637, 7/j/3/a/5; and Petition of John Forbes (1864), Petition of Charles Forbes (1864) and Petition of John Howe (1864), Land Petitions, PANB, RS 272, 45/201.

[15] "Report of the Sunbury County Agricultural Society, Second Annual Report of the Board of Agriculture of the Province of New Brunswick," *Journals of the Legislative Council*, Appendix 2, p. 66. The 1861 Census reported 2,064 sheep as opposed to 1,464 humans living in Blissville.

fashion that his neighbours on the South Branch could find no more explicable a cause for his demise than the immanence of God's presence and judgement in the world.[16] Behind him, he left a large family, to be headed now, in fact as well as in title, by his domineering widow, whose own exalted status amidst the small confines of a horribly minuscule farm in an insignificant corner of one of Her Majesty's least reputable and least glamorous colonies represented an odd, even hilarious, parody of the high Victorian matron at the dawn of the Gilded Age.

Perhaps unable to sustain his morale under the obtuse reign of Penthesilia, the widow Buckingham's son Enoch escaped to the country estate of the Honourable Mr. Perley, where vast gardens and many variety of livestock demanded the constant attention of a small tribe of resident servants. In the forwarding of his timber interests, Perley made good use of his dominable bondsman, apparently putting him to work as a whiting instrument in the rather dubious acquisition of a settlement lot along Three Tree Creek in the Parish of Lincoln.[17] Failure in this endeavour reinforced any opinion Perley may have had of Buckingham's ineffectualness and perhaps contributed to the termination of the young man's employment. Released from Perley's service and possessing, most likely, a cache of accumulated wages, Enoch entered hopefully onto the plane of potentially requitable affection. His eventual marriage to the daughter of the late William Tucker reaffirmed his own familial affiliations, though it held out to him little possibility of inheriting a legacy of any substance.[18] His brother-in-law, William Tucker Jr., had primacy in this regard, but even the latter's fortunes were by no means assured. Uncertainty regarding his

---

[16] Inquest into the Death of Solomon Buckingham, General Sessions, Sunbury County Records, PANB, RS 157, A/2 53a (1853).

[17] Petition of Enoch Buckingham (1861), Land Petitions, PANB, RS 108. A hint of the role Perley played in Buckinghams application is evident in Perley's simultaneous petition for a lot on the same tributary.

[18] Proof of Mrs. Lydia Buckingham's consanguinity has not been found, yet the fact that she shared the same name as Tucker's mother (Lydia Mills) and the fact that Tucker's mother was living with Enoch and Lydia Buckingham in 1871 seems to indicate the strong probability that Mrs. Buckingham was in fact a sister of William Tucker.

ultimate fate led the younger Tucker to seek financial security, first as a farmer on a charred lot in the vicinity of the Rusagonis,[19] and later as a bit labourer on the estates of the elite inhabiting the southern bank of the St. John between the Oromocto and the provincial capital.[20]

Somewhat more prosperously than either Enoch Buckingham or William Tucker Jr., John Anderson tended his several disconnected parcels. Success as a labourer in the woods had allowed him to slowly increase the size of his flock of sheep, thus bringing him into the higher echelons of local animal husbandmen. Unfortunately, this noteworthy feat was accomplished without yielding any clues for the eventual solution of problems endemic to so concupiscent a nature.[21] His many children competed for attention, not only of the routine and necessary paternal kind, but of the sort that would facilitate their eventual liberation from the lamentable burden of a more fully matured sense of hopelessness. Son Charles faithfully joined with his father in the improvement of the family homestead, but son Joseph, already sensing the foreordained limitations of the land, wandered the countryside in search of arable ground until alighting upon that forsaken quarter known as Peltoma.[22]

As stagnant as had become many of the best efforts of the reputed harbingers of some imagined agricultural renaissance, either in Victoria or the older settled portions of the Oromocto's extremities, the South Branch momentarily became the scene of perhaps one of the greatest coordinated efforts to replace the unendurable silence of the uninhabited forests of the watershed with the astatic sounds of permanent human habitation. Calling upon his enormous stores of raw endurance, Deputy Surveyor James

---

[19] Petition of William Tucker (1860), Land Petitions, PANB, RS 108; and Survey Return for William Tucker, Grant Survey Return Plans, PANB, RS 687b, Y6-84.

[20] Journal of George H. Perley, 1864, PAC (Public Archives of Canada), MG 24, C47.

[21] 1861 Census of New Brunswick, Sunbury County.

[22] Petition of Joseph Anderson (1862), Land Petitions, PANB, RS 108.

Kerr outlasted the irascible John Colling,[23] only to find that the responsibilities which he subsequently inherited from his older rival had nevertheless become a shriveled mandate, unpromising as a field for the perdurable exercise of his duty. By 1858 most of the best land along the Oromocto and its tributaries had been alienated to individual settlers, leaving little in the way of arable soil for the location of prospective migrants. A cursory survey by Kerr confirmed the congestion of new tributary settlements such as Clones, Enniskillan and Nerepis Road, not to mention Back Creek and Victoria, and persuaded him of the necessity of again pressing the Crown Land Office to consider enlarging his jurisdiction at the expense of one of his colleagues. An interview with a number of out-of-work mechanics in the city of Saint John served as a pretext for his latest machinations, allowing him to quite legitimately plead for a special sanction to invade Charlotte County in order to help establish his eager petitioners west of the Douglas Valley, not far from the eastern shores of South Branch Lake, where nearly two decades of lumbering had removed many of the barriers to penetration of the once intractable forest.[24] His officious solicitations corresponded with the sympathies of the Surveyor General, who, unimpressed by the perceived lethargy of Kerr's Charlotte County counterpart, granted Kerr license to oversee the formation of what soon came to be known as Creevy Settlement. Requisitioning the use of a farmhouse owned by one Robert Ogden, and surreptitiously enlisting the latter man's assistance in the field, Kerr's natural energies drew headier inspiration from the nervous anticipation of a host of land-hungry onlookers who had made their way (on Kerr's request) to Ogden's domicile to more conveniently await the completion of Kerr's complex calculations.[25] By June of 1859 the ranks of the initial applicants in the new survey had become so swollen and the progress of settlers so impressive that the presentiment of an enormous windfall

---

[23] Robert Gowan to James Kerr, April 27, 1859, Records of the Surveyor General, PANB, RS 637, 2/k/1.

[24] James Kerr to James Brown, August 21, 1858, Records of the Surveyor General, PANB, RS 637, 7/k/3/a/4.

[25] James Kerr to Andrew Inches, September 27, 1858, Records of the Surveyor General, PANB, RS 637, 7/j/3/a/9.

benefiting the Province once the improved lots were sold leapt optimistically into the mind of the exultant deputy and seemingly presaged the advent of a brave and glorious future.[26]

The frightening rapidity of the pace at which new settlers exhausted the limits of the Creevy Settlement soon made it incumbent upon Kerr to cast off the tainted robe of the self-interested beneficiary of patronage and embrace a more authentic concern for the greater fate of the family of man. Unable to squeeze additional 100-acre lots from the surveyed territory and fully convinced of the consumptive quality of the ungranted soil in the immediate vicinity, Kerr hurled covetous glances across to the western shore of South Branch Lake, beyond the old Abbot ground, and onto the vastness of a country that had been ignored even by the ancestors of the near extinct remnants of the region's aboriginal peoples.[27] Early attempts to explore the area were foiled by seasonal inclemency, as snow banks and lack of even the barest of paths barred his movements. Terminating his initial efforts to survey the west side of the lake, Kerr returned to Creevy, only to be enveloped by the obstreperous demands of what by now had become a Malthusian nightmare of unemployed, land-hungry petitioners. The threat of an uninhibited stampede for land and a total contravention of the laws governing settlement impelled the flustered deputy to more earnestly apply his inherent and acquired skills of persuasion. His deftness in speech and desperation in argument won him a miraculous victory over the stubborn procedures and insidious pecking order at Fredericton, and delivered up to him a voucher for supplies and a writ for the comprehensive survey of some 32,000 acres west of South Branch Lake.[28]

---

[26] James Kerr to Andrew Inches, June 20, 1859, Records of the Surveyor General, PANB, RS 637, 7/j/3/a/9.

[27] James Kerr to James Brown, February 21, 1860, Records of the Surveyor General, PANB, RS 637, 7/j/3/a/4.

[28] James Brown to James Kerr, July 30, 1860, Letterbooks, Records of the Surveyor General, PANB, RS 637, 1/a/28, pp. 272-273; and Petition of James Kerr to Executive Council, Records of the Surveyor General, PANB, RS 637, 7/j/3/a/1.

It was a moment of unadulterated triumph for Kerr, but one which, due to the pressures of a hundred expectant souls and the rigours of the task ahead, could hardly have been appreciated with the kind of relish it so lustrously deserved. As Kerr led his expedition, painstakingly routed out the hidden lines of earlier surveys and, with a plenitude of frustration and tedium, sought to harmonize the older plans with the new, Robert Ogden clumsily acted in Kerr's stead at Creevy.[29] Overwhelmed by a task too complex for a man of limited training, Ogden almost at once became embroiled in countless disputes of competing claimants, which he, in ignorance of his master's late activities in the granting of parcels, had unintentionally instigated. Upon his return, Kerr found a cauldron of enmity so calescent that it scalded the sensibilities even of the functionaries in the distant Crown Land Office. With the haughty exaltedness of colonial bureaucrats throughout Britain's perpetually luminated empire, the minions of the Surveyor General blamed Kerr for his lack of judgement and dismissed the laughable efforts of his agent as anything but beneficial to the internal accord of the new settlements.[30] Disillusioned with Kerr's blunders and wholly willing to ignore his real successes, the Surveyor General brandished a fierce indifference in regard to Kerr's repeated claims for additional remuneration for out-of-pocket expenses stemming directly from the prosecution of his late survey. The intervention of the Provincial Secretary, Samuel Leonard Tilley, and the support of Assemblyman John Ferris of Queen's County helped wring a few pounds from the stingy and unforgiving ministry,[31] but it would be another six years before Kerr, with the assistance of a band of legislators that included William E. Perley, would receive a satisfactory response to his incessant claims for provincial

---

[29] James Kerr to John McMillan, January 8, 1862, Records of the Surveyor General, PANB, RS 637, 7/j/3/a/5.

[30] Robert Gowan to James Kerr, January 14, 1862, Letterbooks, Records of the Surveyor General, PANB, RS 637, 1/a/28, p. 420.

[31] James Kerr to Samuel Leonard Tilley, October 24, 1861, Records of the Surveyor General, PANB, RS 637, 7/j/3/a/10.

compensation.[32]

Despite the great controversy generated by the formation of Creevy and the several other settlements encircling the shores of South Branch Lake, Kerr's initiative and steadfastness ensured the conquest by potentially sedentary men and women of the last arable portions of the Oromocto watershed. As soon as the remaining lots in Creevy, Clarendon and the Ferriebanks were taken up, as soon as the land within their bounds was exploited for dwindling sticks of timber and the soil itself made subject to the temperamental whims of a variety of domesticated herbs, the era of progressive land settlement on the Oromocto would be over. For all their momentous implications, the bustle of events on the upper South Branch resonated only vaguely further upstream, where the more well-established portion of the river's population toiled in seeming ignorance of the happenings that boded so deleteriously for the fortunes of their fast-maturing children. In Blissville, Burton and Lincoln parishes, on either bank of the Oromocto and along the river's various tributaries, the struggles of the mechanics of Saint John were almost wholly irrelevant. The advance of farming in so distant a place was only significant as it led to a more complete (and thus ominous) deforestation of a once profitable site of winter employment. Even those old settlers of the river fully suited by disposition to the regularity of the agricultural calendar did not find the ultimate reaches of South Branch Lake particularly appealing, for not only was the region so far removed from the familiar kith and kin of childhood memory and adult experience, but it was also fully outside the bounds of the very municipality to which adhered their entire frame of reference. Little in the way of assistance from the self-appointed agents of agricultural progress, the Sunbury County Agricultural Society, could be expected for such ventures either, as the elite members of that corporation self-indulgently tended their majestic farms in Maugerville and Sheffield and contented themselves less with the aspirations of those individuals desperately seeking release from the turmoil of the timber trade than

---

[32] Petition of James Kerr to the Executive Council, Records of the Surveyor General, PANB, RS 637, 7/j/3/a/1.

with the annual contests for precedence atop the lowly hierarchy of county sod-busters. Puffed up by the real progress made in the breeding of sheep and growing of turnips, Henry Putnam Bridges, the Maugerville-born president of the Society, publicly touted the superiority of Sunbury expertise, only to draw the acrimonious rancour of truly superior agriculturists from throughout the more advanced and productive parts of the Province.[33] Held captive by his own pettiness and pride, Bridges fought the battles in defence of the Society's honour which his own distemper had instigated, while the real needs of the people languished.

Not everyone in the county was so devoid of interest in the expansion of local cultivation. Writing with a weariness contracted after nearly a decade of thankless labours in Victoria Settlement and its immediate vicinity, Deputy Surveyor Stephen Burpee still placed his hopes in the fading possibility of weaning the people away from the so-called chimera of timber and inculcating in them the inestimable virtues of farming. A thorough and accurate survey would be necessary, as well as a parish-by-parish plan of available lots, while a real investment by the presently indolent Agricultural Society in the form of premiums to individuals pioneers would, according to Burpee, prove a real and tangible incentive to the long-neglected practice of the plough.[34] His disillusionment with the corrupt procedures and quarrelsome habits of self-styled settlers and his own boredom with a job that he now attempted to pass off to a number of potential successors (including George Morrow's son David)[35] stifled the effectiveness of his suggestions, as did the continuing disinterest of the leaders of the Agricultural Society in anything smacking beneficial to the denizens of the southern bank of the St. John. Barred by his Maugerville congregation from venturing into the vestibule of the

---

[33] *The Reporter and Fredericton Advertizer*, April 18, 1862.

[34] Stephen Burpee Jr. to Robert Gowan, May 17, 1861, Records of the Surveyor General, PANB, RS 637, 7/n/5/a.

[35] Stephen Burpee Jr. to Timothy O'Connor, September 20, 1861; and Stephen Burpee Jr. to James Brown, June, 19, 1860, Records of the Surveyor General, PANB, RS 637, 7/n/5/a.

new St. Paul's Church in Burton,[36] even the Reverend Wiggins readily acquiesced in the effrontery to all things wrecking of the Oromocto. Directing his surplus energies as a committed agriculturist away from the needs of his forsaken flock in the southern sections of his mission, Wiggins eagerly partook in the administration and affairs of the Provincial Board of Agriculture as that body's recording secretary.[37]

The mutual disdain characteristic for seventy years of the relations between Sunbury's upper districts and the Oromocto and so clearly manifest in the jealous contempt the elite farmers of Maugerville and Sheffield expressed toward their more ineffectual common-stock counterparts in Burton, Lincoln and Blissville did not, at the dawn of this new decade, fail to contaminate additional aspects of county life. Further evidence of enduring sectional divisiveness appeared following the announcement of the impending arrival in New Brunswick of the Prince of Wales. Responding to the implicit appeal to loyalty such royal visitations normally aroused, Charles J. Burpee, a nephew and namesake of Sunbury County's Liberal Party patriarch, resolved to form a volunteer rifle company the ostensible purpose of which was to enhance the splendour of the ceremonies welcoming the Prince upon his arrival at St. John. With the assistance of a young Burton Parish gentleman named Reuben Hoben, Burpee canvassed both sides of the St. John River in an effort to drum up interest. So fertile were the banks of the river in this regard that it was not long before a company of one hundred men was raised.[38]

The bi-sectional cooperation in gathering a county force to pay tribute to the Queen's son, however, soon collapsed, as a Sheffield man by the name of Moses H. Coburn began lobbying for command of the new volunteer force. When Coburn managed with

---

[36] John S. Covert to Bessie Mowat, September 15, 1859, Grace Hellen Mowat Collection, Charlotte County Historical Society (CCHS), Ms. 6/no. 237.

[37] "First Annual Report of the Board of Agriculture of the Province of New Brunswick," *Journals of the Legislative Council* (1861), Appendix 4.

[38] Charles Burpee to Samuel Leonard Tilley, December 21, 1859, Tilley Papers, PAC, MG 27, I/D/15.

unknown powers of enchantment to win the blessing of the leading officers of the county militia, Burpee and Hoben erupted in a
fury that awakened the slumbering dragon of sectional jealousy
and split the heretofore undivided company along geographic
lines. Burpee and Hoben were in part to blame for this, as each
came to realize that the preferment of Coburn nullified their own
aspirations for pre-eminence. Coburn, for his part, only complicated matters further when he refused to acquiesce in a division
of ranks by parish of origin, clinging instead to the hope for leadership of a unified force of men. A vote of no confidence among
the volunteers of Sheffield (undoubtedly acting under Burpee's
tutelage) and a quickening spirit of rebelliousness among new de-
tachments forming in other parts of the county soon forced the
would-be commander to recognize the insurmountable obstacles
his candidacy posed to martial solidarity. Yet his relinquishment
of command came too late, as the divided regiments had already
established independent hierarchies and autonomous existences
based on the comforting and convenient peculiarities of physical
geography and communal insularity.[39] Division, thus, was irre-
versible, providing further encouragement to the complete
institutionalization of an already unhealthy degree of sectionalism — though, in a more positive light, it spared the county as a
whole the rueful embarrassment and scorn of perceived disloyalty that might otherwise have occurred if even this unsatisfactory
solution had not been forthcoming.[40]

The idea of perseverance in a now largely superfluous royal
cause, though subject to the modifications of traditional county
rivalries, was nowhere more strong than on the Oromocto, where
the many lineages sprung from Loyalist forebears flourished in

---

[39] Charles J. Burpee, once an avid supporter of a united company, later
justified division on the grounds that most of the Sheffield volunteers
lived in the lake district, several miles from the St. John and thus hardly
in a place allowing of easy or convenient transit to Oromocto, where the
company headquarters was located.

[40] Charles Burpee to Samuel Leonard Tilley, December 21, 1859;
Charles Burpee to Samuel Leonard Tilley, January 16, 1860; Coburn
Burpee to Samuel Leonard Tilley, April 9, 1860; Charles Burpee to Sam-
uel Leonard Tilley, April 14, 1860; and William E. Perley to Samuel
Leonard Tilley, April 23, 1860, Tilley Papers, PAC, MG 27, I/D/15.

mutually reinforcing proximity. At French Lake and Geary, the King William Lodge was still expanding its ranks, and though its founding master had retreated to the back benches of membership, its internal accord had only improved following the embarkation of the Reverend Garrity on an ill-fated evangelical tour of the lower St. Croix.[41] Further upstream from French Lake, on the North West and South branches of the river, the tenets of Orangism were being expounded by agents who capitalized on the latent affinities of the dissenting populace for sacred mysteries and declarations of hereditary loyalty. Prominent in this work was George Kingston. While his brother sank into anonymity in Geary, George steadily rose in the estimation of the large numbers of expatriate Irish and native-born Protestants who, since 1855, had periodically gathered at his home to tend to the affairs of their own newly established lodge. His efforts in the hinterland were assisted by Free Will Baptist Deacon Richardson Boone, who established a third lodge at Hartt's Mills in 1859.[42] When the latest clamour for incorporation of the Provincial Lodge arose in 1860, so widespread had Orange sympathies on the river become that nearly two hundred and fifty well-wishers from Geary, French Lake, and the North West and South branches lobbied with the government for consideration of that long withheld privilege.[43] Responsive to his people as always and still cherishing the trappings of professed loyalty since his recent promotion in the

---

[41] Joshua N. Barnes, *Lights and Shadows of Eighty Years: An Autobiography* (Saint John: Barnes and Company, 1911), pp. 66-68. Garrity succeeded in establishing a small congregation of Disciples on Grand Manon, only to run headlong into the stout resistance of his former Free Will colleagues and the infectious appeal of the Mormons.

[42] Edward Steele, *The History and Directory of the Provincial Grand Orange Lodge of New Brunswick* (Saint John: by author, 1934), p. 112.

[43] Petition of Jeremiah Smith et al., Records of the Legislative Assembly, PANB, RS 24, 1860/pe/file 2/no. 36, Petition of James Kirkpatrick et al., Records of the Legislative Assembly, PANB, RS 24, 1860/pe/file 3/no. 49, and Petition of Aaron Hartt et al., Records of the Legislative Assembly, PANB, RS 24, 1860/pe/file 4/ no. 68.

county militia,[44] William Edward Perley listened with receptive ear to the eloquent ramblings of his colleague, David Tapley, as the latter tried to convince his fellow legislators of the utility and innocuousness of a yea vote.[45] For all of Tapley's locquacious efforts, and for all of Perley's own less exaggerated sympathy, the motion made for a more thorough consideration of the bill before the House was treated to a swift, though hardly conclusive, defeat.

Regardless of their collaboration in the furtherance of the Orange cause and their joint position as leaders in the county branch of the Liberal Party, the partnership of William E. Perley and David Tapley was less attributable to happy design and ideological affinity than to unalloyed convenience. Necessity had paired the two on a strange platform encompassing the complaints and demands of constituencies on either side of the St. John River — an almost unnatural alliance that, like the old Reform coalition of the 1840s, had the makings of inevitable dissension, faction and dissolution. In spite of the sparrings of their supporters over such matters as the militia, regardless of the natural arrogance of either man that compelled each one to presume priority over the other, William E. Perley and David Tapley remained, throughout much of their shared term in office, inextricably lashed to a single Liberal yoke by their common sense of deference to Samuel Leonard Tilley. Perley in particular had managed to cultivate a servile empathy for the Provincial Secretary that soon elevated him to a position of influence disproportionate to his actual prominence and productiveness in the legislature. Private contacts and intimate persuasions rather than grandiloquent speeches on the floor of the House of Assembly were Perley's preferred means of winning recognition for his people. And Tilley appreciated such subtle supplications, apparently going so far as to intervene with the Board of Works on Perley's behalf in order to acquire great road status for the Douglas Valley Road.[46] Far from being a soft

---

[44] Perley received a commission as a Captain in the Sunbury Militia on June 9, 1860.

[45] *The Headquarters*, April 4, 1860.

[46] William E. Perley to Samuel Leonard Tilley, August 23, 1859, Tilley Papers, PAC, MG 27, I/D/15; and "Sixth Annual Report of the Chief

touch, Tilley had more practical motivations in bestowing upon Perley his favour. Perley's peculiarly gossipy nature and zealous capacity for gathering intelligence on the grassroots level throughout the lower St. John basin made the Blissville worthy an extremely useful tool — as did Perley's blindly committed support of Smasher supremacy.[47]

For all their mutual, yet delitescent, animosity, Perley and Tapley adequately fulfilled the aspirations of the electors by extending patronage to the party faithful and assuring, or attempting to assure, a steady flow of public employment on the county's increasingly elaborate web of highways.[48] The brazenness of their petty tyranny over the political spoils was not completely satisfactory to everyone, least of all to legendary lumberman John Glasier, who now began to direct his indomitable gaze to the yet unvanquished sward of politics. The humiliation of his friend Charles Fisher served as a pretext for his own announced pretensions of popularity, while a nearly inexhaustible treasury made it unlikely that any could outdo him in the acquisition of support from among the less committed partisans of either political faction. Almost obscene in physical appearance, his hook nose and hook chin, his ill-fitting black wig ineffectually disguising the embarrassing defoliation of his scalp and crowned

---

Commissioner of Public Works," *Journals of the Legislative Council* (1861), Appendix 2, p. 24.

[47] William E. Perley's letter to Samuel Leonard Tilley, April 7, 1860, Tilley Papers, PAC, MG 27, I/D/15, provides a window on Perley's relationship with the Provincial Secretary. In this letter, Perley reported what actions would likely prove favourable on the grass roots level and what actions would likely antagonise the populace.

[48] William E. Perley and David Tapley to the Executive Council, March 28, 1860, Executive Council Cabinet Series, PANB, RS 9, 1860/9; William E. Perley to Samuel Leonard Tilley, June 18, 1860, Executive Council Cabinet Series, PANB, RS 9, 1860/3; and David Tapley to Samuel Leonard Tilley, December 3, 1860, Executive Council Cabinet Series, PANB, RS 9, 1861/1. The most ambitious of all the schemes hatched by the assemblymen was a bill to elevate all byroads in the county to the status of great roads. The bill was rejected by the legislature. See Records of the Legislative Assembly, PANB, RS 24, 1861/bi/file 2/no. 25.

perpetually by an ancient beaver pelt cap, caused perhaps as much hilarity as authentic disgust in his peers, but even this mingling of jocular and revulsive provocations could not dismiss the authority and respect his wages and wealth naturally accrued him.[49] A certain inherited eccentricity and eclecticism in his spiritual predilections somewhat dampened the enthusiasm of the dissenters, from whose ranks his family had sprung, but conversely allowed him to circumvent the offended sentiments of the most fanatical of sectarians. A liberal bias diluted his ideological protest against Liberal hegemony, but as the Liberals had betrayed the great Fisher and as the local party machine rigidly backed the incumbencies of Perley and Tapley, the determined Glasier committed himself to a candidacy that placed him, by default, in the camp of the Tories. Thus, as the legislative elections scheduled for the spring of 1861 approached, Glasier formally offered himself at the polls, joining Enoch Lunt at the steps of the Burton Court House on a Conservative platform, the most strident and emphatic plank of which was a belief in the infinite purchasing power of the colonial currency.

The overtly corrupt and well-nigh criminal approach to the ballot box anticipated by Sunbury's reputably conservative candidates for the legislature was in fact perhaps the only logical one in a time when general satisfaction with the reigning Liberals was unbesmirched by the kinds of economic misfortunes that had fueled the successful campaigns of past challengers. As an election strategy it had a certain potency that became especially formidable when George Morrow, an old compadre of both Lunt and Glasier, pledged his support to the Conservative ticket. Of less immediate importance was the avowal of fealty by County Councillor John Sterling Covert. A successful commercial farmer residing in Maugerville who was consumed by an urgent sense of self-righteous populism so typical of the not completely reconstructed elite, Covert had made a love match that was not without favourable political implications. Indeed, his wife's consanguineous ties with R.D. Wilmot gave him entry into the latter's Belmont estate, and quickly allowed him a degree intimacy with the great

---

[49] D.M. Young, "John Glasier," *Dictionary of Canadian Biography*, Volume XII, pp. 376-377.

man that soon transcended their mutual obsession with politics.[50] Despite his own Tory affiliations, familial loyalty to Charles Fisher helped secure him the enviable position as a road inspector in apparent contravention of the recommendations of the county's Liberal establishment.[51] Fisher's subsequent fall naturally aroused his anger, at the same time instilling in him a sense of fear for his continued tenure in a choice position in the county hierarchy. Emerging from a protracted period of mourning over the tragic death of his wife and infant child, Covert eventually became an avid partisan of Conservatism. Largely irrelevant to the fight to win over the supremely important constituencies residing along the Oromocto, Covert nevertheless prosecuted a fierce advocacy of the Conservative cause that would help to broaden his own credentials in any future race for higher office.

The fortunes of the Conservative challenge to Liberal hegemony were enhanced not only by the bottomless quality of its war chest and the strength of its appeal on both sides of the river (particularly at the mouth of the Oromocto), but also by the fissures apparent within the Liberal Party itself and, even more fortuitously, the infirmity of William E. Perley. Stricken by a lamentable ailment that even the venomously partisan Covert (a neighbour of Perley's son, Dell) could not help but deem pitiable,[52] Perley found it impossible to rise from his sick bed for the purpose of rallying local supporters.[53] Unmindful of Perley's distress and what many took to be the fearful and imminent arrival of the reaper, David Tapley sought to exploit his colleague's misfortune

---

[50] Covert's wife once reported that "Mr. Wilmot sends for John on all occasion when he has any 'deep thing' to talk about."

[51] Annie Covert to Miriam Mowat, June 5, 1857, Grace Hellen Mowat Collection, CCHS, Ms. 6/no. 164; and Annie Covert to David John Mowat, June 12, 1857, Grace Hellen Mowat Collection, CCHS, Ms. 6/no. 166.

[52] John S. Covert to Bessie Mowat, March 27, 1861, Grace Hellen Mowat Collection, CCHS, Ms. 6/no. 249.

[53] *The Headquarters*, June 7, 1861.

by taking a more prominent role in the legislature.[54] So useful did he prove himself to Tilley that the Provincial Secretary even briefly considered elevating Tapley to the Executive Council, the rumour of which momentarily broke the debilitating spell of illness and energized Perley, after some discomfort, to scrawl a note discounting Tapley's worth in receiving so exalted an honour.[55] A quibbling over precedence on the ballot further inhibited the internal accord of the Liberals, preventing them from fully addressing the success of Conservative money in attracting large and enthusiastic crowds.[56] Indeed, Glasier's and Lunt's progress through the county had the makings of a veritable circus, complete with entertainment, food, drink and less pardonable forms of refreshment, in addition to the largely gratuitous and ideologically vacuous sloganeering of the candidates themselves.[57] Shameless in his own illegalities, thoroughly reveling in his predictions of a coming revolution in county affairs, all the while engaging in verbal combat with the most fervent of Liberal partisans, Glasier could hardly have helped but to inculcate his own excesses into the malleable skulls of his underlings. Failing to persuade the more intransigently Liberal members of the electorate to drop their prejudicial attitudes, Glasier's thugs soon resorted to outright bribery and threats of physical violence to assure victory at the polls. Worried that the internal difficulties of the Liberal Party might well foment a collapse and result in the succumbing of an otherwise reliable county to the varied blandishments of his political opponents, Tilley sent his trusted lieutenant James

---

[54] Tapley in fact assumed most of Perley's duties, even taking up bills his colleague had prepared and presenting them to the Assembly (see *The Reporter*, March 22, 1861). In an attempt, perhaps, to establish a more distinct identity for himself, Tapley sponsored a move to annex the western shore of Grand Lake to his native parish of Sheffield. Like the earlier effort to upgrade the counties roads, it failed.

[55] William E. Perley to Samuel Leonard Tilley, April 3, 1861, Tilley Papers, PAC, MG 27, I/D/15.

[56] William E. Perley to Charles Burpee, June 16, 1861, Burpee Family Papers, York-Sunbury Historical Society Collection, PANB, MC 300, Ms. 5/no. 3.

[57] Petition of Charles Brown et al., Records of the Legislative Assembly, PANB, RS 24, 1862/pe/file 1/no. 14.

Steadman to the Oromocto to shore up support.[58] The ill-omened and ill-chosen location of Steadman's appearance, the Burton Court House, placed him firmly in the most visceral of Conservative bastions, assuring him of a barrage of jeers that prevented him from completing his well-intentioned political soliloquy on the virtues of the Liberal creed.

When the polling finally commenced, violence erupted and a host of impersonators on the Conservative payroll cast their spurious ballots in compliance with the dictates of their employers. Surprisingly, William E. Perley survived the fray, winning solidly in Blissville where even the momentary blight upon his mortal frame could not dissuade a grateful populace from their traditional commiseration with him. David Tapley, however, for all his manipulations and machinations, fell from collective grace, due less to any local animosity than to the inexhaustible appeal of the contents of Glasier's purse— a wrenching outcome that only became more unbearable when it was discovered that Glasier's margin of victory was a mere three votes. As for Enoch Lunt, he had only the consolation of a respectable second-place finish in Burton Parish (behind Glasier) to ease the burden of yet another lost campaign and a forever unknown amount of expended cash.[59]

The tumultuous upset of the Liberal establishment that had ruled the county since the summer of 1856 naturally provoked a swift and livid reaction. The day after the public declaration of the results, the supporters of David Tapley submitted a protest to the provincial government, citing not only the gross criminality of Glasier's candidacy— the bribery, implied venality, coercions and impostures— but also the less partisan irregularities of the County Revisers, High Sheriff James White and Municipal Warden Charles H. Clowes.[60] Incensed that his reputable facade could be so derisively smeared by the embittered friends of a defeated candidate and that his own name could be linked with the

---

[58] *The Headquarters*, May, 29, 1861.

[59] *The Reporter and Fredericton Advertizer*, June 7, 1861.

[60] Petition of James Hamilton et al., Elections Administration Records, PANB, RS 816, B/12.

electoral outrages of the victorious, Clowes joined ranks with the hardly disinterested Conservative David Morrow and formally rejected the protest on a series of technicalities that cleverly and conveniently circumvented the necessity of investigating the veracity of the Liberals' specific complaints.[61]

The problems facing Perley in the aftermath of victory were not less vexing. Miraculously purged of the invisible demons that had wreaked havoc upon his internal constitution by a providential return to office, he shook off the last vestiges of infirmity and rose from his bed, undoubtedly relieved that his troublesome associate was now disposed of, but hardly oblivious of the new challenge posed by the fire-eating Glasier. The vortex of Tapley's insatiable vengeance, however, could not be ignored either. Thus, almost immediately, Perley was engaged in combating a guerrilla campaign of bickering, sniping and accusation that in time placed over him the ban of the very same criminal complaint under which were pitched the forces loyal to his new colleague.[62]

The alliance between the two besieged victors that was the natural outcome of such a shared predicament never materialized. Too committed to Fisher's return and too anxious to usurp the senior position in the riding despite his freshman status, Glasier managed to drive into perpetual exile any charitable feelings that may have resided in his new colleague's heart. Proscription by Perley of all of Glasier's political supporters from the rolls of official patronage was now in order. Glasier himself attempted to intervene, particularly in the case of his useful subordinate, John S. Covert, but when the Honourable William Henry Steeves somewhat jocularly suggested to Perley the possibility of Covert's retention as road supervisor, he ignited the shortened fuse of the volatile assemblyman and caused a heated explosion of words laced with vitriol and acerbity.[63] Covert was sacrificed for the sake

---

[61] Petition of Charles H. Clowes et al., Elections Administration Records, PANB, RS 816, B/12.

[62] Petition of James Hamilton et al., Elections Administration Records, PANB, RS 816, B/12.

[63] William E. Perley to Charles Burpee, June 16, 1861, Burpee Family Papers, York-Sunbury Historical Society Collection, PANB, MC 300, Ms. 5/no. 3.

of placating the temper of Perley,[64] who, nevertheless, under the strain of an awkward two-fronted conflict with Liberals on the one side and Conservatives on the other, began to waver between the extreme positions of formal resignation from office and outright desertion of the Liberal cause. In his stabler moments Perley recognized the possibility of winning Glasier over to Tilley's camp, and even recommended that Tilley offer the disgruntled Fisher a place on the Provincial Bench as a means of diffusing the intestinal acuity of Glasier's opposition.[65] A real terror that Glasier could prove a threat to his own preferential position in the county was diminished by a strange spirit of cooperation that was in part the result, undoubtedly, of Tilley's selection of Perley for a place on the Executive Council— a selection that prompted at least one of Tilley's Sunbury informants to speculate adversely on Perley's innate worth when the time came, inevitably, to meet the challenge of the legislative opponents of Smasher rule.[66] A mellowing of hostilities among the divided Liberals of Sunbury County eventually removed from Perley's shoulders the burden of Tapley's nettlesome complaint, while Tapley himself bided his time, longingly waiting for a legislative investigation that was ultimately disqualified due to the sophistic wrangling of Glasier's superior legal representation.[67]

Throughout the fractious political contest of 1861, the people of the Oromocto, however momentarily distracted by the food and drink flowing unstoppably from the cornucopia of the Glasier candidacy, thoughtfully regarded the ominous unfolding of a

---

[64] John S. Covert to Bessie Mowat, July 14, 1861, Grace Hellen Mowat Collection, CCHS, Ms. 6/no. 271.

[65] William E. Perley to Samuel Leonard Tilley, July 15, 1861, Tilley Papers, PAC, MG 27, I/D/15.

[66] J.B.C. Burpee to Samuel Leonard Tilley, August 27, 1862, Tilley Papers, PAC, MG 27, I/D/15.

[67] *The Reporter and Fredericton Advertiser*, March 14, 1862. David Tapley left the county soon afterward, settling in Saint John where, through the influence of Mr. Tilley, he became Police Magistrate for Portland Parish. He remained at this post until 1889, all the time resisting solicitations on the part of friends to re-enter political life. He died in Saint John in 1894.

more bellicose and bloody struggle much further to the south. The disruptive effects of the American Civil War had already begun to work their way through the watershed by the summer of 1861. As foreign demand suffered temporary coronary obstruction, employment along the river fell. By June of 1862 the amount of land under license for timbering purposes had plummeted to one hundred and six square miles.[68] The malaise creeping through the settlements from Oromocto Village to the South Branch equally affected George Morrow, who, for the first time in the better part of two decades, failed to occupy the position as the county's largest timber merchant. Apparently concentrating his family's resources, culling profitable reserves while disposing himself of the burden of what were probably more superfluous berths, Morrow made way for William E. Perley. Flush with victories over seen and unseen adversaries, Perley responded to Morrow's deferment with a vitality that allowed him, after two decades of ravenous and fitful climbing, to mount the pre-eminent position atop the hierarchy of the Oromocto's timbermen. Other ventures in Madawaska and various parts of the Province diluted any displeasure Morrow may have harboured over Perley's twofold triumph, while lesser successes, such as the reacquisition by his old partner's son of the alienated portion of the Geary milling establishment, may well have acted as an intoxicant, inducing a sense of nostalgia for his lost days of unquestioned and incontestable local ascendancy.[69]

Morrow's mastery was not restored in the subsequent year, when a marked increase in demand resulting from the insatiable needs of the belligerent factions of America returned older levels of prosperity to the river economy.[70] Perley continued in his novel role as preeminent magnate, enjoying, along with his many employees, the quickening of local consumption that was only intensified when the river's indolent shipyards finally resumed their former energetic guise. In these now heady days of profit, so rambunctious did the press for the marketplace become that the overseers of the annual Oromocto timber-drive abandoned basic

---

[68] *The Royal Gazette*, June 17, 1863.

[69] Sunbury County Registry Office Records, PANB, RS 95a, 22/68.

[70] *The Royal Gazette*, June 15, 1864.

civility and civic duty and recklessly drove the produce of the woods into the long-suffering pillars of the several bridges that spanned the river's width.[71]

Though the Morrows may have suffered a degree of degradation, their prominence in the forest industry of the Oromocto had by no means evaporated. Most of the family's berths lay on the main branches of the river, but a sizeable concern in the Victoria area, bolstered greatly by the recent acquisition of a number of land grants, continued to satisfy the demand of the Morrows' customers abroad. The last remaining sticks of tamarack were the target of the Morrows' craving, and as the supply dwindled they found themselves with little choice but to ignore the boundaries of what now constituted an overwhelming number of granted parcels. Resuming most of his former duties as seizing officer in Burton Parish after the retirements of John Colling and Stephen Burpee, James Kerr acted upon the complaints of the victims of young George D. Morrow's depredations.[72] Confusion at the Crown Land Office led to less conscious wrongdoing on the younger Morrow's part, as poorly kept records allowed at least one license to be issued to him in total ignorance of the reality that much of the land in question had in fact already been granted to settlers.[73] Joining Morrow in his various outrages, yet operating under a competing and irreconcilable set of assumptions, was that ancient despoiler of the Victoria woods, Archibald McLean. Still disdainful of law and order, McLean entered a loose partnership with William Howe that ended in the clandestine confiscation by Kerr of their cache of Rockwell timber.[74] A familiar intransigence

---

[71] Bye Law to Protect the Bridges Across the Several Rivers and Streams Throughout the County of Sunbury, Executive Council Cabinet Series, PANB, RS 9, 1864/3.

[72] Robert Gowan to James Kerr, March 24, 1864, Letterbooks, Records of the Surveyor General, PANB, RS 637, 1/a/30, p. 225.

[73] Robert Gowan to George D. Morrow, December 12, 1864, and December 24, 1864, Letterbooks, Records of the Surveyor General, PANB, RS 637, 1/a/30, pp. 273-274.

[74] James Kerr to John McMillan, March 11, 1863, Seizing Officers' Records, Timber and Sawmill Records, PANB, RS 663d, 30/a.

in the face of criminal prosecution fostered a shamelessness that went so far as to provoke an angry rejection of Kerr's subsequent insistence on the payment by McLean for damages to the Crown. McLean's activity in and around Victoria, however, would soon be at an end. Extinction of marketable timber eventually spawned his indifference and allowed him a restful retirement to Oromocto Village, surrounded by the energy of his sons and wholly unheedful of the dislocations yet to occur at the scene of his late transgressions.

Kerr's renewed activity in the Victoria area helped alleviate any objections the government may have had to his assumption of the duty of overseeing land settlement following Stephen Burpee's retirement. The difficulties Kerr initially encountered as a result of his role in the accommodation of a former Oromocto ship's carpenter by the name of William Fleet paled in comparison to the controversy involving a number of Victoria's older, permanent inhabitants. Two decades of confusion and non-uniformity in the drawing and marking of boundaries, beginning with Amasa Flaglor and culminating with Kerr himself, at last fulfilled its latent promise as a source of contention for the unwitting pioneers who had been so unfortunate as to settle within Victoria's ken. A search through the woods for evidence of Flaglor's old base-line in the form of rotting stakes and painted tree trunks proved successful enough to allow for a comparison of Flaglor's original survey with the subsequent work of Burpee. Noting discrepancies in the division line between the fifth and sixth tiers of lots, Kerr surmised that Flaglor's conclusions were the most plausible cause of the confusion. For most of the settlers the incompetence of one Deputy Surveyor half a generation ago was of little consequence, but for Daniel James Wood, for whom the discrepancies meant the reduction of his lot by half, the shortcomings of the agents of the Crown were an occasion for lament only marginally consolable by the ever diminishing epiphanies of the forest industry.[75]

The eternal minuet performed alternately by Crown agent and lumberman, by lumberman and settler, and by settler and Crown

---

[75] James Kerr to John McMillan, March 19, 1863, Records of the Surveyor General, PANB, RS 637, 7/j/3/a.

agent proceeded as if according to the will of an omniscient choreographer, hidden by a cloak of invisibility that his own amusement over the mystification of the hapless dancers might forever remain unknown to them. Bankrupt of any real powers to combat the malicious design of fate, whether it be vaguely manichean or expressly economic in nature, the Reverend Wiggins continued to ignore the plight of the unfortunates living within the bounds of his sprawling mission. When he retired, an awful legacy remained behind for his successors. The Church of England, once the dominant sect on the Oromocto, was now only a minor contender for the souls of the unredeemed, trailing in appeal behind the Catholics and Methodists and all but drowning in the turbulent wake of the irrepressible Baptists.[76] To restore the wretched condition of the county mission the Anglican hierarchy decided upon the personage of the Reverend Henry Pollard. Arriving from his previous assignment in Saint Stephen after much anticipation on the part of the faithful, Pollard was shocked by the apparent ignorance of the majority of its now dissenting and spiritually indifferent inhabitants.[77] The condition of the back settlements of the Oromocto, in particular, he singled out as proof of the neglect of his predecessors. With an iconoclasm that would soon ruffle the sensibilities of the fogies occupying the ranks of his Maugerville vestry, he set out with the intention of winning back the church's prodigal offspring. The Irish population of Victoria Settlement proved unusually responsive to Pollard's calls for a spiritual renewal, but they were hardly exceptional in this regard.[78] Harbouring an essential sympathy for the lacklustre glories of the Established Church on account of his upbringing

---

[76] In 1861 (according to data in the 1861 census) there were 2,281 Baptists (both Free Will and Calvinist), 542 Roman Catholics, 425 Methodists and 391 Anglicans dwelling in the Oromocto River parishes of Lincoln, Burton and Blissville.

[77] R.P. Gorham, "Notes on the History of the Church of England in the Parish of Maugerville, Sunbury County, N.B." (1937), Archives of the Diocese of Fredericton, PANB, MC 223, M3-16, p. 32-33.

[78] Register of Burton and Maugerville; 1787-1878, Archives of the Diocese of Fredericton, PANB, MC 223, M3-6.

within its less than smothering embrace, and indisposed to show much confidence in a brand of dissent adherence to which had coincided with the regrettable loss of half his homestead, Daniel James Wood heeded Pollard's weekly remonstrations and returned to the Anglican fold. Attending the regular meetings of the faithful at the home of his friend Robert Touchbourn, he presented his children to the enthusiastic reverend for the purpose of bestowing upon them the eternally refreshing ritual of baptism.[79]

Wood's desertion of the Baptist sect did little to disconnect him from the largely Baptist populace of the river, with whom he continued to share the unbreakable bond of kinship and common fortune. And even as the ultimate implications of Pollard's evangelical resolve now seemed ready to polarize the people of the river, his actions, in truth, merely contributed one more variable to the common fold of experience of Baptist and non-Baptist alike. To a large extent, though, the magnitude of the task at hand forced Pollard to limit his activity to the region close to the heart of the old stronghold of Oromocto Anglicanism. Here, at the mouth of the river, Pollard's zeal encouraged the local people to tear down old St. John's and rebuild it stone by stone.[80] A trek up the branches of the Rusagonis likewise met with positive response, and it was not long before a permanent outpost in that ancient Baptist country was established.[81]

Pollard's expanding cultivation of the surprisingly fertile evangelical fields of the Oromocto inevitably prevented the good missionary from satisfying the vain indulgence of the people of Maugerville, who had been too long spoiled by the sustained presence of the county parson. When Pollard perceived that residence at Oromocto Village was more practical given the number of missions now flourishing nearby, and then announced to his incredulous hosts that his wife's health required him to board with an Oromocto doctor by the name of Edmund Cougle, the

---

[79] Ibid.

[80] The new St. John's Church, paid for in part by subscriptions raised by R.D. Wilmot, was consecrated by Bishop Medley on October 26, 1864.

[81] Gorham, op. cit., p. 32.

response was infuriatingly petty.[82] The old trans-St. John jealousies came to the fore. The vestrymen and congregation at Maugerville refused to further subsidize Pollard's salary, while the vestry clerk, John S. Covert, unable to tolerate disputations that were largely irrelevant to his political ambitions, resigned his post.[83] Pollard thus abandoned Maugerville. His new Oromocto congregation, grateful for his ecumenical imminence, and feeling exultant over the favour bestowed upon them at the expense of their rivals, conscientiously undertook to fulfill the responsibility for satisfying the material needs of the Reverend and his family which the vindictive people of Maugerville had so shamefully renounced.

Largely unaffected by the controversies engulfing the church, the affairs of Sunbury County's municipal government entered a ofttimes discordant period of adjustment. Low electoral turnouts stemming from the Council's unfortunate decision to hold the annual elections in the month of December, during which a majority of the electors were busy in the woods, was finally corrected early in 1861, though the Council's arbitrary rescheduling of balloting for the fall prompted a mystifying controversy over the polls that could only be surmounted by appeal to the provincial legislature.[84] Charles H. Clowes remained Warden throughout this minor uproar, but for reasons not particularly clear he was entirely swept from Council membership in the elections held in October and replaced by David Morrow.[85] Clowes' role as Warden was filled by Maugerville's George Horatio Nelson Harding. In the succeeding year, Clowes returned to office, and was able to reassert himself as leader of the municipal corporation. Resuming

---

[82] "A Brief History of the Associated Parishes of Maugerville and Burton, by a Senior Church Warden," Archives of the Diocese of Fredericton, PANB, MC 223, M3-16B.

[83] John S. Covert to Bessie Mowat, April 2, 1864, Grace Hellen Mowat Collection, CCHS, 6/309.

[84] Petition of the Municipality of Sunbury, Records of the Legislative Assembly, PANB, RS 24, 1861/pe/file 1/no. 16.

[85] Harold G. Kimball, *History of Oromocto* (Fredericton: Unipress, 1966), p. 42.

his stewardship of the county, Clowes oversaw the spread of municipal authority along the Oromocto, bringing its inhabitants into greater dependence on the will of the governing order through the imposition of stricter rules upon the use of public and private interval lands.[86] Some resistance to the Council's dictates of course arose, particularly among the people of the North West and South Branches, who resented the Council's designation of the river as a lawful fence, not only for the reason that the river was hardly adequate to constrain the liberty of local cattle, but also because of the Council's failure to consult either of the district's two councillors.[87] The abuse of the pylons of the river's bridges, perpetrated by local river drivers, also attracted the Council's regulatory attention.[88] A series of fines imposed for varying degrees of licentiousness, however, had little effect in deterring damage to the great Oromocto bridge resulting from normal wear and tear. The temperamental draw once again acted up, inhibiting the passage of vessels and requiring the intervention of Assemblyman William E. Perley and County Road Commissioner Charles Hazen before its health and integrity could be restored.[89]

As the bridge defied the Council's authority in the good governance of the county, so too did the last remaining vestiges of the old sessional order. Resisting the incremental and inevitable decay of their old powers, a number of the Justices of the Peace refused to acknowledge the right of the Council to administer

---

[86] "A Bye Law, In Addition to a Bye Law Relating to the Low Lands and Islands within the Limits of the Municipality of Sunbury," Executive Council Cabinet Series, PANB, RS 9, 1861/6; and A Bye Law to Regulate the Going at Large of Cattle in a Portion of the Parish of Lincoln, Executive Council Series, PANB, RS 9, 1865/5.

[87] Petition of David W. Smith et al., Records of Lt. Governor John Henry Thomas Manners-Sutton, PANB, RS 347, C/9.

[88] "Bye Law of Sunbury County," Executive Council Cabinet Series, PANB, RS 9, 1864/3.

[89] "General Report of the Chief Commissioner of Public Works for the Year 1859," *Journals of the Legislative Assembly*, Appendix, p. 292-3; and Charles Hazen to Samuel Leonard Tilley, May 27, 1863, Tilley Papers, PAC, MG 27, I/D/15.

county revenues.[90] The levying and collection of fines remained within the mandate of the justices, but when the Council attempted to appropriate the monies thus collected, they met with a less than satisfactory response. Upset over the contemptuous attitude of the justices, and resenting the latter's dismissal of the authority of the county's popularly elected officers, the Council passed an ordinance requiring termination of any rebelliousness and the immediate surrender of the controverted funds. Continued defiance forced Warden Clowes to appeal to the Executive Council, whose lukewarm suggestion that provincial intervention might be forthcoming proved inadequate to instill in the wayward justices a more submissive attitude.[91] A year later the justices were still recalcitrant in their opposition to the expanding authority of the Municipal Council, and continued not only to discharge duties no longer theirs to discharge, but also to retain portions of the monies they collected. Imminent intervention by the Executive Council of a more substantial sort ultimately presaged the end of the Sessions' last resistance to the lapsing of their executive and administrative function.[92]

While the County Council expanded its control over the Oromocto, the old ways characterized by the Council's largely autonomous and largely unaccountable predecessors met a more symbolic end with the death of George Hayward in September of 1862.[93] His body buried, his memory eulogized by hundreds of mourners who flocked from throughout the Province to attend his funeral, Hayward left behind a large estate which, according to the stipulations of his last will and testament, devolved upon a select number of close friends and relations. His warm affection for and close filial bond with former Emigrant Agent Moses Henry Perley impelled Hayward to bequeath to Perley's son his

[90] Petition of the Warden and Municipality of Sunbury County, Executive Council Cabinet Series, PANB, RS 9, 1864/6.

[91] Robert Fulton to Charles Clowes, July 14, 1864, Letterbooks, Provincial Secretary Correspondence, PANB, RS 13, Volume 10/p. 556.

[92] Petition of the County Council of the Municipality of Sunbury, Records of Lt. Governor Arthur Hamilton Gordon, PANB, RS 348, C/5

[93] The Headquarters, October 1, 1862.

Lincoln Parish home.[94] But while Hayward may have intended that the granting of his manor might also have the effect of extending to his great nephew his own legacy as one of several traditional patrons of the people of the Oromocto, George Hayward Perley could not, despite any nominal resemblance to his uncle, very easily don his uncle's prestigious mantle of formal and informal authority. Having been reared in the city of Saint John and conditioned by his father's status as a privileged member of the Provincial elite, Perley was ill-suited to life in the country, where peculiar deferential attitudes and dependent relationships sharply contrasted with the more rigid demarcations characteristic of the urban social order. Even his marriage to a daughter of a Maugerville-born hero of the Napoleonic Wars could little mitigate the awkwardness of his foray into the countryside. Thus, it was perhaps appropriate that his capacity as his father's personal secretary in the surveying of the Maritime fisheries prevented him from fully establishing himself on the Oromocto's banks. His father's unexpected death did little to effect the status of his employment, since his father's successor as Fishery Commissioner, Joseph Howe, retained his services,[95] but the sorting out of his father's indecipherable journals and official papers soon required a profounder sense of quietude than could be found either at sea or amidst the distracting bustle of Saint John.

George H. Perley's life in the vicinity of the Oromocto commenced following his return from his autumnal exploration of the Newfoundland coast in November of 1863. Transferring himself, his wife, two sons and his aged father-in-law to the old Hayward estate, Perley oversaw the administration of his late father's private and public affairs, laboured over his report on the survey of the fisheries conducted under Howe's aegis and struggled beneath a burden of want arising in part from a confusion over his salary that had its origins in his father's faulty accounting skills. An inherited hankering for alcohol predisposed him toward regular states of clandestine inebriation that understandably

---

[94] Will of George Hayward, Sunbury County Probate Court Records, PANB, RS 72.

[95] George H. Perley to Joseph Howe, May 8, 1863, Howe Papers, PAC, MG 24, B-29, Volume 15, p. 210.

confounded his performance of his official duties. And while he found it most difficult to locate sympathetic companions in debauchery in the temperate vale of the Oromocto, the oppressive attraction to the less countrified environment of Fredericton satisfied the social demands of his peculiar addiction. His familial background obviously placed him in the top ranks of Oromocto society, but an absence of any sense of local social responsibility, largely due to the urbanity of his upbringing and the nonparochial nature of his experience, did little to facilitate his assimilation. Even in the realm of the spirit he displayed a marked indifference toward integration into the larger community. An infrequent attendant at Anglican services in Oromocto, Perley remained unmoved by the admirable example of his father-in-law's walk to St. John's Church each Sunday. Shunning such exaggerated displays of piety, Perley indulged himself in the simpler joys of ice-skating and solitary ornithological treks through the Lincoln woods. Aside from the members of his family, Perley's only steady companion was the son of the elder Sheriff John Hazen, James King Hazen, with whom he periodically forsook all serious considerations of the day for the quiet joys and challenges of chess.[96]

Ultimately, Perley would not remain in his rural haven, for the regular, outrageous effects of his unfortunate habit finally disposed Joseph Howe, after repeated warnings, to terminate his services in July of 1865.[97] Poor financial planning, combined with his rather licentious lifestyle, only complicated his affairs following his dismissal from the Imperial service. A series of loans he could not repay and mortgages on his Lincoln estate he could not honour hardly helped to salvage his ruinous fortunes.[98] His income curtailed, his finances in ruins and the demands of his family far too exhausting to satisfy any longer without significant

---

[96] Journal of George Perley, 1864, PAC, MG 24, C27.

[97] Joseph Howe to George H. Perley, September 8, 1864 and Joseph Howe to George H. Perley, July 31, 1865, Howe Papers, PAC, MG 24, B-29, Volume 12, p. 423.

[98] See Sunbury County Registry Office Records, PANB, RS 95, 22/101, 22/503, 22/526, 24/106, 24/116, 24/139, 24/161, 24/166, 25/32.

change in his situation, Perley sold his inheritance to pay off his enormous debts[99] and returned to the city of his birth. Here, after an attempt to gain employment as a Deputy Surveyor with the Crown Land Office,[100] he took ill and shortly died.[101]

George H. Perley was an anomaly on the Oromocto: a nominal Anglican in a predominantly Baptist countryside; an elitist who remained ignorant, even oblivious, of the ethos of rural society; outward looking rather than parochial; a landed gentleman of urban sensibilities who shunned the irresistible allure of timber; the heir of one of the Oromocto's great patrons, but nevertheless too preoccupied with his own concerns to involve himself with the affairs of his inherited clientele. It is not surprising that when the sound of the debate over Confederation began to resonate from the halls of government and waft fitfully across the land, breaching the collective tympanum and swaying the allegiance of the people of the Oromocto, George H. Perley remained characteristically inattentive. Odd coincidence thrust him into the entourage of the Canadian delegation on its way to Charlottetown, and while all of British North America was held transfixed by the anecdotes and speculations reported by the print media, George H. Perley desperately longed to be rid of his bothersome companions and experience a happier conveyance to his destination off the coast of Newfoundland.[102]

Less susceptible to ennui in the matter of the fate of half a continent was Perley's assemblyman cousin, William, whose political indenturement to Samuel Leonard Tilley could suffer no other attitude than unwavering support for Union. The personal magnetism emanating from him on account of his privileged status and economic clout provided him with a solid core of support

---

[99] Id., 24/154 and 25/32.

[100] George H. Perley to Charles Connell, January 7, 1867, and John H. Grey to Charles Connell, January 7, 1867, Records of the Surveyor General, PANB, RS 637, 2/q/1; and Charles Connell to George H. Perley, Letterbooks, Records of the Surveyor General, PANB, RS 637, 1/a/33, p. 74.

[101] M.V.B. Perley, *History and Genealogy of the Perley Family* (Salem: published by author, 1906), p. 586.

[102] Journal of George Perley, 1864, PAC, MG 24, C47.

among his Oromocto constituents for an idea that could only be expected to be innately popular anywhere that Orangism and the messianic rapture of the Free Willers intimately conspired to wed the popular resolve and imagination to anything smacking of a more Imperial, perhaps more benign, version of the American innovation known as Manifest Destiny.[103] Mesmerized by the facility Union might extend his activities in Quebec along the most extreme tributaries of the St. John River and undoubtedly convinced of the hopelessness of political survival amidst a largely pro-Confederation electorate, John Glasier, once a committed opponent of everything having to do with the Tilley regime, finally fulfilled Mr. Tilley's long-standing faith in his inherent liberalism and measurably softened the tenor of his opposition. In secret consultation with William E. Perley he pledged his support to the government in any vote to be taken on the issue of Union and promised solidarity with his former enemies ever afterward.[104] Hearing word of the terrible betrayal in the midst of his plans to campaign in opposition to Perley, John S. Covert openly announced, with all the rhetorical hyperbole he could summon for the occasion, his intention to single-handedly depose both incumbents. Perley, himself, could only laugh at the dubious nature of Covert's exaggerated claims, and, after ruminating over the popularity of Confederation in his riding,

---

[103] On page 69 of his book *Orangism, The Canadian Phase* (Toronto: McGraw-Hill, Ryerson, 1972), Herewood Senior attests that Orangemen in New Brunswick generally favoured Confederation. Voting patterns along the Oromocto likewise tend to support Senior's assertion— generally it seems to have been those who belonged to or had sympathy for the lodge who voted for Unionist candidates. That Free Will Baptists similarly became advocates of the Confederation cause cannot be confirmed by any modern authority, yet on the Oromocto, a large number of Free Will Baptists, many of whom were also Orangemen, likewise seem to have cast their ballot in favour of pro-Union candidates. That Covert received his greatest support at the mouth of the river, where there were fewer Free Will Baptists, as well as fewer Orangemen, seems to uphold this.

[104] William E. Perley to Samuel Leonard Tilley, January 30, 1865, Tilley Papers, PAC, MG 27, I/D/15.

reported to his liege the likely prognosis for victory in the impending elections.

Affecting the outcome of any legislative contest on the Oromocto was the question of the railway. The improbable vision of William Scoullar seemed ready to finally take more tangible form as the backers of the long-heralded Western Extension of the European and North American Railroad prepared to prosecute the line's construction. Seven years' study of the problems involving the surveying and fabrication of railways, in addition to an intimacy with the major investors on either side of the international border, helped secure Charles S. Burpee's nephew, Egerton Ryerson Burpee, the task of exploring a route through the New Brunswick wilderness as far as the St. Croix.[105] The Douglas Valley was the natural course of the lower section of the proposed line, and after passing through Hartt's Mill Settlement, skirting the north bank of the North West Branch of the Oromocto and piercing the western Oromocto divide, the initial stage of Burpee's labour was complete.[106] Pregnant with a litter of previously unfathomable possibilities, and ready to impart to the upper Oromocto a degree of importance and prosperity the contemplation of which was a dizzying prospect, the Western Extension quickly became susceptible to the endemic controversies of the watershed. In the maelstrom of the Confederation debate, the traditional biases of the region plotted against what might otherwise have been a unanimously popular innovation and induced, instead, a suspicion that the railway was perhaps designed less for the benefit of the subjects of the Queen than for the inestimable pleasures of the Yankee.[107] Making one last public appearance before succumbing to his own mortality, Calvin Hatheway remonstrated against the project, calling instead for a central route, perhaps through his beloved Maugerville, totally bypassing the hated Oromocto and depriving the Americans of the boon

---

[105] E.R. Burpee to Samuel Leonard Tilley, April 11, 1864 and April 12, 1864, Records of Warrants, Appointments and Commissions, PANB, RS 538, D/15, 1860-1864.

[106] E.R. Burpee to Samuel Leonard Tilley, January 5, 1865, Executive Council Cabinet Series, PANB, RS 9, 1865/2.

[107] MacNutt, op. cit., p. 411-412.

of provincial trade.[108] An historical sense of wary insularity, a manifold of attachments to their assemblymen and the overwhelming popularity of Union seems to have inclined the people of the river toward a state of strange accord with the codgerly figure they had repeatedly repudiated as their chosen representative. Thus, despite any benefits the Western Extension might bring, the people of the Oromocto, in these earliest days of the campaign of 1865, stood staunchly opposed to its completion.

Having adopted a rigid position made all the more intransigent by his personal animosity toward his opponents, John S. Covert blundered into the political snare of Western Extension. As if ignorant of its implicitly anti-Confederate onus, Covert tacked it onto a platform from which he denounced the inequity and corruption practiced by the incumbents in the allocation of by-road grants.[109] It was a poorly conceived strategy, but one which the inherent polarity of politics irresistibly impelled him to embrace. With Lemuel Allen Wilmot pronouncing at the Burton Court House upon the glories of a great and unified nation extending from the Atlantic coast to the Pacific,[110] and the formerly divided and mutually antagonistic political machines of Perley and Glasier functioning in a state of amity and common purpose, Covert's hopes for even a poor showing on election day paled. So desperate did the anti-Unionists become that York County Assemblyman George Hatheway, somewhat estranged from his father in the matter of British North American Union, began to stump the Oromocto. Guided by an impetuous streak, as well perhaps as resentment over Perley's role as a member of a government that was preparing to surrender the Province into the clutches of Upper Canada, Hatheway took particular pleasure in a prearranged meeting of partisans of his cause held virtually within sight of Perley's home in the heart of the latter's private

---

[108] Calvin Luther Hatheway to Samuel Leonard Tilley, September 28, 1862, Tilley Papers, PAC, MG 27, I/D/15.

[109] *The Headquarters*, March 1, 1865.

[110] MacNutt, op. cit., p. 428.

Blissville domain.[111] The unexpected appearance of the most vocal of anti-Confederates on his doorstep so unnerved Perley that his private spending to secure the loyalty of the people escalated beyond the limits of his personal resources, forcing him to solicit a loan from his mentor, Samuel Leonard Tilley.[112] Retaliation against the impudence of Hatheway was required as well, and it came in the form of several sleigh-loads of bogus voters gathered from the ranks of Perley's supporters and raucously transported to Fredericton to take fraudulent part in the legislative contest of York County.[113]

Perley's gesture to subvert the election in favour of the cause of Confederation ultimately failed. Confederation lost, Tilley was cast from office and the opposition gained control of the Assembly.[114] The Oromocto proved to be more merciful to the great Confederation cause, as both Perley and Glasier were returned to their seats, though not without some difficulty experienced along the way.[115] Despite the odds against him, Covert had made a stubborn race of it in the traditionally more conservative parish of Burton, out-polling Perley and coming within thirty votes of Glasier. A fourth contender, Sunbury County's Secretary-Treasurer James Hamilton, also fared better in Burton than did Perley, though his lack of support in populous Blissville dismissed his hopes for final triumph. Blissville, the fount of Perley's greatest personal strength and the source of his margin of victory over Covert, did not, however, uniformly vote in his favour. As elsewhere throughout the county, Glasier took precedence atop the poll, forcing Perley into a very insecure position and compelling him to further tap his finances in an effort to stay apace in order that his seniority, let alone his seat, might be preserved. In the end, Perley managed to maintain his place in Fredericton, though his rank soon came into question and his once sound finances were

---

[111] *The Headquarters*, March 15, 1865.

[112] William E. Perley to Samuel Leonard Tilley, May 29, 1865, Tilley Papers, PAC, MG 27, I/D/15.

[113] *The Headquarters*, March 15, 1865.

[114] MacNutt, op. cit., pp. 430-1.

[115] *The Headquarters*, March 8, 1865.

reduced to an utter shambles. Even the steady revival of the timber trade, that surest indicator of electoral outcomes, could not rescue him from his pecuniary difficulties. Unable to purchase more than ten square miles of reserves following the election,[116] Perley bemoaned his sorry state to his former patron Tilley and begged for leniency in the latter's expectations regarding the prompt repayment of debts.[117]

As Covert's margin of defeat reveals, the ambivalence of the people of the Oromocto to Confederation was significant. Despite the success of the pro-Union candidates represented by Glasier and Perley, the region's Anti-Confederates could find some consolation in the narrow possibility of a more complete conversion of the watershed to their cause. In truth, the likelihood of such a conversion was scant, while speculation over its prosecution was essentially irrelevant. The Anti-Confederates controlled the Assembly, the Confederates controlled the county and there was no immediate prospect of altering either of these two indisputable realities. For the people of the Oromocto, benefits streamed in regardless of the apparent paradox of their subordination to a legislature hostile to their vague ideological orientation. Not only did their old, reliable patrons still sit in Fredericton, but the Western Extension now loomed on the southeastern horizon, preparing to open a new avenue to the outside world and provide new stimulus to the arrested energies of a countryside slowly enervated over the course of several decades by the steady recession of opportunities in the traditional staple industries. But before the first ties could be laid and the first spikes driven the political climate drastically changed. Fenian outrages, the threat of American belligerence and an economy victimized by American retribution following the surrender at Appomattox purged the idea of Confederation of its more noxious attributes and convinced many of its most staunch opponents of its necessity.[118] The elections scheduled to take place in June of 1866 to test the popularity of the new

---

[116] *The Royal Gazette*, June 20, 1866.

[117] William E. Perley to Samuel Leonard Tilley, May 29, 1865, Tilley Papers, PAC, MG 27, I/D/15.

[118] MacNutt, op. cit., p. 441.

government's resolution to embrace Union represented a kind of anticlimax. On the Oromocto the results were predictable. Still recovering from the wounds incurred during his all too recent bout at the polls, John S. Covert abstained from participation, leaving the opposition to the unlikely candidacy of Henry Bridges, whose fanaticism in the improvement of the county's livestock ill prepared him for the more profoundly nuanced dealings of a dissevered human polity. Faced with only token opposition, Glasier and Perley again marched to victory, though yet another third-place finish for Perley in Burton Parish undoubtedly gave rise to speculation that his appeal was largely a parochial one.[119] Appropriately, Tilley refrained from asking him to resume his place on the Executive Council. Demoralized by this indignity, Perley began to nurture a precious resentment of the entire Liberal establishment that would only grow more intense and embittered as events unfolded.

The immediate aftermath of the resolution in favour of Confederation was not particularly pleasing for the Oromocto community. Perhaps begrudging his constituents their greater display of preference for his running mate, Perley sponsored an initiative to expand the authority of the Municipal Council in the selection of parish officers. And though opposition in Oromocto Village, French Lake and Geary was strong, the controversial legislation survived the scrutiny of the provincial Assembly.[120] Of less trivial consequence was the rapid downturn in the economy following the vengeful revocation by the Americans of the Reciprocity Treaty. The entire Oromocto lumbering industry stagnated and declined, reaching its lowest level in decades. Perley's brief heyday on the river, already on the decline, was now finished. Into the vacuum left by Perley's demise stepped Assemblyman William Todd of St. Stephen, though he had a strong and wily competitor for local hegemony in the person of George D.

---

[119] *The Reporter and Fredericton Advertizer*, June 1, 1866.

[120] "Bill to Provide for the Election of Councillors and the Appointment of Parish Officers," Records of the Legislative Assembly, PANB, RS 24, 1866/bi/file 4/no. 36; and Petition of Rate Payers and Freeholders of Sunbury, Records of the Legislative Assembly, PANB, RS 24, 1866/pe/file 2/no. 29.

Morrow. For the time being, Morrow prevailed, seizing for himself the not necessarily hereditary legacy of his father and emerging through the dank misery diffused by depression as the premier lumberman of the Oromocto.[121] Denominational affinity with York County's High Sheriff Thomas Temple helped him cement a partnership that resulted in the launching of the brigantine, *Susanna Temple*.[122] Yet while joint ventures of this sort were certainly profitable, Morrow suffered the effects of limited cash reserves that prevented him from gaining legal access to the basic resources required for the conduct of his business. When lumber was scarce on lands he controlled, Morrow had little compunction in continuing his long-standing habit of raiding the Victoria woods.[123] His disreputable culling of the stands watered by the Brizley, Rockwell and Geary streams stirred James Kerr and several younger colleagues to take up the all too familiar pursuit of the evidence of arboreal depredations.[124] Forced by the vagaries of the timber economy to resort to similar acts of abject piracy, yet unable to sell at decent price the products of their necessary vice, the poor of the river scratched pathetically at the earth in hopes of uncovering nutritional treasures. The peculiar dependence upon the scanty rewards of the lumber camp and the ailing constitution of the economy, however, imposed a ban on a more sustainable indulgence in farming. Despite a rise in the number of subscriptions, lack of resolve among the leaders of the local Agricultural Society continued to inhibit the proffering of cash incentives and the circulation of tools, seed grains and stud animals. The eradication of the ancient and once near lethal potato rot and a growing acknowledgement of the wonders of manure

---

[121] *The Royal Gazette*, June 12, 1867.

[122] Hancox, op. cit., p. 49.

[123] James Kerr to Charles Connell, July 1, 1867, Records of the Surveyor General, PANB, RS 637, 7/j/3/a/7.

[124] Charles Connell to James Kerr, February 8, 1867 and Charles Connell to James Kerr, April 13, 1867, Letterbooks, Records of the Surveyor General, PANB, RS 637, 1/a/33, p. 242 and p. 369; and James Kerr to Charles Connell, April 15, 1867, Records of the Surveyor General, PANB, RS 637, 7/j/3/a/7.

were only small triumphs in an otherwise dismal agricultural epoch.[125] And while travelers marveled at the picturesque quality of the scenery at the river's mouth and sectarian excursionists made advantageous use of its banks for Sunday afternoon diversions,[126] the awful truth of the countryside's relative decay could not be obscured.

The prostration of the river economy was further compounded by the political aftershocks of the Confederation vote. Seeking a restorative cure for the injuries recently suffered, William E. Perley discovered the potential salve in the upcoming Dominion elections. Seniority in the local Liberal hierarchy automatically thrust him into position as the leading contender in the riding of Sunbury, but the ambitions of Charles Sidney Burpee, long gestating in the smoke-filled room of caucus politics, suddenly overcame any instinct the latter man may have had to defer in Perley's favour. His appetite whetted by executive appointments to the Provincial Board of Agriculture and the Provincial Fishery Commission, Burpee now prepared himself for greater honours. The immediate result was a division in the almighty Liberal Party— each contestant bringing squarely behind him a loyal cadre of supporters deeply committed to the selection of their man for the distinguished status of Commoner. The parochial character of Perley's faction boded ill for his chances, as did Burpee's control of the county party machinery, but a hastily drawn-up accord giving Perley precedence seems to have temporarily ended the brief internecine conflict.[127]

The terms of the agreement, however, were tenuous, and when the siren call of glory on a continental scale failed to relent in all its alluring sonances, Burpee could not refrain from repudiating his pledge and reaffirming his intention to capture a seat in the Dominion Parliament. Neither man could criticize the other on

---

[125] "Seventh Annual Report of the Board of Agriculture of the Province of New Brunswick," *Journals of the Legislative Assembly* (1867), Appendix VI, pp. 75-76.

[126] *The Reporter and Fredericton Advertiser*, August 24, 1866 and August 23, 1867; and *The Headquarters*, September 2, 1868.

[127] *The Reporter and Fredericton Advertiser*, August 16, 1867 and August 23, 1867.

grounds of policy. With regard to the great consuming issue of the Intercontinental Railway both men advocated a southern route that would link it with the Western Extension, thus diverting through the county a welter of national traffic.[128] Without ideological or political differences to kindle the embers of serious debate, the conflict gravitated toward the personal. Money, of course, had a prominent role to play as well, and though Burpee himself did not possess the kind of inexhaustible wealth that had so well served the candidacy of John Glasier several years before, his network of high-standing friends easily eclipsed the insufficiency of his accounts. The Morrows in particular, having been drawn into the Liberal Party through their affiliation with Glasier, proved especially useful by contributing their personal resources to the election effort and converting a large number of their Oromocto clients to partisanship in Burpee's cause. His riches depreciated by recent events and his own prestige on the river thoroughly deflated, Perley could not compete with the formidable coalition fronted by his opponent; thus, when the ballots were counted, it hardly came as a surprise that Perley trailed in every voting district save his home parish of Blissville.

Perley's defeat in the Dominion election induced a schism in the ranks of the Liberals that was formalized by Perley's sulking defection to the camp of the provincial Tories. No longer able to tolerate the slights against him by an unappreciative party, and already sympathetic to the Conservatives for reasons of Tilley's own prior desertion, Perley left the responsibilities incumbent upon victory to the triumphant Burpee and soulfully ruminated over an offer tendered by the new Conservative Premier, his one-time opponent Andrew Wetmore, to resume his place on the Executive Council.[129] The nature of the task in Ottawa was no more than monumental, even to one, such as Burpee, so resolute in his determination to lift the fortunes of his constituents. The likelihood of the Intercolonial Railway taking a northern route seemed

---

[128] Ibid., September 13, 1867.

[129] John Glasier to Charles Burpee, February 12, 1869, Burpee Family Papers, York-Sunbury Historical Society Collection, PANB, MC 300, Ms. 5/no. 25; and *The Reporter and Fredericton Advertizer*, February 12, 1868.

strong, but the desperate longings of the people of Sunbury County nevertheless impelled Burpee to apply himself in the fight for a more amenable alternative. Fears that the people would turn on him in any subsequent election further bolstered his efforts,[130] despite the failure of his operatives at home to conjure up more than four hundred and thirty-six supporters in a petitioning campaign intended to impress upon the new national government the advantages of running the railway through the St. John River Valley.[131] The success of a staunch anti-Confederate in the Saint John by-elections forewarned of imminent difficulties, presaging for some the repudiation by a hostile province of the Act of Union and the overturning of the uncertain Liberal conventions of Sunbury County.[132] When John Glasier vacated his seat in the Assembly following an appointment to the Dominion Senate, the threat of electoral revolution understandably demoralized and divided an already fractured party and spread seeds of strife that quickly germinated in the Oromocto's fertile red interval.

In the forefront of contention for Glasier's vacant seat was Glasier's own brother, Duncan. It was certainly plausible to expect that the existence of a sympathetic bond for a particular family might allow for the continuity of Liberal success, but the truth of the matter was that Duncan's own failings were too many for even his brother to overlook. Proprietorship of a line of steamboats notorious for their hazardous decrepity had already given rise to a certain disreputableness. When his steamer, the *Sunbury*, exploded and sank, killing eleven passengers, including the daughter of Sheffield's Congregational minister, his chances of a

[130] Reuben Hoben to Charles Burpee, March 26, 1868, Burpee Family Papers, York-Sunbury Historical Society Collection, PANB, MC 300, Ms. 5/no. 10.

[131] Moses Coburn to Charles Burpee, March 23, 1868, Burpee Family Papers, York-Sunbury Society Collection, PANB, MC 300, Ms. 5/no. 6; and Petition of James Holden et al, *Sessional Papers, First Session of the First Parliament of the Dominion of Canada, Session 1867-8*, Volume 6 (no. 18), p. 9-10.

[132] R. Babbit to Charles Burpee, April 13, 1868, Burpee Family Papers, York-Sunbury Historical Society Collection, PANB, MC 300, Ms. 5/no. 13.

rapid rehabilitation were drastically reduced.[133] John Glasier himself favoured young David Morrow, but despite his intervention to encourage Morrow to become his successor in the House of Assembly, Morrow deferred.[134] The death of his father in January of 1868 held his emotions captive, debilitating his enthusiasm and preventing him, presently, from taking up a vocation perfectly suited to his temperament and social standing.  Ducking Glasier's solicitations, Morrow gave his blessing to Sheffield farmer Archibald Harrison, who likewise had the support of his uncle, Charles S. Burpee.[135] Only Reuben Hoben, who had risen to the rank of Warden of the Municipality of Sunbury following the retirement of Charles Clowes[136] and won appointment as Lieutenant Colonel in the newly formed 2nd Battalion of the county militia stationed at Oromocto,[137] contested for Burpee's favour with any real vigour.

In the end, however, consanguineous attachments were too compelling for Burpee to resist. Brushing aside Hoben's claims as to his likely virility at the polls, and apparently convinced that

---

[133] *The Reporter and Fredericton Advertizer*, November 20, 1863. Glasier himself was deeply grieved by the tragedy, and was on hand to assist the survivors in any way he could. Still he did nothing to improve the quality of his boats, which *The Carlton Sentinel*, on November 5, 1864, decried as "old rattle traps."

[134] John Glasier to Charles Burpee, March 25, 1868, Burpee Family Papers, York-Sunbury Historical Society Collection, PANB, MC 300, Ms. 5/no. 6.

[135] Reuben Hoben to John Glasier, May 4, 1868, Burpee Family Papers, York-Sunbury Historical Society Collection, PANB, MC 300, Ms. 5/no. 23. Harrison's background placed him in an enviable position from which to launch a political career. His father, Charles Harrison, served in the legislature for Queen's County from 1827 to 1834. His father's sister had married Calvin Hatheway, thus making him a cousin of Hon. George L. Hatheway. And his wife was a daughter of former Sunbury MLA Whitehead Barker.

[136] Kimball, op. cit., p. 44.

[137] David Facey-Crowther, *The New Brunswick Militia: 1787-1867* (Fredericton: New Ireland Press and The New Brunswick Historical Society, 1990), p. 154.

Hoben honestly stood little chance of victory, Burpee threw his support to his nephew — pinning on him the hopes of his party in a showdown with none other than John S. Covert. Recovered from his recent political misfortunes, Covert was undoubtedly confident of victory. Marriage into the Saint John-based shipbuilding Hawes family allowed him to contemplate new ventures. With the Morrows and Brysons effectively retired from ship construction along the Oromocto, Covert pressed his kinsmen for a contract to build the *E.B. Hawes*.[138] Employing men once obligated to the old, now largely extinct patrons of the Oromocto, and thus able to identify himself with the route by which the people's own meagre needs might find fulfilment, Covert filled the vacuum of patronage on the river and naturally positioned himself to assume the unclaimed yet somewhat diluted distinction once possessed by men the likes of the late George Hayward and the elder George Morrow. Covert won by over a hundred votes, very likely accruing the support of the disaffected Liberals loyal to William E. Perley. Faced with a partisan of the presently reviled Burpee, they could no doubt overlook the fact that the man to whom they allocated their preference had once been the object of their deepest scorn.[139]

The Assembly race of 1868 brought to a close a decade of political strife that had fractured traditional opponents and traditional allies alike and produced a schism within the ranks of the Liberal Party that was less conducive to bitter feelings and recrimination than to a general state of confusion. With the near extinction of the old-style politico who was assured of office by the economic and social dependence of his constituents, and the rise instead of party organizations that were able to operate without recourse to the traditional cult of heroic personality so characteristic of the early days of river politics, the people of the Oromocto found themselves deprived of yet another recognizable point of reference. Meanwhile, the changes taking place in communications and transportation did little to restore order to the increasingly complex and disorderly lives of the river's inhabitants, even as the

---

[138] Hancox, op. cit., p. 51.

[139] *The Headquarters*, September 23, 1868; *The Reporter and Fredericton Advertizer*, September 25, 1868; and *The Headquarters*, September 30, 1868.

changes themselves offered opportunities of a pronouncedly positive variety. By the fall of 1867, in the immediate wake of Charles
Burpee's tanning of William Perley and the latter's departure into
the wilderness of Conservatism, the organizers of the Western Extension prepared for the culmination of all their plans and
fatiguing negotiations. The special significance of the railroad to
the Oromocto naturally piqued the interest of the river's inhabitants, who not only found some diversion in the anticipation of its
arrival, but employment as well in the crews hired by sub-con-
tractors John Glasier and George D. Morrow to prosecute the
railway's construction.[140] Within a year's time the route had
reached the river's banks, and the bridge that now spanned the
Porcupine Stream (not far from Tracy's Mills) and the shanties lin-
ing either side of the excavations— inhabited by the more
transient labourers and their superabundance of dependents—
foreshadowed the time when the small lumber settlement
founded over seventy-five years before would be freed of its slav-
ish affiliation with the shabby entrepot at the river's mouth,
allowing it to assume what one correspondent predicted would
be "grander proportions." More work was yet required before this
could come to pass— the breaching of the troublesome western
perimeter of the Oromocto divide and the grading of the road
beds as far as the Maine border— but the two hundred souls at
work on the route, laying ties and driving spikes, in addition to
the men separately employed several miles away on the far side
of the North West Branch in the quarrying of gravel, intimated the
prediction's imminent fulfillment.[141]

While the builders of the Western Extension prepared, somewhat inadvertently, to alter the social and economic orientation of
the Oromocto community, the elite inhabitants of Fredericton
plotted means to connect their fair city with the emerging network
of rails that so far seemed designed to prevent them from sharing
in the related boons of modernity and increased trade. Promises
of money grants from the Province, the government of York
County and the City Council of Fredericton helped instill life into

---

[140] *The Reporter and Fredericton Advertizer*, August 30, 1867.

[141] Id., September 4, 1868.

a corporate body headed by Sheriff Temple.[142] To the cheers of the local populace, the good Sheriff declared his company's intention of pursuing the completion in a year's time of a new branch line that would join the Western Extension at a junction near Hartt's Mills.[143] Alarmed by the necessary erosion of the importance of the Nerepis Road as the main conduit of overland traffic between Fredericton and Saint John,[144] the people of the lower Oromocto naturally shuddered at the prospect of the branch's construction. At a fete sponsored by the assorted magnates of the city, Sunbury Councillor George Harding obligingly commended Temple on the admirable resolve of his company and the benefits the railroad would bring the Province at large, though he could not help but report that sympathy for it in his locale was less than enthusiastic.[145] Work ultimately got underway, though disputes with the owners of expropriated lands, the demands of the proprietor of a gravel pit, a brief pitched battle between a contingent of Fredericton gendarmes and striking workers on the outskirts of town and the ineptitude of the subcontractors intermittently punctuated and stalled the Railway's progress.[146]

By October of 1869 a group of dignitaries, including a somewhat subdued William E. Perley, set out on a pilgrimage to Hartt's Mills via carriage for the purpose of surveying the progress of the nearly completed line, only to suffer the annoyance of a muddy and athletic conveyance by foot once the dirt path they were following became impassable due to a recent bout of precipitation.[147] The distemper of the river further delayed formal opening of traffic on both the Western Extension and its Fredericton tributary,[148] but once a temporary bridge over the North West Branch was

---

[142] *Journals of the Legislative Assembly* (1867), pp. 200-202; and *Journals of the Legislative Council* (1867), pp. 77-78.

[143] *The Reporter and Fredericton Advertizer*, October 30, 1868.

[144] *The Reporter and Fredericton Advertizer* of April 2, 1869 virtually gloated over the imminent termination of the Nerepis Road's usefulness.

[145] Id., November 8, 1867.

[146] Id., June 11, 1869, June 4, 1869, August 20, 1869 and August 27, 1869.

[147] Id., October 8, 1869.

[148] Id., November 12, 1869.

erected to replace another carried away by a jam of logs, the elegance and grandeur of unfettered celebration escaped its confining prison and swept the entire route from Fredericton to Hartt's Mills and all the way, in either direction, to Bangor and Saint John. In early December the great men of the province converged by rail on the little junction. And though the Lieutenant Governor occupied the most privileged rank among the gathered throng of notables, it was John Glasier who received the greatest tribute when the train, on its way to its rendezvous near the forks of the Oromocto, stopped along that section of the track in the rear of the Senator's home in order that he and his one-time mentor, Charles Fisher, might board.[149]

As the engine coursed its way along a route that bisected the Oromocto watershed, the little farm settlements of Grassville, Bunkers and Three Tree Brook flitted by in rapid succession, revealing to the rare observer, underwhelmed by the ingestion of spirits or bored to distraction by the antics of his fellow passengers, the full bloom of a countryside whose degenerate fruits could little sustain the appetite of its poorest and most ancient Caucasian inhabitants. Despite a gradual rejuvenation of the local economy, the ravages originating in the vindictiveness of the American government continued. During the 1867-68 season only one hundred and fourteen square miles of Crown timber land was under license to individual proprietors.[150] Though this was evidence of sagging productivity, it hardly accounted for all of the deficiencies associated with the faltering progress of the industry. A markedly foreign element, beginning with the arrival of William Todd in 1866, had further intruded into the watershed, depriving local entrepreneurs and more regionally oriented magnates of their traditionally intimate role as resident patrons within the community. Even George D. Morrow had little choice but to bow in homage to the newcomers. When Alfred Robinson completed the consolidation of the North West Branch through the establishment of a Crown corporation known as the Oromocto River Driving Company, Morrow was lucky enough to join with

---

149. Id., December 3, 1869.

150. *The Royal Gazette*, July 22, 1868.

him as a member of the company's Board of Directors.[151] The continuing vitality of their business and their own traditional alliance with the Morrows allowed the Tracys to resist the ravenous hunger of the new cartel, but the tired old Hartt and Kelley establishments on either branch of the river represented nothing more than appetizing little morsels to be gobbled up at leisure between more satisfying entrees of processed boards and planks.[152] The reduced market for forest products naturally diminished the demand for the articles manufactured from timber. Shipbuilding survived, but the scale on which it was prosecuted was smaller than in years past — its longevity on the river owing simply to the family commitments of the river's last active shipbuilder, John S. Covert. When the advantage of relocating in Saint John and the American States at last outweighed the expense of conducting business in inland New Brunswick, Covert's kinsmen would revoke their covenant and disappear from the Oromocto forever.[153]

For the poor man, dependent for his livelihood on the vitality of the shipyards and lumber camps, agriculture offered an obvious solution to the quandary of unsatisfied material need, but even here the solution was not a really viable one. Very little unsettled, arable territory remained, and as the incentive of timber that had stimulated the settlement urge in the past had been removed by the long-term downward slide of the economy, few

---

[151] "Bill to Incorporate the Sunbury River Driving Company," Records of the Legislative Assembly, PANB, RS 24, 1867/bi/file 4/no. 117.

[152] Robinson and Company, did in fact purchase the Kelley Mills on January 20, 1873. According to the deed of sale, the Robinsons had already been conducting business at the old Hartt Mill for some time.

[153] The last ship the Hawes family built on the Oromocto was the 1191 ton *Canon Harrison*. It was launched in 1876. In 1883 Fredericton poet Martin Butler visited the village and found it a shabby place, where several stores and rum shops inadequately filled the vacuum left by the decline of manufactures. According to him, the days when "the proud old shire town of Sunbury County could point with pride to her ships in every port of the world" were over, and that it was "now but a relic of by-gone glory." Ten years later, however, shipbuilders on the Oromocto attempted a comeback with the launching of the schooner *Alfred Bartlett*. Unfortunately, the comeback did not last. See *The York Gleaner*, August 29, 1883 and *The Daily Gleaner* July 25, 1892.

there were who could fathom the prudence of resorting to the land. Even if the option was still an attractive one, the old bottleneck remained. Land clearance and farm development required money. The poor man had none. As for the authorized arbiters of land settlement, the Sunbury Agricultural Society, they continued to indulge in their own personal exigencies, leaving those few inhabitants of the Oromocto willing to try their hand at farming without proper leadership and inspiration. The old sectional jealousy between the Oromocto and the settlements of Sheffield and Maugerville did, however, offer some potential for alleviation of the problems in this regard. Intended to correct the "malpractices and corruption of the past years" perpetrated by the old society against the Oromocto, the elite members from Burton seceded — the irony of the name of their new society, the Sunbury Union Agricultural Society, becoming all too evident when the members of the old society flew into an uproar over their colleagues' insurrection.[154] Rejecting the pretentious annual fairs that had been used by the self-satisfied planters of the St. John to arrogantly display the products of their leisurely vocation, the new society adopted the long-recommended practice of granting premiums to meritorious farmers.[155] But even though the new society's innovation finally began to address the needs of the Oromocto's people, it was, in the end, for a certain segment of the river's population, a gesture that came all too late.

For the poor of the river, the periodic visits of the expatriate Hugh McMinn seemed more laden with promise than any potential boon offered by the railroad or the new agricultural society. Successful in his own humble way as a lumberman-farmer, bringing word of new prospects elsewhere for employment in the traditional business of the river, Hugh McMinn undoubtedly took on the proportions of some minor prophet, relegated to the dingier pages of the book of life, yet possessing the keys to the locked door behind which reposed a trove of precious mysteries. The

---

[154] "The Tenth Annual Report of the Board of Agriculture of the Province of New Brunswick," *Journals of the Legislative Assembly* (1870), Appendix, pp. 49-55.

[155] Id., pp. 125-127.

recent history of the river had been marked by severe discombob-
ulation: reorientation of local government; disappearance of the
great patrons in favour of disinterested outsiders, political parties
and new social institutions; ideological ferment; factionalism;
and, perhaps most important of all, prolonged economic prostration. With the sprouting of new highways, the building of the
railway and the depreciation of the importance of the timber
drive, even the river itself was becoming less relevant in the lives
of the people. Though the jaded divinity immersed within its waters might lash out and attempt to destroy the outward
manifestations of its irrelevancy, the supreme role the river
played in uniting a diverse community made up of numerous little settlements strung out over a thirty-mile distance was all but
done with. The gravity binding the redundant population to the
river's banks thus weakened, and the river itself entertaining little
in the way of continuing fascination for the bulk of its inhabitants,
the moment was ripe for the thoughtful consideration by the people of the Oromocto of the option to leave the watershed and
relocate someplace where the possibilities for continuing on in a
more or less familiar fashion were not only assured, but ebul-
liently demonstrated by the success of one of their own.

The option to leave was nowhere more pronounced than
among those members of the lower orders of Oromocto society
who possessed an intimate bond of affiliation with Mr. McMinn.
Family connection, both inherited and acquired, represented the
most potent of prerequisites for finding admittance into the small
migratory body that departed for North Lake. Historical affinity
and common experience on the river of a markedly less familial
nature were also determining factors. A universal adherence to
the Free Will Baptist creed, a sympathy for the Orange Lodge, if
not for temperance, and a common (yet lately diluted) economic
and social dependence on a small group of river patrons had
bound the migrants up almost inextricably. And though politics
may have occasionally relegated some of them to competing factions, the essential similarity of their experience within a single
political dynamic was hardly conducive of long-term malediction.
A largely unknown number of minor personal reasons also contributed to the general climate favouring group migration.

For Hugh McMinn's brother-in-law, Daniel James Wood, the

decision to leave was an easy one. Deprived of half his land through the incompetence of the agents of the Crown, and denied his traditional employment by the unfeeling dictates of the market, Wood prepared his family's passage to a more promising locale.[156] Victimization by market trends likewise impelled McMinn's brother George, George McMinn's father-in-law James S. Frost, Wood's son-in-law Stephen Howe, Howe's cousin Andrew Howe and three sons of John Anderson— Joseph, Frederick and David— to heed Wood's example. Taking temporary leave of their dependents, the men journeyed to the St. Croix in the winter of 1868-69, where they apparently took up residence in the Hills' Forest City boarding house until private lots could be staked out, trees cleared and permanent homes erected.[157] Obediah Buckingham, who was intimately connected with this initial group of migrants (being a brother-in-law of Andrew Howe and a cousin of Stephen Howe), momentarily refrained from going with them, though it seems clear that had it not been for the timing of his marriage to a daughter of Charles DeWitt, and perhaps the shadowy dictates of his mother, who seems to have controlled the family finances, he certainly would have joined them in the first difficult days of settlement.

The arrival of the Oromocto contingent in North Lake could not have been more auspiciously timed. Having just purchased the tannery from the Hill brothers for $30,000, Thaxter Shaw was in the midst of planning a series of renovations intended to enhance its current level of production.[158] Constrained by the terms

---

[156] While Daniel was away preparing a home in North Lake for his family, the infamous Saxby Gale swept through Victoria Settlement. His daughter Almara, the wife of Stephen Howe, was staying with her mother when the storm hit and only narrowly escaped injury when a portion of the roof fell inches away from her and her sleeping baby.

[157] Their presence in North Lake in the spring of 1869 is attested to by their signatures on a petition of North Lake settlers requesting the creation of a new parish, to extend from the Narrows to Eel River and to be called Wilmot. See Petition of Patrick Selvage et al., Records of the Legislative Assembly, PANB, RS 24, 1869/pe/file 1/no. 11.

[158] *The Saint Croix Courier*, March 4, 1869 and March 18, 1869.

of his purchase from marketing alcohol or promoting any other variety of immorality normally associated with large groups of men unencumbered by the responsibilities of family life, Shaw fostered the habits of sobriety among his employees. Still retaining the New Brunswick portion of the Forest City township, where they were already preparing to erect a new store and install new machinery in their sawmill, the Hills likewise contributed to the cultivation of clean living— opening up the top floor of a new meeting hall to the newly organized Society of Templars, building a Methodist chapel and encouraging the establishment of a parochial school for the edification of the young. The completion of the Western Extension put rail traffic to within ten miles of the thriving little community at the Narrows, and though overland travel in general in and out of Forest City was still somewhat difficult, Shaw's intention to sponsor a steamer between Vanceboro and the outlet at the base of Grand Lake offered the real potential for more facile connection with the outside world.[159]

Forest City, however, for all its many conveniences, was not the ultimate destination of the wayward tribe from the Oromocto. Most likely with McMinn's assistance, the emigres located lots at Green Mountain and its environs, overlooking and abutting the various bays and inlets that accentuated Grand Lake's eastern flank. Once the immediate needs for shelter were met, a larger stream of dependents from the Oromocto commenced, creating a current that finally dislodged the dawdling members of the Buckingham family from their moorings on the river. Obediah and his brother James came first, charged by their mother with the task of purchasing suitable land for the entire clan to settle upon with money obtained through the sale, in 1870, of a portion of the family's South Branch estate.[160] Once done, mother Buckingham made her way to North Lake, followed by her son Enoch, who was accompanied by his kinsman William Tucker.[161]

---

[159] Id., March 18, 1869.

[160] Sunbury County Registry Office Records, PANB, RS 95, 26/137; and York County Registry Office Records, PANB, RS 98, 61/372.

[161] His presence in North Lake, while not verifiable by any documentary source, is confirmed by the great-granddaughter of Enoch Buckingham, Ella (Buckingham) Kasson, who reported that "uncle Bill

As the final consequences of the partial dissolution of the Oromocto community unfolded, others, not initially involved in the migration, also made their way to North Lake. John Boone's son, William Joseph, abandoned Victoria around 1870. His cousin Alexander, who had left Geary for Fredericton some years before and found work there as a carpenter, followed in 1872, bringing with him his brother, Joseph Albert Boone, his wife and a large brood of children. Having inherited nothing following his father William's death, Ozias Carr sold off a second-rate parcel of land and made the journey west, conveying with him his wife (a sister of Alexander Boone) and the awful, as yet unrealized, implications of overt vice and secret perversion.[162] Unable to properly care for her two children alone, the widow of George Henry Howe (George having died in 1863) sent her son Abner to live with her former neighbour, Daniel James Wood, establishing in this way an alliance that would be formally cemented with young Abner's marriage to Wood's daughter Mariah. Several members of the family of James Till (including, at one point, James himself) Joseph, son of Yankee John Howe, Gideon Hamilton DeWitt (son of Charles DeWitt), Gideon's blind cousin, Salome, and even Charles Tapley, a near kinsman of Assemblyman David Tapley and distant relation of the Geary Carrs, rounded out the migration, so that by 1881 there were over a hundred former residents of the Oromocto, representing most of the river's main settlements, congregated around that great geological prominence at the centre of the North Lake district known as Green Mountain. Contacts

---

Tucker" accompanied the latter from the Oromocto. He did, not, however, stay very long. Before the census of 1871 was taken he had returned to the Oromocto.

[162] Ozias was a strange and unfortunate man. Springing from a family in which alcoholism was both rampant as well as accepted (his mother had a vision of his late, and perpetually intoxicated, brother entering heaven with a bottle in his back pocket), Carr was adept in the manufacture of moonshine. It is said that after his wife turned him out of the home when she discovered an incestuous relationship between Ozias and one of their daughters, Carr retreated into the woods around North Lake, making his livelihood by occasional veterinary ministrations to sick livestock and the sale of his home-grown liquor to local lumbermen.

between the new residents of North Lake and their old homes on the Oromocto continued for years to come, as the inestimable power of a thousand seen and unseen bonds existing between the migrants and the river could not help but compel many of them to make occasional sojourns to the countryside of their birth. Intermarriage between members of the two distant communities naturally occurred, as did periodic shifts in residence that would continue well into the middle decades of the twentieth century.[163]

The former residents of the Oromocto who settled Green Mountain constituted, in essence, a colony. It was a colony existing within an older community, focused around the personage of Hugh McMinn and made up of individuals drawn by the existence in their new home of opportunities no longer available to them in their place of origin. By no means a man of great historic accomplishment, McMinn nevertheless represented the promise of life on the frontier. He conveyed to his people a sense of reward to be found abroad, away from an increasingly stultifying, unattractive existence on the banks of the Oromocto, and led them, in a fashion less heroic than Moses, into a land flowing, if not with milk and honey, then with waters polluted by the organic and inorganic by-products of the tanning process. Romantic allusions aside, McMinn was simply a man. What he did, while interesting, was not profoundly remarkable. The forces at work in the Oromocto watershed, whether taking political, spiritual, economic or social form, more than adequately account for the peculiarity of a group of Oromocto residents following the path taken by one of their kinsmen. It is these forces, simultaneously binding the migrants together over the course of a generation's time and ultimately driving them from their home, that are the dominant protagonists of this protracted story. Regardless of the vibrant and romantic allure of the river's hidden genius, in spite of the intriguing experience of the great patrons, and however amusing might be the foibles of humanity perpetrated over a period of

---

[163] Between 1881 and 1940 Guy Tracy Boone, Leslie DeWitt, Charles Howe, Frederick William Howe, Philip Newton Howe, Roxanna Howe, Hanford Kingston, Ida Kingston Rachel Kingston, Henry Till, Hugh Allen Till, John Almon Till are known to have moved back and forth between Oromocto and North Lake.

forty years, it is the irresistible progress of time, the girding effects of common experience, the limitations of geography and the dictates of the market that must claim the highest accolades. Time, common experience, geography and the market had all conspired to create the Oromocto community. And, as far as one particular segment of the river's population was concerned, time, common experience, geography and the market dissolved it. They will ever prevail. As it was on the Oromocto, so it would be on the St. Croix.

# APPENDIX A

# MAPS

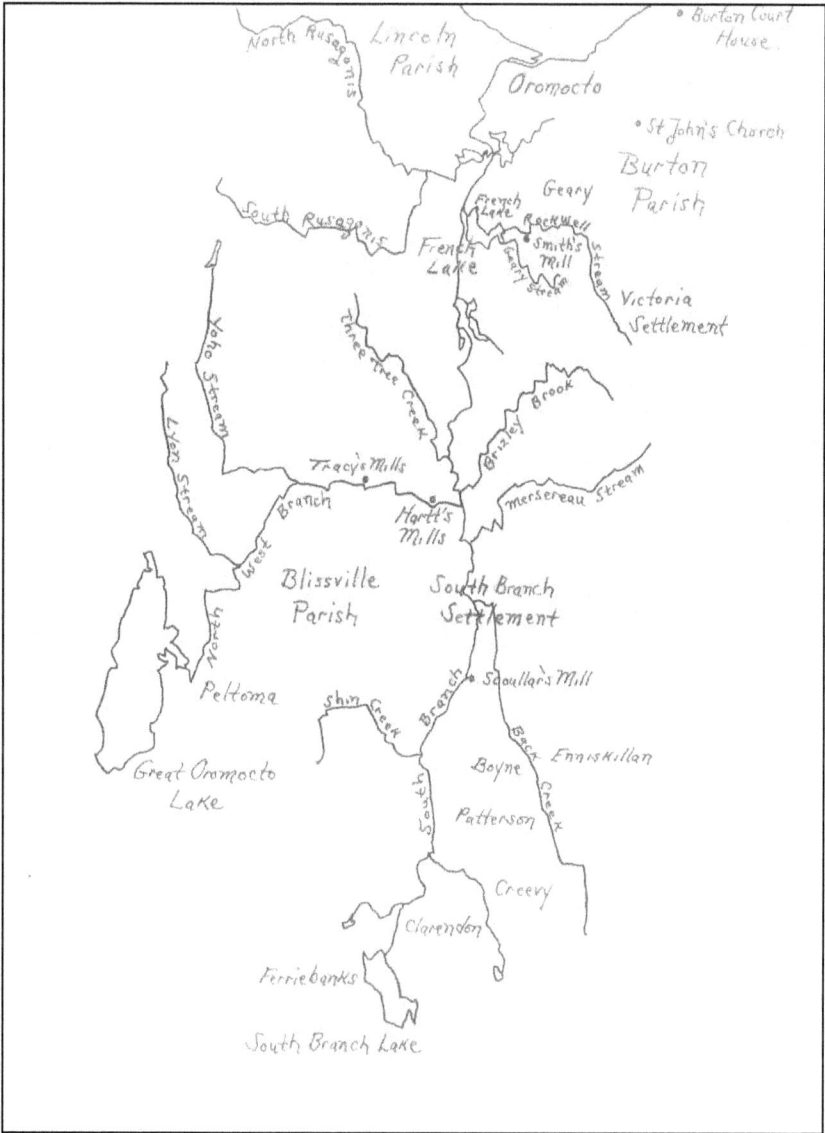

THE OROMOCTO WATERSHED

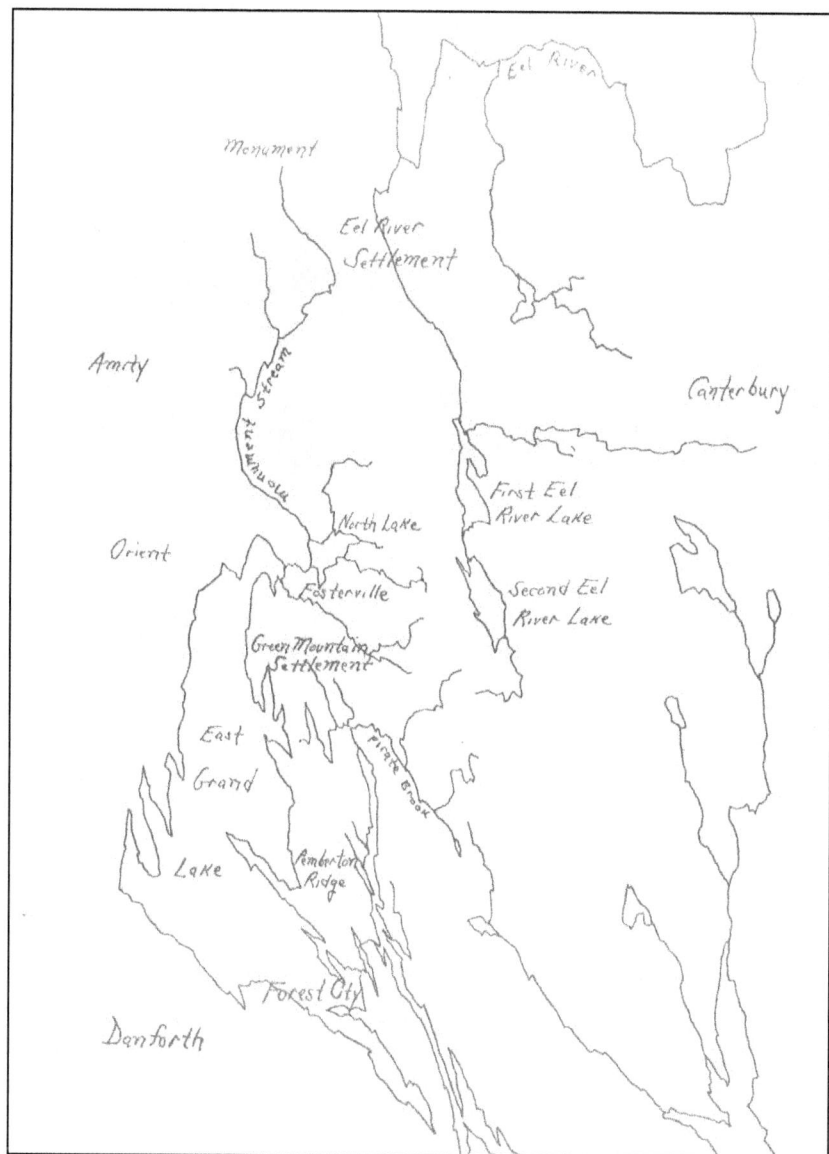

NORTH LAKE

# APPENDIX B

# GENEALOGICAL TABLES

BUCKINGHAM-FROST-HOWE-MILLS-McMINN-TUCKER-WOOD FAMILY NETWORK

BOONE-CARR-TILL FAMILY NETWORK

George Hayward=Anne Drury

William Boone=Anne Hayward

William Boone=Ruth Hill

Samuel Boone=Catherine DeWitt
d/of Everet

Alexander Tapley=Abigail Hood

Hannah Tapley=William Carr

Sarah Nason=Everet
d/of Lemuel Boone

Samuel Boone=Hannah
Boone Jr

Sarah Tracy=John E. Boone
grd/of Solomon

Minnie Gray=Samuel K. Boone

Guy Tracy Boone

Asa Ann William=Mary A.
Carr Boone Carr Whelpley

Ebenezer Carr

Amesa Carr

Edward=Martha
Carr Boone

Ruth=James
Boone Till

John=Elizabeth
Boone Haines

William=Margaret
Boone Morrell

George=Mary
Boone Haines

Nathan
Boone

Alexander=Sarah
Boone Perry

Joseph Albert
Boone

Sarah Boone=William A.
Carr

George Ozias Carr=Charlotte
Boone

Gilderoy Alex. Sam. James W. Gg.A. Sarah Wm.
Carr Carr Carr Carr Carr Carr Till

Margaret Howe=Alexander
d/of George Till

John E.=Mary N. Mills
Till d/of James

John Aimon
Till

John Henry Till=Alice Howe
d/of Stephen

John=Martha James=Eliza A. Wm. Joseph=Mary Howe Mary A.=Yenkee
Till Till Boone Boone d/of Wm Sr Boone

Ariana 2.=George N. 1. Margaret
Boone Till McMinn
d/of George

James
Till

Melissa A.=Joseph
Till Howe

Hugh Allen Till

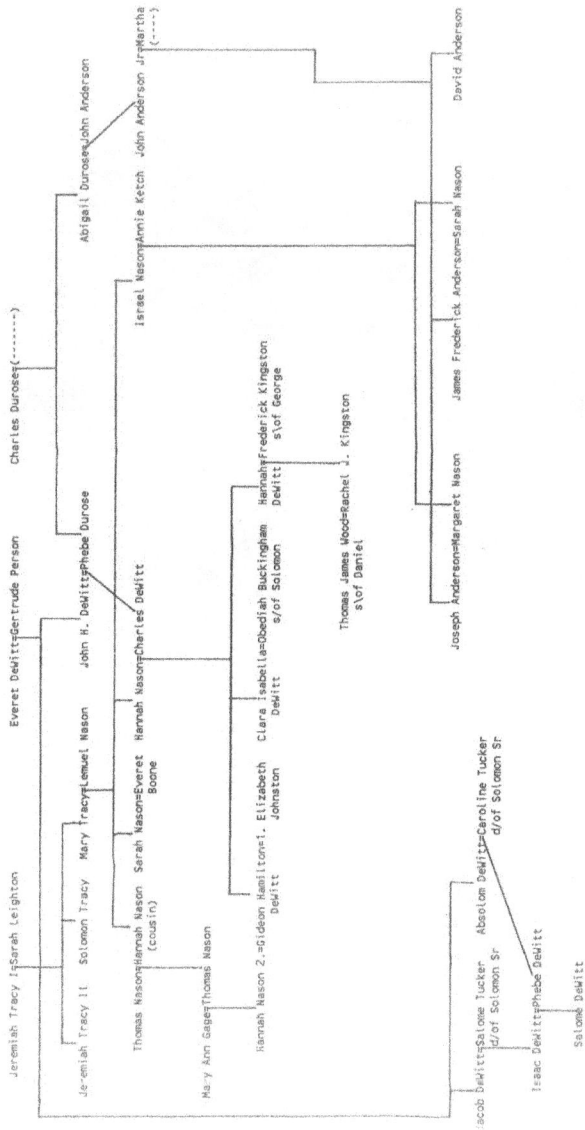

ANDERSON-DEWITT-DUROSE-NASON-TRACY FAMILY NETWORK

BIBLIOGRAPHY

## I. Primary Sources

## A. Public Archives of New Brunswick

**1. Government Records**

RS 1 Journals of the Proceedings of the Legislative Assembly of New Brunswick (1830-1870)

RS 2 Journals of the Proceedings of the Legislative Council of New Brunswick (1830-1870)

RS 4 Synoptic Reports of the Debates of the Legislative Assembly, 1837-38, 1852, 1854-58, 1860-62, 1865-67.

RS 6 Minutes and Orders in Council.

RS 7 Executive Council Records (PAC microfilm series).

RS 9 Executive Council Cabinet Series

RS 13 Provincial Secretary Correspondence

RS 22 Railway Administration Records

RS 24 Records of the Legislative Assembly

RS 42 Supreme Court Records, 1785-1835

RS 55 Chancery Court Records

RS 60 Clerk of the Chancery: Election Court Records

RS 66 King's County Probate Court Records

RS 71 St. John County Probate Court Records

RS 72 Sunbury County Probate Court Records

RS 89 King's County Registry Office Records

RS 92 Queen's County Registry Office Records

RS 94 Saint John County Registry Office Records

RS 95 Sunbury County Registry Office Records

RS 98 York County Registry Office Records

RS 107 Department of Natural Resources: Crown Lands

RS 108 Land Petitions

RS 126 Department of Public Works Administration Records

RS 157 Sunbury County Council Records

RS 184  New Brunswick Museum Branch Records
RS 272  Land Petitions
RS 344  Records of Lt. Governor Sir John Harvey
RS 345  Records of Lt. Governor Sir William McBean George Colebrooke
RS 346  Records of Lt. Governor Sir Edmund Head
RS 347  Records of Lt. Governor John Henry Thomas Manners-Sutton
RS 348  Records of Lt. Governor Arthur Hamilton Gordon
RS 538  Records of Warrants, Appointments and Commissions
RS 555  Records of Immigration Administration
RS 566  Records of Old Soldiers' and Widows' Pensions
RS 598  Statute Labour Administration Records
RS 625  Agricultural Societies Administration Records
RS 637  Records of the Surveyor General
RS 656  Crown Lands Branch Maps and Plans
RS 663  Timber and Sawmill Records
RS 686  Land Grant Records
RS 687  Grant Survey Return Plans
RS 816  Elections Administration Records

## 2. Private Sector Records

MC 80  Published Holdings (see Works Consulted)
MC 223  Diocese of Fredericton Records.
MC 230  Society for the Propagation of the Gospel Records.
MC 267  Bell Genealogical Collection.
MC 300  York-Sunbury Historical Society Collection.
MC 361  New Brunswick Agricultural Societies' Records.
MC 382  Frost Papers.
MC 416  Colonial Office Papers.
MC 431  John Nason Collection.
MC 451  Diary of Thomas O. Miles.
MC 493  Audit Office, War Office.
MC 1001  Hill Family Papers.
MC 1162  Rusagonis United Baptist Church Records.
MC 1396  The George Hayward Collection.
MC 1706  Fredericton Junction Family Histories.
F 7822  Records of the Lincoln Baptist Church.
F 8114  Records of the Patterson Baptist Church.

### 3. The Census

1851 Census of New Brunswick, Carleton County
1861 Census of New Brunswick, Carleton County
1851 Census of New Brunswick, St. John County
1851 Census of New Brunswick, Sunbury County
1861 Census of New Brunswick, Sunbury County
1871 Census of New Brunswick, Sunbury County
1881 Census of New Brunswick, Sunbury County
1891 Census of New Brunswick, Sunbury County
1851 Census of New Brunswick, York County
1861 Census of New Brunswick, York County
1871 Census of New Brunswick, York County
1881 Census of New Brunswick, York County
1891 Census of New Brunswick, York County

### 4. Newspapers

*The Carleton Sentinel* (Woodstock)
*The Headquarters* (Fredericton)
*The Morning News* (St. John)
*The Morning Telegraph* (St. John)
*The New Brunswick Courier* (St. John)
*The Provincial Patriot* (St. Stephen)
*The Reporter and Fredericton Advertizer* (Fredericton)
*The Royal Gazette* (Fredericton)
*The Saint Croix Courier* (St. Stephen)
*The York Gleaner* (Fredericton)

## B. Public Archives of Nova Scotia

RG 1  Land Grants.
RG 5  Petitions for Claims.
1827 Census of Nova Scotia.

## C. Public Archives of Canada

MG 24 C/47  Journal of George H. Perley.
MG 27 B/29  Joseph Howe Papers.
MG 27 I/D/15  Tilley Papers.

## D. Charlotte County Historical Society

Grace Hellen Mowat Collection.

## E. Allen Boone Collection

Letter, John Smith to Jeremiah Smith, September 16, 1852.

Letter, Lena E. (Smith) Phillips to "Friend," February 6, 1953.

Robina (Harper) Brown, "Lauvina Settlement: An Account Written for Presentation to a Meeting of the Geary-Lauvina Women's Instititute, 1952."

Allen Boone, "History and Records of King William L.O.L. #114, Geary, New Brunswick."

## F. John A. Wood Collection

Letter, Abner Mersereau to "Wife," September 13, 1852.

## II.  Secondary Works

Acheson, T.W. *Saint John: The Making of a Colonial Urban Society*. Toronto: University of Toronoto Press, 1985.

------------------. "Hugh Johnston." *Dictionary of Canadian Biography*. Toronto: University of Toronto Press, 1988. Volume VII, pp. 444-445.

------------------. "John McNeil Wilmot." *Dictionary of Canadian Biography*. Toronto: University of Toronto Press, 1988. Volume VII, pp. 915-916.

----------------. "Andrew Rainsford Wetmore." *Dictionary of Canadian Biography*. Toronto: University of Toronto Press, 1990. Volume XII, pp. 1096-1098.

Baker, William M. "Isaac Burpee." *Dictionary of Canadian Biography*. Toronto: University of Toronto Press, 1982. Volume XI, pp. 133-135.

Baillie, Thomas. *Report of the Surveyor General of New Brunswick Upon the Present State of the Crown Lands*. Fredericton: J. Simpson, 1849.

Banta, Theodore M. *Lineage of Thomas Sayre, A Founder of Southhampton*. New York, 1901.

Barnes, Joshua N. *Lights and Shadows of Eighty Years: An Autobiography*. St. John: Barnes and Company, 1911.

Bates, Walter. *Kingston and the Loyalists of the Spring Fleet of 1783 with Reminiscences of Early Days in Connecticut: A Narrative*. Ed. William Obder Raymond. Reprint; Woodstock: Non-Entity Press, 1980.

Bell, David Graham. "The Confederation Issue in Charlotte County, New Brunswick." Unpublished M.A. Thesis, Queen's University, 1976.

-------------------------. *Early Loyalist Saint John: The Origin of New Brunswick Politics-- 1783-1786*. Fredericton: New Ireland Press, 1983.

Bell. E.W. *Israel Kenny and his Descendants*. Published by Author, 1944.

Bill, Ingraham E. *Fifty Years with the Baptist Ministers of the Maritime Provinces of Canada*. Saint John: Barnes and Company, 1880.

Bitterman, Rusty. "Middle River: The Social Structure of Agriculture in a Nineteenth-Century Cape Breton Community." Unpublished M.A. Thesis, UNB, 1987.

---------------------. "The Hierarchy of the Soil: Land and Labour in a 19th Century Cape Breton Community." *Acadiensis*, Volume XVII, No. 1 (Autumn, 1988), pp. 33-55.

Boone, Allen. "Boone Family Records." Typescript by author, 1988. Housed in the PANB. MC 80/no 1409.

Boone, Allen and Gerald Carr. "Some Geary Carrs." Typescript by authors, 1986. Housed in the PANB. MC 80/no. 1469.

Boone, Lloyd G. "Boone Family Records, 1686-1987." Typescript by author, ca. 1987. Housed in PANB. MC 80/no. 1383.

British Military and Naval Records Index. Copy on microfilm in possession of the Harriet Irving Library at the University of New Brunswick, RG 8, I, Series C.

Brookes, Alan A. "Out-Migration from the Maritime Provinces, 1860-1900: Some Preliminary Considerations." *Acadiensis*, Volume V (Spring 1976), No. 2, pp. 26-55.

Buckingham, James Silk. *Canada, Nova Scotia, New Brunswick and Other Brittish Provinces in North America With a Plan of National Colonization.* London: Fisher, Son and Company, 1843.

Buckner, Phillip. "Sir William McBean George Colebrooke." *Dictionary of Canadian Biography.* Toronto: University of Toronto Press, 1976. Volume IX, pp. 145-148.

--------------------. "George Ludlow Wetmore." Dictionary of Canadian Biography. Toronto: University of Toronto Press, 1987. Volume VI, p. 810.

Bumstead. J.M. "Seth Noble." Dictionary of Canadian Biography. Toronto: University of Toronto Press, 1983. Volume V, pp. 627-628.

Campbell, Eugene. *French Lake.* Oromocto: Published by author, 1981.

------------------------. *Oromocto in View.* Oromocto: Roger's Publishing, 1982.

Campbell, Eugene, Ellen A. Wright and G.S. d'Avray Bailey Jr. *From Timber to Brick: Oromocto Heritage Houses — to 1950.* Oromocto: H. Randall Press, 1979.

Campbell, Gail. "'Smashers' and 'Rummies': Voters and the Rise of Parties in Charlotte County, New Brunswick, 1846-1857." *Historical Papers.* Ottawa: Canadian Historical Association, 1986. Pp. 86-116.

-----------------. "Disenfranchised but not Quiescent: Women Petitioners in New Brunswick in the Mid-19th Century." *Acadiensis*. Volume XVII, No. 2 (Spring, 1989), pp. 22-54.

Canada, Government of. Sessional Papers. *First Session of the Parliament of the Dominion of Canada, 1867-8*. Volume 8.

Clark, S.D. *Church and Sect in Canada*. Toronto: University of Toronto Press, 1948.

Clowes, Raymond S. *The Clowes Family Tree*. 2 Volumes. Published by author, 1985.

Coldham, Peter Wilson. *American Loyalist Claims*. Volume I. Washington: National Genealogical Society, 1980.

Creighton, Donald. *The Road to Confederation: The Emergence of Canada, 1863-1867*. Boston: Houghton Mifflin Company, 1865.

Davis, Harold A. *An International Community on the Saint Croix: 1640-1930*. Orono: University of Maine Press, 1950.

DeWitt, Katherine and Norma Alexander. *Days of Old: A History of Fredericton Junction*. Fredericton: Sunbury West Historical Society, 1987.

Elliot, Bruce. *Irish Migrants in the Canadas: A New Approach*. Kingston: McGill-Queen's University Press, 1989.

Facey-Crowther, David. *The New Brunswick Militia: 1787-1867*. Fredericton: New Ireland Press & The New Brunswick Historical Society, 1990.

*Free Christian Baptist General Conference of New Brunswick. Extracts from the Rules and Minutes of the Free Christian Baptist General Conference of New Brunswick, Held at Lincoln, N.B., 6th, 8th and 9th July, 1850.* Saint John: George W. Day, 1850.

Gesner, Abraham. *First Report on the Geological Survey of the Province of New Brunswick*. Saint John: Henry Chubb, 1839.

----------------------. *Fourth Report on the Geological Survey of the Province of New Brunswick*. Saint John: Henry Chubb, 1842.

------------------------. *Fifth Report on the Geological Survey of the Province of New Brunswick*. Saint John: Henry Chubb, 1843.

------------------------. *New Brunswick: With Notes for Emigrants*. London: Simmonds and Ward, 1847.

Godfrey, W.G. "James Glennie." *Dictionary of Canadian Biography*. Toronto: University of Toronto Press, 1983. Volume V, pp. 347-358.

Grady, Rex. "From Oromocto to North Lake: Rural Decline and Migration in Nineteenth Century New Brunswick." Unpublished M.A. Thesis, University of New Brunswick (Fredericton), 1993.

----------------. "'With Unfeigned Regret': New Brunswick's Response to the Great St. John's Fire of 1846." *Newfoundland Quarterly*, Volume 88 (1994), No. 4, pp. 51-54.

Graves, James C. and Horace B. Graves. *New Brunswick Political Biography*. 11 Volumes. Typescript by authors. Housed in the PANB as MC 1156.

Hancox, Brent. "Five Decades of Wood and Sail: The Shipbuilding Industry of Oromocto." Typescript by author, 1984.

Hannay, James. *History of New Brunswick*. 2 Volumes. Saint John: John A. Bowes, 1909.

Harper, J. Russell. *Historical Directory of New Brunswick Newspapers and Periodicals*. Fredericton: University of New Brunswick, 1961.

Hatheway, Calvin Luther. *The History of New Brunswick, From its First Settlement*. Fredericton: James P.A. Phillips, 1846.

Hayward, George H. Carleton County, New Brunswick Marriage Volume I: 1832-1887. Fredericton: Published by author, nd.

--------------------------. *1851 Census, Sunbury County, New Brunswick, Canada*. Fredericton: published by author, 1974.

--------------------------. *York County New Brunswick, Marriage Register, Volume 1: 1812-1837-- A Transcription of the Original*. Fredericton: Published by author, 1986.

----------------------. *The Nevers Family of Sunbury County*. Fredericton: Published by author, 1991.

Hazen, Tracy Elliot. *The Hazen Family in America*. Thomason, CT: Published by Robert Hazen, 1947.

Hill, Louise. *Maugerville: 1763-1963*. Fredericton: Published by Author, 1963.

Jack, David Russell. *Biographical Data Relating to New Brunswick Families Especially of Loyalist Descent*. Saint John: Saint John Free Public Library, 1980.

Jack, Isaac Allen. *Jack's Biographical Review*. Boston: Biographical Review Publishing Company, 1900.

----------------------. *History of the Saint Andrew's Society of Saint John, New Brunswick: 1798-1903*. Saint John: J. and A. McMillan, 1913.

Johnson, Daniel F. *New Brunswick Vital Statistics From Newspapers*. 45 Volumes. Fredericton/Saint John: Published by author, 1982-1992.

Johnston, J.F.W. *Report on the Agricultural Capabilities of the Province of New Brunswick*. Fredericton: J. Simpson, 1850.

Kimball, Harold G. *History of Oromocto*. Fredericton: Unipress, 1966.

Knorr, Sharon. "Hoyt Pioneer Cemetery." Typescript by author, 1986. Housed in PANB.

Knowlton, I.C. *Annals of Calais, Maine and Saint Stephen, New Brunswick, Including the Village of Milltown, Maine and the Present Town of Milltown, New Brunswick*. Calais: J.A. Sears, Printer, 1875.

Lawrence, Joseph Wilson. *The Judges of New Brunswick and Their Times*. Reprint, 1905; Fredericton: Acadiensis Press, 1983.

Lovell, John. *Hutchinson's New Brunswick Directory for 1865-66*. Montreal: John Lovell, 1866.

----------------. *Lovell's Province of New Brunswick Directory for 1871.* Reprint, 1871; London, Ontario: The Genealogical Research Library, 1984.

MacNutt, W.S. "The Politics of the Timber Trade in Colonial New Brunswick: 1825-1840." *The Canadian Historical Review,* Volume 29 (1949), pp. 47-65.

----------------. *New Brunswick, A History: 1784-1867.* Reprint; Toronto: University of Toronto Press, 1985.

----------------. *The Atlantic Provinces: The Emergence of a Colonial Society: 1712-1857.* Toronto: McClelland and Stewart, 1965.

----------------. "Thomas Baillie." *The Dictionary of Canadian Biography.* Toronto: University of Toronto Press, 1976. Volume IX, pp. 21-24.

----------------. "John Richard Partelow." *Dictionary of Canadian Biography.* Toronto: University of Toronto Press, 1976. Volume IX, pp. 622-623.

McAlpine's Publishing. *McAlpine's New Brunswick Directory.* Saint John: McAlpine's Publishing Company, 1903.

McFarland, C. Tracy. "Genealogy of the Tracy Family." Typescript by author, 1966.

McGrand, Samuel. *Backward Glances at Sunbury and Queen's.* Fredericton: The New Brunswick Historical Society, 1967.

McKinnon, William. *Over the Portage: Early History of the Miramichi.* Fredericton: New Ireland Press, 1989.

Moffitt, Mrs. George Webb. "DeWitt Family History." Typescript by author. Housed in PANB. MC 80/no. 1360.

Monro, Alexander. *New Brunswick; With a Brief Outline of Nova Scotia and Prince Edward Island.* Halifax; Richard Nugent, 1855.

Moore, William D. "Sunbury County: 1760-1830." Unpublished M.A. Thesis, UNB, 1977.

New Brunswick Baptist Association. *Minutes of the Meetings of the New Brunswick Baptist Association.* Saint John: Henry Chubb, 1822-1844.

New Brunswick Society for the Encouragement of Agriculture, Home Manufactures and Commerce Throughout the Province. *Report of the New Brunswick Society for the Encouragement of Agriculture, Home Manufactures and Commerce Throughout the Province.* Fredericton: James Hogg, 1851.

Nova Scotia Historical Society. *Collections of the Nova Scotia Historical Society.* Volume 13.

Parsons, Stanley. "Hoyt Baptist Church Cemetery, 150 Years: 1838-1988." Typescript by author, 1988. Housed in the PANB. MC 80/no. 642.

Patterson, Stephen E. "Israel Perley." *Dictionary of Canadian Biography.* Toronto: University of Toronto Press, 1983. Volume V, pp. 665-667.

Payzant, Joan M. "'Mc' Loyalists: McMinn, McMane, McMain, M'Minn." *The Nova Scotia Genealogist.* Volume 1 (1983), No. 2, pp. 50-56.

Perley, M.V.B. *The History and Genealogy of the Perley Family.* Salem: Published by author, 1906.

Phillips, Miriam L. *Facts and Folklore: Tracy and Little Lake Area.* Fredericton: Published by author, 1985.

Provincial Archives of New Brunswick. *The New Brunswick Census of 1871, Sunbury County.* Fredericton: The Queen's Printer, 1989.

Rayburn, Alan. *Geographical Names of New Brunswick.* Ottawa: Surveying and Mapping, Department of Energy, Mines and Resources, 1975.

Raymond. William Obder. *The River Saint John: Its Physical Features, Legends and History from 1604 to 1784.* Reprint 1910; Sackville: The Tribune Press, 1950.

Renfree, Harry A. *Heritage and Horizon: The Baptist Story in Canada.* Mississauga, Ontario: Canadian Baptist Federation, 1988.

Russell, Loris S. "Abraham Gesner." *Dictionary of Canadian Biography.* Toronto: University of Toronto Press, 1976. Volume IX, pp. 308-312.

Sabine, Lorenzo. *Biographical Sketches of Loyalists of the American Revolution*. 2 Volumes. Boston: Little, Brown, 1864.

Saunders, S.A. *The Economic History of the Maritime Provinces*. Ottawa: Royal Commission of Dominion-Province Relations, 1939. Reprint Ed.; Fredericton: Acadiensis Press, 1984.

See, Scott W. "The Fortunes of the Orange Order in 19th Century New Brunswick." *New Ireland Remembered*. Ed. Peter M. Toner. Fredericton: New Ireland Press, 1988. Pp. 90-105.

Senior, Herewood. *Orangism, The Canadian Phase*. Toronto: McGraw- Hill, Ryerson, 1972.

Sewell, Elizabeth. *Sunbury County, New Brunswick, Marriages: 1767-1888*. Volume I. Fredericton: Published by author, 1987.

Spray, W.A. "Moses Henry Perley." *Dictionary of Canadian Biography*. Toronto: University of Toronto Press, 1976. Volume IX, pp. 628-632.

----------------. "Robert Duncan Wilmot." *Dictionary of Canadian Biography*. Toronto: University of Toronto Press, 1990. Volume XII, pp. 1104-1106.

Steele, J. Edward. *The History and Directory of the Provincial Grand Orange Lodge of New Brunswick*. Saint John: Published by author, 1934.

Tapley, Harriet Silvester. *Genealogy of the Tapley Family*. Danvers, Mass: The Endecott Press, 1900.

Toner, Peter M. *An Index to the Irish Immigrants in the New Brunswick Census of 1851*. Fredericton: The Queen's Printer, 1991.

Tracey, John C. *The John C. Tracey Book*. Two Volumes. Unpublished Manuscript housed at the PANB. MC 80/no. 601.

Tracy, Lucy. "Genealogy of the Tracy Family." Typescript by author, 1959. Housed in the PANB. MC 80/no. 895.

Vincent, Thomas B. "Samuel Denny Street." *Dictionary of Canadian Biography*. Toronto: University of Toronto Press, 1983. Volume VI, pp. 739-741.

Waite, P.B. *The Life and Times of Confederation, 1864-1867: Politics, Newspapers, and the Union of British North America*. Toronto: University of Toronto Press, 1962.

Wallace, C.M. "Sir Samuel Leonard Tilley." *Dictionary of Canadian Biography*. Toronto: University of Toronto Press, 1990. Volume XII, pp. 1051-1060.

Wetmore, James Carnahan. *The Wetmore Family of America*. Albany: Musnell and Rowland, 1861.

Whalen, J.M. "Calvin Luther Hatheway." *Dictionary of Canadian Biography*. Toronto: University of Toronto Press, 1976. Volume IX, pp. 374.

White, John D. "Speed the Plough: Agricultural Societies in Pre-Confederation New Brunswick." Unpublished M.A. Thesis, UNB, 1976.

Wicks, E.M. and V.H. Olson. *Stamford's Soldiers: Genealogical Biographies of Revolutionary War Patriots from Stamford, Connecticut Area*. Stamford: Stamford Genealogical, 1976.

Wood, John Allen. "John Mercereau: Loyalist." *Generations*. No. 32 (June, 1987), pp. 28-34.

------------------------. "Daniel Wood of French Lake: Chronology." Typescript by author, 1990. Housed in the PANB. MC 80/no. 1513.

------------------------. "John Wood of French Lake: Chronology." Typescript by author, 1990. Housed in the PANB. MC 80/no. 1513.

Wright, Esther Clark. *The Loyalists of New Brunswick*. Fredericton: Published by author, 1955.

--------------------------. *The Saint John River and its Tributaries*. Published by Author, 1966.

--------------------------. *St. John Ships and Their Builders*. Published by author, 1976.

Wynn, Graeme. "Administration in Adversity: The Deputy Surveyors and Control of the New Brunswick Forest Before 1844." *Acadiensis*, 7 (1977), pp. 49-65.

--------------------. "'Deplorably Dark and Demoralized Lumber-ers'?: Rhetoric and Reality in Early Nineteenth Century New Brunswick." *The Journal of Forest History*, 24, (1980), no. 4, pp. 168-187.

--------------------. *Timber Colony: A Historical Geography of Early Nineteenth Century New Brunswick*. Toronto: University of Toronto Press, 1981.

Young, D.M. "Elijah Miles." *Dictionary of Canadian Biography*. Toronto: University of Toronto Press, 1987. Volume VI, pp. 504-505.

----------------. "James Taylor." *Dictionary of Canadian Biography*. Toronto: University of Toronto Press, 1987. Volume VI, pp. 755-756.

----------------. "David Burpe." *Dictionary of Canadian Biography*. Toronto: University of Toronto Press, 1988. Volume VII, pp. 120-121.

----------------. "John Glasier." *Dictionary of Canadian Biography*. Toronto: University of Toronto Press, 1990. Volume XII, pp. 376-377.

# INDEX

## ABOUT THE AUTHOR

Rex Grady is a native of California and a graduate of the University of California at San Diego, the University of New Brunswick (Canada) and Empire College School of Law in Santa Rosa, California. He possesses B.A., M.A., M.A. and J.D degrees from those institutions. For many years he worked as an ocean lifeguard for the State of California, in the southern and then northern parts of the State. He is a trial lawyer and, since the year 2007, has been Professor of Constitutional Law and Legal History at Empire College. In addition to this volume, he is the author of *Let Ocean Seethe and Terra Slide: A History of the Sonoma Coast and the State Park that Bears Its Name*, the two volume *Cases & Controversies: A Student's Guide to Law School Exams in Constitutional Law*, and *What is This Freedom? Law, Faith and History in the Time of Trump*. He lives in Santa Rosa, California with his wife and children.